D1368543

this
business of
INTERNET
LAW

this business of

business of

INTERNET
LAW

Tools for navigating the
evolving business and
legal landscape of today's
Internet environment

X. M. FRASCOGNA, JR.

H. LEE HETHERINGTON

SHAWNASSEY HOWELL

BILLBOARD BOOKS
An imprint of Watson-Guptill Publications
New York

To Rufus and Leon (X. M. Frascogna, Jr.)
To Michelle for your love, support, and laughter (H. Lee Hetherington)
To Lauren, my second generation cyber-guru (Shawnassey Howell)

Senior Acquisitions Editor: Bob Nirkind
Editor: Tom Cohn
Book design: Cheryl Viker
Production Manager: Ellen Greene

First published in 2001 by Billboard Books,
An imprint of Watson-Guptill Publications
A division of BPI Communications, Inc.
770 Broadway
New York, NY 10003

Library of Congress Cataloging-in-Publication Data for this title can be obtained by
writing to the Library of Congress, Washington, D.C. 20540

Library of Congress Card Number: 2001094181

ISBN: 0-8230-7735-7

Printed in the United States of America

First printing, 2001

1 2 3 4 5 6 7 8 9 / 09 08 07 06 05 04 03 02 01

Acknowledgments

Many people have generously shared their expertise and knowledge with us during the course of the development and completion of this book. We are grateful for the many ideas, suggestions, and experiences provided to us by so many individuals in such diverse professions as law, medicine, entertainment, manufacturing, sports, insurance, gaming, and financial services. Also, a special thank you to our clients. Thank you for asking us to solve your legal and business problems—especially those problems related to the Internet. Searching for answers to your problems provided us with many valued new approaches and solutions, and in doing so, generated real world material for our book.

We wish to acknowledge and thank the following individuals:

David Britt
Janice Carden
Damon Howell
Marcy Lee
David Maddox
Charlie Malouf
Brenda Marsalis
Valerie Meredith
Tim Nielander
James Powell
Bette Lou Reeves
Joseph Sclafani
Stuart Silfen
Elizabeth Thomas
Mary Jacq Watson

Further, we wish to acknowledge the special contributions of the following companies:

Blackberry Records, Inc.
D2 Interactive, LLC
Frascogna Courtney, PLLC
Speed City International, Inc.

Finally, a special thank you to Bob Nirkind and Harriet Pierce and all the staff at Watson-Guptill. We are most fortunate to have had a business relationship grow into a friendship. Thank you for all your support over the last two decades.

Contents

CHAPTER 12
Criminal Liability on the Web

CHAPTER 13
Jurisdiction: Whose Law Applies in the Borderless World of Cyberspace?

PART ONE

Introduction

CHAPTER 1

The Internet:
A Double-Edged Sword

Like the advent of radio, television, satellite, and computer technology, the Internet is a technological advance so grand in scope and transformative in concept that it is literally changing the way we live, work, play, learn, and interact at the commercial equivalent of the speed of light. The Internet is a worldwide network of computers conceived in the 1950s as a tool for the military and developed in the late 1960s with the assistance of the academic world, which used it as a communications medium to share research. It has since evolved into the bridge that links the manufacturing and service economies of the twentieth century to the quickly unfolding information economy of the twenty-first century. Its potential is almost limitless and its evolution into an integral part of our existence is an undeniable fact of modern life. The development of legal and business norms in the face of constant technological refinements and increasingly more innovative and sophisticated new applications will surely prove to be a roller-coaster ride. And because traveling in uncharted territory is always a daunting challenge, we have written this book specifically to help you mark the trail as you integrate this life-changing technological tool into your professional and personal lives.

The Internet is many things to many people. It is a research tool that offers unprecedented access to great universities, libraries, and databases of the world. It is also an easy and economical way to purchase an airline ticket, a book, or even a computer and have them delivered to your doorstep. The World Wide Web also provides you with a relatively effortless means of meeting people or a cost-effective approach to conducting business from the virtual office that is your home. Moreover, with e-mail and instant messaging, the personal letter has become an endangered species with little or no downside, unless of course you are the postal service.

The possibilities for practical application are truly unlimited. In a word, the Internet has become an all-purpose synonym for speed, choice, efficiency, and economy. Unfortunately, such a powerful tool comes with a learning curve that can, at times, be steep. Besides keeping you up to date on the latest legal, business, and technical developments, a primary purpose in writing this book is to reduce that learning curve by helping familiarize you with this dazzling new technological innovation. Likewise, we seek to help you to make the most efficient use of this evolving technology from the perspective of your unique circumstances.

As with any new powerful technology that possesses so many positive attributes, the Internet can also be a place to be avoided at all costs. Just as we want to help you make the most of its potential, we also want to warn as well as educate you against falling victim to the potential pitfalls of this new electronic innovation.

WINNERS AND LOSERS IN THE ONLINE ECONOMY

What are some of these downside considerations? There is no one answer—it all depends on your particular vantage point. Economically, the big winner stands to be the individual consumer. However, for every consumer who is empowered by the Net, there are many traditional businesses whose very existence is suddenly threatened by online applications. It is no exaggeration to say that the Internet is displacing or reshaping entire sectors of the economy. Stockbrokers, travel agents, and a host of old-line brick-and-mortar retailers, to mention only a few, are feeling its effects. One of the distinct trends caused by the e-revolution is to cut out the middleman in many transactions, thereby lowering the ultimate cost borne by the consumer. The ability to go direct to the source eliminates, or at least reduces, the role of brokers in much the same way that automatic teller machines have displaced bank tellers and personal computers have reduced the ranks of white-collar middle managers and clerical workers.

Another disadvantage of the Internet is the learning curve. Traditional businesses are accustomed to conducting themselves in an established manner. Steering businesses onto a new course involves more than just installing a computer and hoping for the best. As with any other business strategy, moving onto the Internet involves research, planning, and education. To be successful, you have to know your industry within the context of the evolving online environment. That requires you to stay abreast of your own business, but everything the competition is doing as well. You also have to understand and appreciate the dynamics of the online community of users for whose business you are competing. And finally, you have to keep up with the constant changes in technology within the context of industry and company specific applications. This almost certainly guarantees some level of frustration and resistance from both a financial and a human resource standpoint. In a word, playing in the high-tech world can come at a substantial cost measured in dollars and also in employee and customer morale.

Of course, this is not to say that businesses cannot profit from the emerging online environment. Notwithstanding the failure of many Internet start-ups, the power to interact directly with customers, to reach individuals on the other side of the globe, and to conduct business in the time it takes to click your mouse are undeniable and unprecedented advantages offered by e-commerce. In cyberspace, business can operate 24 hours a day, seven days a week with minimal supervision. Furthermore, the Internet provides a flexible, comprehensive, and interactive advertising and marketing medium like none other. The time limitations imposed by television and radio ads are nonexistent. Web sites also provide more room for detail than a print advertisement could ever hope to offer. Unlike any other medium, customers can choose which parts of a site to view and which parts to ignore, and the companies can track their customers' progress as they move through the site. This gives businesses the tangible feedback they need to improve their web site. Moreover, the Internet allows companies to interact with their customers, no matter where they are.

Security Concerns

In matters related to security, there are very real concerns that have been fostered by the Internet. Matters of personal privacy, identity theft, pornography, and damage to one's personal and professional reputation are foremost in the minds of many who have chosen to or are considering joining the new electronic economy. Likewise, novel issues relating to the protection of intellectual property rights under the law of copyright, trademarks, and trade secrets have been raised by advances in technology. In extreme cases, stalkers, thieves, scam artists, and all sorts of imaginative cyber-criminals have discovered innovative ways to intrude into people's lives through the virtual electronic window that exists in every home and office with an online computer connection. In addition, business security problems have arisen regarding theft of customer credit cards and other sensitive information, invasion of networks by hackers, and destruction of vital information by viruses. Even national security issues are beginning to surface thanks to the ease of access that the Internet represents in the hands of an experienced user determined to compromise military and national security interests.

Who Is Winning the Race between Technology and Law?

Congress, the courts, and law-enforcement agencies are all struggling to keep pace with technology. As one might expect, technology has outpaced many of the legal and business conventions that developed in the slower pre-electronic environment. This results in uncertainty, frustration, and in extreme cases, fear, depending upon the specific application involved. The good news is that law and business will catch up. But meanwhile, confronted by unlimited choice and an uncertain business, legal, and personal security environment, what is the prudent Internet user to do?

This book proceeds from the proposition that knowledge is power. Understanding how you can use the Internet most effectively, while avoiding legal and technical traps that may snare you, can open up an exciting new world of endless possibilities. With a little planning and creativity, anyone can use this medium to research, promote, inform, and profit from any enterprise. Because the Internet never closes, requires no travel, and, with the click of a button, offers consumers information and products from around the world, the playing field has been instantly leveled for the entrepreneur, the small business person, and the aspiring artist. It is equally available to the dot-com start-up company and the household names of the commercial world like General Electric, IBM, Microsoft, and others that are traded on the NASDAQ and New York Stock Exchanges. In sum, everyone with a basic knowledge of Internet business, law, and technology stands to dramatically increase both their productivity and bottom line, while those who choose business as usual do so at great peril.

A common initial reaction to the Internet is one of near disbelief at the seemingly limitless amount of free information that is suddenly available to anyone in the world with a computer, modem, and Internet Service Provider (ISP). This newfound ability to access such a vast new storehouse of information can be both exhilarating and overwhelming. Depending on your imagination, specific goals, and aspirations, it seems as if there is nothing you can't learn, experience, or do from the comfort of your own home or office, all at very little cost. Planning a vacation, listening to and downloading music, contacting people around the world, and running every aspect of a business without the limitations of bricks and mortar are but a few of the possibilities. But, before you run out to build your web site and take on the world, stop and consider that as with most other things in life, success, or the lack thereof, lies in the details.

While the Internet can be a powerful tool, it can also be the source of vexing and seemingly unending problems. To help you gain a better appreciation for all the possibilities, both good and bad, consider the following example. It is designed to alert you early on to a whole new world of possibilities, complete with the challenges and frustrations that always crop up once the glow of promise meets the cold hard light of reality. You may have already encountered some or all of what follows. And if you haven't, we are confident you will. We strongly believe that by looking at someone else's problems first, you will be in a much better position to use the information in this book proactively to avoid or circumvent problems that may interfere with your ability to maximize your success. And as to the inevitable problems that are lurking just around the corner, you can't make them vanish but you can at least take steps to minimize or eliminate their downside with the peace of mind that comes from knowing what you are doing rather than just guessing.

THE CYBERSAGA OF MUSIC-CENTER.COM

Music Center is a fictional business owned and operated by its sole proprietor, Jimmy Powell, in New River, North Carolina, a tourist and college town located in the Blue Ridge Mountains. Jimmy has run his business with a degree of comfortable success for the last ten years, selling compact discs, cassettes, concert t-shirts, posters, key chains, and related items to local patrons. Jimmy frequently plays the music that he sells over the loudspeakers in his store for his patrons' listening pleasure. He also showcases local talent, often playing and selling their music in his store and advertising their concerts by posting flyers in his windows.

After doing some basic hardware and software research, Jimmy finally bought a new computer, signed onto the Internet, and was instantly enthralled. All he could think about was the unlimited potential that his business would have if he placed it on the web. He could run the whole operation himself from the shop that he already owned. He already had the inventory, he wouldn't need any additional employees, and his name was already well established in the community.

Jimmy's first step was to hire a web designer, Allison. He handed her a check for $4,000 and told her to "come up with something" that would attract customers on the web. Allison browsed around Music Center to get a feel for Jimmy's business and went right to work creating a site for him. She assured him that his site would be spectacular.

Two weeks later, Allison called Jimmy to advise him that his site was complete. She told him that he would need to pay the monthly fee for the host immediately so that she could transfer the site onto the web. "Host? What host?" Jimmy asked. Allison explained that their contract had required her to procure the domain name on his behalf and design the site. She said that she would be glad to set up an account with a web host to lease him server space, then he could just forward the monthly payments directly to the host. Jimmy told her that would be fine.

After the account was set up, Jimmy pulled up the site, anxious to view his business from the new perspective. However, after a few minutes of browsing, he was less than pleased. Although the site was informative, it was tacky and rather dull. His home page was little more than his name (in flashing neon lights), a picture of his storefront, and a link to view all of his products on other pages. The color scheme was all wrong, and many of the words and names were misspelled. There was an itemized listing of all of the products, complete with pictures and a search function to find them, but there was no place for customers to place orders from the web site—only a fax number.

He called Allison to tell her that this was not what he had in mind. She told him that she was sorry he wasn't pleased. She offered to fix the typos for him but told him that he had not asked her to set his site up to take orders and since he hadn't given her any guidance, she had done what she thought was appropriate. She offered to redesign the site for an additional fee, explaining that their contract had provided that she would design a site and she had done so. She had put a lot of effort into the site and didn't feel that she should be the one to suffer if he didn't like it.

Frustrated, Jimmy explained that he understood her position, but said that if he had to pay additional fees anyway, he would prefer to allow someone else to redesign. He asked her to remove the site from the Internet and to send him a copy of the site's source code so that he could turn it over to another designer. Allison agreed to remove the site but refused to turn over the source code. She directed him to review their contract and explained that she had created the site and had retained all rights in the program. Although she had granted him a license to use the site for the purpose of posting it on the web, he was not entitled to alter it in any way without her permission, and she was not obligated to turn it over to him.

Angry, Jimmy hung up the phone, trying to decide whether he needed a lawyer. He decided to put off that decision and deal with the more immediate problem—what to do about his web site. He called some friends to get a reference for another web designer and started over, this time a little wiser for the experience. He began to think about what he wanted in a web site, putting together a list of things he liked and didn't like for the next designer he hired. After meeting with his new designer, Aaron, providing him with specific directions concerning the style and content of the site, and carefully reviewing the proposed agreement, Jimmy set Aaron to work. He checked progress regularly, suggesting changes along the way, until the site looked exactly the way he wanted it.

However, when Aaron went to post the site, he discovered a few problems. When Allison registered the domain name and set up the account with the web host, she had done so in her own name. Aaron had contracted with Jimmy to provide a host and monthly maintenance for the new site, but he could not load the web site to the new host under Jimmy's domain name unless Allison assigned the name to Jimmy, and Jimmy listed Aaron as his administrative contact. Jimmy's contract with Allison gave him the right to his domain name, so Jimmy contacted Allison to ask her for an assignment, which would vest all rights in the domain name in Jimmy's name. After getting the assignment from Allison, Aaron contacted the domain name registrar to have the registration information changed. However, Aaron told Jimmy that this process could take quite a while and suggested that they register a different domain name for now so that they could go ahead and post the new site. Jimmy was upset that he could not use the first name, music-center.com, because it was the exact name of his business.

Aaron told Jimmy that, once the registration information was changed, they could set it up so that requests for either web site would take the user to Jimmy's page. Aaron registered music-center.com and posted the new site.

Although a little irritated with his bumpy start, Jimmy was thrilled with his new site. Aaron had designed the home page with pictures of him, his business, his customers, and some assorted photos of the local bands that he promoted in his store. The site had links to some of the bands' home pages, as well as tour schedules and a link to pages of some other sites that sold tickets for the bands' concerts. It had separate pages for featured products, with pictures of the product, detailed descriptions, and sound clips from the albums so that the user could hear the music before purchasing it. In addition to featured products, the site had a search function for users to find albums by a specific group or with a specific title, which the site would then display with a picture, a price, and other pertinent information. Best of all, the site had an area for customers to purchase products online by entering their name, address, and credit card number.

Next, Aaron put the web marketing plan in place. Through strategic placement of banner ads, registration with specialty search engines, and purchasing of keywords (words that were related to the items contained on the web site), Jimmy's web site was soon a big success. He suddenly found himself taking orders not only from customers in North Carolina, but also from Texas, California, British Columbia, Brazil, Japan, France, and Australia. Jimmy could not have been more pleased.

Jimmy started to compile a list of all of his customers, along with their e-mail addresses, home addresses, and phone numbers. It was not long before he had a substantial list, and he began to consider how he could use that to his advantage. He started a monthly newsletter, which he e-mailed to all of his existing customers. He then approached another local businessman, Steve, a video-store owner, and asked if he would be interested in purchasing a copy of the list for use in his own business. Jimmy sold the customer list to the video store for $400.

Jimmy's web business was off to a good start. One day, however, he got an e-mail from a local photographer. The photographer, Lionel, was upset because there was a picture on Music Center's home page that had been taken by him: a publicity shot of a local band. Lionel explained that he held the copyright to the picture and that Jimmy's web site was infringing his copyright. Jimmy sent Lionel an e-mail, apologizing profusely for the error, and promising to remove the photograph immediately. Jimmy called Aaron, instructing him to remove the picture and to check the ownership of all of the other pictures just to be safe. The next day, Jimmy received another e-mail from Lionel, offering to accept $500 from Jimmy in order to avoid suit for infringement.

It appeared that Jimmy's problems were just beginning. In the mail later that day, Jimmy received a certified letter. It was a summons resulting from a lawsuit filed against him in Idaho. The complaint stated that a customer of Jimmy's purchased a glass key chain from his web site that had shattered and injured the customer. "Idaho?" Jimmy wondered aloud. "Can they do that? I've never even been to Idaho."

Still reeling from the suit, he began to wonder what else could go wrong. It wasn't long before he found out. In the next day's mail, there was a letter from an attorney in California. The letter stated that Soundslike Records, Inc. had discovered that Jimmy was playing music from one of their artist's albums on his site. Jimmy was slightly confused. He had always kept his ASCAP and BMI licenses current because he played music in his store, too. Wasn't that supposed to cover the music that he played? Besides, he reasoned, the sound clips were less than thirty seconds. No problem. He would just write the attorney and explain that Music Center had performance licenses from ASCAP and BMI, so he was entitled to play the music. He tossed the letter aside.

A week went by before more problems presented themselves. First, Jimmy received a letter from a company, TicketAgent, that sold tickets for live performances. TicketAgent took issue with Jimmy's practice of linking into their subpage to sell tickets, rather than through their home page. TicketAgent informed him that this practice deprived them of income because customers were allowed to skip the advertising on TicketAgent's home page. TicketAgent demanded that he cease this practice immediately or face a suit for trademark infringement and unfair competition.

Jimmy then got a phone call from the lead singer of "Iliad," a fairly popular regional band that always sold out shows whenever they came to Jimmy's town. The singer informed Jimmy that Iliad had its own web site and in order to market the site, Iliad had approached a search engine to purchase their name as a keyword. Iliad wanted a banner ad for their site to appear at the top of the page any time their name was entered into the search engine. However, Iliad had discovered that Music Center had already purchased the name and was using it to advertise its own site. The singer informed Jimmy that Iliad had obtained a federal trademark registration for its name and that Jimmy's use of the name in this manner infringed on the band's trademark.

Jimmy even received several e-mails from very irate customers. Apparently, they were displeased because a copy of Jimmy's newsletter had been e-mailed to their accounts more than 25 times the day before. The customer e-mails ranged from mildly annoyed to caustic and even furious. Jimmy called Aaron to ask what had happened. Aaron explained that a program he was using had a computer virus, causing the program to e-mail the same message repeatedly to each customer on the mailing list. Aaron also informed him that he was concerned about some other problems he was having with the system. As part of his duties as Jimmy's host, Aaron collected and compiled all customer information and gave it to Jimmy so that he could fill orders. This information was stored on Aaron's computer, which maintained a permanent connection to the Internet. Aaron told Jimmy that someone had accessed the system and tampered with some of the information, including the customers' credit card numbers.

Amidst the barrage of angry e-mails was a message from a customer who lived in France. The customer had been contacted by e-mail with a solicitation by the video store. She had e-mailed Steve to find out where he had obtained her name and e-mail address only to discover that she had been listed on the customer list sold to the video store by Music Center. The woman demanded that her name be removed from his list and swore never to make another purchase from his web site.

By this time, Jimmy was seriously concerned about the stability of his business. With complaints and threats coming from all sides, he wondered if he should remove the web site from the Internet until he could dispose of the multitude of problems that his little venture had caused. He was certain, with all of the successful Internet businesses out there, that there had to be a way to minimize the risks. He just didn't know how.

Jimmy called an attorney, who suggested that he write out a list of questions, then bring them in for a consultation. He sat down at his desk and created the following:

1. Did he have any recourse against Allison for not properly designing his web site?
2. Did he have any recourse against Allison for failing to turn over the source code for his web site?
3. Was he liable to Lionel for copyright infringement, even though he hadn't known the picture was copyrighted, and he had removed it as soon as Lionel had brought it to his attention?
4. Could his customer bring suit against him in Idaho, even though he had never had a business there? Could the customer hold him liable personally since he was not incorporated?
5. Could Soundslike Records sue him for copyright infringement even though his performance licenses were current?
6. Was he liable to TicketAgent for "deep linking" into their site?
7. Was he liable to Iliad for using its name to draw customers to his page?
8. What about his customers? Would he be liable for the possible theft of their credit card numbers? The sale of his customer list? The accidental "spamming" of their accounts?

When Jimmy met with his attorney a few days later, the lawyer read the list of questions, frowned, and explained that there was potential exposure, from either a legal or business standpoint, in every area listed on the page. "Jimmy, the Internet is a great place to conduct business," he explained, "but there are some safeguards that you simply must take, or, as you can see, you can end up in a lot of trouble. You have a potentially lucrative business, and I don't want to see you take it off of the web. I think you just need a little education."

HOW TO GET THE MOST OUT OF THIS BOOK

As the story of Jimmy Powell and Music Center suggests, the Internet, with all of its power and promise, is still subject to all the same restrictions and challenges that have always applied to businesses and individuals, along with more than a few new wrinkles never encountered by anyone in the pre-Internet world. So how could Jimmy have avoided all or at least most of his problems? More to the point, how can you avoid ending up like Jimmy? That is what the rest of the book is about. For now, we ask your patience as we begin with Part Two, where we will cover some Internet basics with which you may or may not be familiar. We feel this is necessary to build a solid foundation that will prepare you for Part Three, which is devoted to an in-depth consideration of current law as it applies to the Internet. In Part Four we will deal with Internet business and e-commerce issues that are interwoven into the law of commerce. These range from practical considerations that are often based on common sense to highly complex business norms that are the product of statutes, administrative regulations, and evolving business custom and usage. We conclude with other reference material calculated to reduce your learning curve while forming the basis of the reference library you will need to get the most out of your Internet experience.

Before we get started, however, allow us to issue a final blanket caveat. As in other aspects of law, business, and technology, some questions don't yet have answers. Some never will. In addition to the unresolved issues, let us warn you ahead of time that there will be substantial areas of ambiguity characterized by many more questions than answers. These unsettled areas of law and business usage will require you to adopt approaches and positions in the absence of definitive rules and authoritative precedents. Please understand that while this isn't always preferable or comfortable, it is simply part of the game for anything new and evolving.

The same considerations apply to the problem of obsolescence. As with microprocessors and monitors, the shelf life of information varies dramatically. Some of what we will have to say is based on rock-solid principles that haven't changed in a hundred years and are not likely to change in another hundred.

But then there will be crucially important information that arrived on the scene as recently as this morning's newspaper. As with any new developments and applications, there will be rules and doctrines that will almost certainly be radically altered by the time this manuscript hits the presses. We urge you to monitor newspapers, magazines, journals, and newsletters to stay current. You simply have no other choice if you want to take full advantage of all the Internet has to offer. If it is any comfort, know that we will never stop tracking, analyzing, and processing information, but due to the uncertainty that surrounds the online environment, you may not read it until a new edition of this book comes out. In the meantime, we urge you to keep up with all that is new to the best of your ability.

For up-to-the-minute information, please see our website at www.tbointernetlaw.

PART TWO

Internet
Basics

CHAPTER 2

A Quick Tour of the Internet

The first step toward using the Internet to its best advantage is to become familiar with the basics of its technology along with some of the common terms used to describe this rapidly developing electronic innovation that is transforming the way we live and work. The following is a brief overview designed for those who have had little or no exposure to the Internet. If you're an old hand, please bear with us. But if you are like so many who are finding their way cautiously through the quickly changing electronic landscape, this will be a good way to get started. We assure you that the concepts discussed below will be explained in much greater detail in later portions of this book. For now, we just want to concentrate on helping you see the big picture of what has popularly become known as "cyberspace."

THE INTERNET DEFINED

The *Internet* is nothing more than a series of computers, called *servers,* linked together to form a large network. The servers have the ability to transmit and receive data to and from each other. These servers, in turn, are linked to individual users, who utilize them as their starting point to tap into the Internet.

It is possible for individual users to have direct access to the Internet, especially through a college or university or other governmental or commercial entities that maintain, high-speed, dedicated lines with plenty of capacity to handle a wide range of data transmission. However, most individual users are connected through an *Internet Service Provider* (ISP). An ISP is a company that provides both individuals and companies with access to the Internet through its own servers and high-speed connections to other servers. The ISP may provide services both on and off the World Wide Web. When an ISP provides services off of the Web, it allows you access to features on its own server without sending you onto the Web to view information on other servers.

FEATURES AND FUNCTIONS

When you think of Internet use, some of the more popular features to come to mind are e-mail, messaging services, search engines, and chat rooms. There are many other components of Internet use that you should be aware of as well. Multimedia, hyperlinking, framing, and meta tags are all features with business and legal implications. Furthermore, as discussed above, some of these features are available on a limited basis without venturing onto the Web. For instance, some large ISPs allow their customers to engage in instant message transmissions, to talk in chat rooms, to play games, or to send e-mails to other members of the service without ever accessing the Internet—all members can communicate within that ISP's server. However, the cost of the service is generally not affected by your choice to stay off the Web, and the usefulness of restricting your communications to the community of other users of your ISP is not readily apparent. Let's take a look at each of these features.

E-Mail

In the past few years, e-mail has become a widely accepted fact of modern life. *E-mail* is a method of communication that involves typing a message into your computer, then transmitting it to another person's account for pickup at that person's leisure. An e-mail can include attachments, such as music, pictures, or documents created on a word processor. For instance, you may sit down at your computer and type the following message to a friend: "I'm going to the beach next weekend. Want to come along?" As soon as you type in your e-mail address and click the "send" icon, the message appears in your friend's account. Your friend has the option of reading your e-mail immediately or at a later time. If you've thoughtfully included a map and directions as an attachment, your friend can then click an icon for attachments and receive the material you've sent. Different e-mail programs generally carry out the same general functions, although the terminology or specific icons may vary. For instance, some use a paperclip icon to attach a file, while others have a button that says "attachments."

A useful feature of most e-mail programs is the ability to transmit the same e-mail to multiple persons at the same time. The advantages to e-mail are obvious—it is quick and cheap. However, sending unsolicited e-mails to very large numbers of users is usually prohibited by most ISPs. This practice is called *spamming,* named for a Monty Python sketch where the performers sang the word "spam" over and over again. Spam is generally the Internet equivalent of the so-called junk mail—sale flyers and letters addressed to "postal patron" or "occupant" that plagues everyone's mail box from time to time.

Instant Messaging

Instant messaging is a service provided by some of the larger ISPs, and some other online companies, that allows users to hold conversations with each other from their respective computers. The first user simply enters the second user's address and a message to initiate contact. A box appears on the second user's screen with a place for a response. This is an extremely useful tool for people who live far away from each other and want to avoid expensive long-distance calls.

Even if you don't check your e-mail for several hours, or days, when you do, your messages are still waiting for you. However, unlike e-mail, instant messaging is real-time communication that requires both users to be online at the same time.

So, if you and a friend are both online, you can type your friend a message, click "send," and the message instantly appears on your friend's screen—it doesn't have to be retrieved. He can then type a reply and send it immediately back to you. If your friend is not online, most instant messaging programs do not allow you to send the message, although some instant messaging programs simply store the message until the recipient logs on, just like e-mail.

Chat Rooms

Chat rooms are nothing more than electronic meeting places. A chat room can be public, meaning that the room is open to anyone who wishes to enter and "talk" (type messages) with the others already in the room, or private, meaning that the room is restricted to a group of people who are specifically invited to be there. Most public chat rooms are set up by subject, such as "music," or by demographics, such as "thirtysomething."

Chat rooms serve many useful purposes for businesses as well as individuals. Businesses may set up private chat rooms for employee meetings, rather than requiring employees to meet at a remote location. Employees sign into the chat room at the designated time and participate in the discussion by typing messages into the message box and clicking "send." Chat rooms are also frequently used for online education or distance learning, as will be discussed in Chapter 3, because they allow both for simultaneous instruction of multiple users and for real-time discussion.

Multimedia Transmission

Imagine *surfing the web* (browsing around on the Internet) and finding nothing but page after page of text. That doesn't sound very exciting, does it? Fortunately, the hardware that comprises the Internet is enhanced by the use of software that makes possible the transmission of pictures, video, music, and other graphics. This is commonly referred to as *multimedia*. The capacity of the Internet to transmit sound and visual images greatly enhances its value and attractiveness to potential users by making this a truly multidimensional media transmission platform with endless commercial possibilities. Recall our example in Chapter 1. Music Center's web site contained text describing each product. However, a picture of the products and some clips of music from the albums are far more effective marketing tools than a paragraph of text.

MP3 and Other Sound File Technology

A certain type of sound file, *MP3,* is worth noting at this point. MP3 technology has provided a method of compressing sound files into a manageable size for convenient transfer and use. MP3 files, and video files, can be *downloaded* for later use or *streamed.* Downloading involves copying a file from the Internet (or some other source) to your computer. Streaming audio and video is a real-time transmission of the file. Through this method of transmission, no copy of the file is permanently stored on your computer. MP3 technology has sparked a great deal of continuing controversy, as will be discussed in Chapter 7.

Web Sites

Images, sounds, and text can be grouped together to form a web site. A web site is a document on the Internet where individuals, businesses, and other organizations store information for others to access. The access can be public or restricted to "members only."

Web sites can be relatively simple, comprised of just a page or two, or extremely elaborate sites that can rival a commercial television or multimedia studio. All web sites are located the same way, by the use of a unique domain name. The domain name is an address that the web site owner registers with one of several registration companies. The web site owner may add extensions to the domain name if the web site is comprised of more than one page. This allows you to access a particular page or series of pages according to predetermined categories set up by the web site owner. For instance, a site displaying real estate listings for a particular city or region may have a particular home page domain name, while each advertiser or listing would have a more specific address which allows users to access directly without the inconvenience of navigating through the entire site.

Hyperlinks

Moving from web site to web site can be accomplished in two ways. You can type the web site's address into an address bar provided for that purpose, or you can use your mouse to click on a hyperlink. A *hyperlink* is a picture, graphic, or line of text, usually colored and underlined, that takes you to another section of the current web site, or to another web site entirely. *Linking* occurs when the link delivers the user to another site.

Deep Linking

A similar practice, called *deep linking,* occurs when a link delivers you directly to a certain spot on another web site without stopping at that web site's home page. Many web site owners do not like for other sites to deep link to their site. Why would you think this a problem? After all, isn't the first site referring users?

At first glance, this wouldn't seem to be a problem. However, imagine spending thousands of dollars developing a home page with all the bells and whistles. This is your portal to the site, and you've researched every possible aspect of your page to come up with ideas that will attract the maximum number of users. You've sold ad space based on the traffic that you expect on your home page. You have a menu that tells users all about all the great things that your site has to offer.

Then imagine some other company sending users directly to one of your product pages. The user skips the advertising, skips the menu listing the other products that you are offering, bypasses your hit-counter (a program designed to count the number of visits, or "hits," to your web site) and lands on a periph-eral page. Worse yet, the originating site's entire business, and profit, is achieved by piggybacking on your hard work. Now it doesn't sound so harmless, does it?

Framing

Some site owners have similar views toward *framing*. Framing is a method of displaying several pages on the screen at one time. As you travel through cyber-space, you may notice that some hyperlinks deliver you to a new site, but the border containing the headings from the old site remains. Framing is a common way for one web site to forward users to other sites without losing those users entirely. This can be important for advertising purposes. Linking, deep linking, and framing, therefore, have raised some important copyright and trademark issues that are discussed in Chapters 6 and 9.

Search Engines

A useful tool for surfing the web is a *search engine*. A search engine is a feature of a web page that searches the web in order to find material that is similar to the terms you tell it to look for. In a relatively short time, some of these search engines have become household names. Yahoo!®, AltaVista®, and Go are among the most widely used.

A search engine provides you with the means of finding a source of specific information by surveying the vastness of cyberspace in a matter of seconds to connect you with web sites that provide information similar to what you requested. You can type in several words that describe what you are looking for, and the search engine returns a list of sites that contain similar information. Generally, the listings contain a hyperlink, a short summary of what is included on the web site, and a web address.

To illustrate, when you enter the term "MP3 Players," you might receive a listing for an online store that sells electronics with a link to its home page and a short summary of its offerings; a similar listing for another corporation; a listing for the "Diamond Rio" MP3 player with a description and a link directly to that product's page; and so on.

There are far too many search engines to name them all. Some of the most well known include WebCrawler™, Excite℠, AltaVista®, Lycos®, Go, and NorthernLight. Most of these engines can be found by entering "www," the name, and a ".com" extension in the address bar of your browser (e.g., www.webcrawler.com). If you use a service such as America Online® or MSN™, the service usually provides a search function of its own.

Another search engine worth noting is metacrawler®. Metacrawler® has a feature called a "power search" that submits your search to a number of other search engines. This provides a broader range of results, since not all sites are registered with the same search engines. Most of the more well-known search engines have a mechanism by which they register new sites automatically. However, some search engines will not pick up a site unless the site owner actively registers.

Specialized search engines provide a more concise method of locating the specific information for which you are searching. Specialized search engines only register web sites within a particular area. For instance, AltaVista®, among others, has a special search engine for MP3 files. Other examples include the Dow Jones Business Directory, a search engine that searches and rates business web sites, and ditto.com, a search engine that searches for pictures.

Meta Tags

A search engine often returns web sites that have seemingly nothing to do with words you have entered. Although novice users often think this is a mistake, it is clearly not. The search engine looks for more than just the text on the web page in order to compile its list. Some search engines, in addition to searching the domain name, the page summary, and the page's text, also search the page's program, called the *source code,* to find the words entered by the user. The words in the source code that the engine searches are called *meta tags.*

For example, suppose that you have a business named SoftwarePlus that sells software online. Your greatest competitor, Discount Software, Inc., sells similar software products with different names. If your competitor enters the name "SoftwarePlus" into his web page's program as a meta tag (meta name="keywords" content="SoftwarePlus"), then the user never sees that name when she accesses Discount Software's web site. However, when that same user enters "SoftwarePlus" in the search engine in order to find your web site, if the search engine checks the meta tags, it returns Discount Software's site in addition to yours.

For obvious reasons, raising your web site's status on the list returned by a search engine has certain advantages. If you have a list of 165,000 sites that may match the words you entered, chances are you will only look at the first ten to fifteen sites. "Meta-tagging," or entering particular words in the source code, provides the web owner with some extra control over where their site falls in the list when certain words are entered into the search engine. It also provides opportunity for abuse, as will be discussed in Chapter 10.

Web Hosting and Webmasters

If you own a web site, chances are you have a *web host* for your site. A web host is the server that holds your site. Sometimes the company that provides the server space also provides other services to the site owner. In contrast, some web site owners have their own server. However, in most instances, the web host is an independent company that leases space on its server.

A *webmaster* is a person, or group of people, that maintains the site. The webmaster may both monitor the site to ensure that its policies are being honored and update the site as necessary. Businesses that sell products online may use independent companies to take orders and other information from the customers and forward them to the business for processing.

Webmasters can analyze other data that is collected from users as well. Files, called *cookies,* can be used to collect data from visitors to the site without any deliberate action from the user. Cookies are used for several purposes, including online shopping, password storage, and collection of specific types of information in order to develop user profiles.

User profiles can be valuable to advertisers. Information such as age, gender, and subject matter of interest to each user can show an advertiser whether a particular web site would be a good spot to place a banner ad. For instance, suppose you sell women's running shoes. Further suppose that an online magazine that is visited largely by women between 25 and 40 approaches you to advertise on their site. If the magazine has tracked each user as they have perused the site and a large percentage of the users read the articles about health and fitness, then you might be interested in placing a banner ad on the site. You would want to know how many users visit the site over a specific period of time and how many of those users gravitate toward the areas that contain articles and discussions about fitness.

However, some users object to the collection of this information without their knowledge or consent. Therefore, some *web browsers*—that is, the software that allows you to move around on the Internet—can be set to notify you when a web site is attempting to install a cookie. The browser then allows you to either accept or reject the cookie. While this helps to protect your privacy, it also interferes with your ability to use certain aspects of some web sites, such as "shopping carts" used for online shopping. Online shopping carts are intended to mimic the shopping carts you use when you go to a grocery store. When you select an item for an online purchase, the site will use a cookie to store a list of your items until you are ready to complete the purchase. Once you are ready to check out, the site will retrieve the list from the file and finish the transaction.

Usenet

Usenet is another popular Internet feature. The Usenet is a collection of very large discussion groups, called *newsgroups*. These newsgroups are used primarily for the exchange of opinions and ideas. Although Usenet can be accessed on the Internet, the Internet is not the only place where the Usenet can be found. Some newsgroups are located on servers not connected to the Internet. The only way to access them is through a direct connection.

You may choose to participate in one or more newsgroups based on your interest in specific subject matter. Once you choose a newsgroup, you may "post" messages to the newsgroup for other users to read and respond to, either by posting a response, or by e-mailing the author of the original message.

Suppose you join a newsgroup for people who are office administrators. If you are having a problem deciding what kind of copier to buy, you can post a message asking users about their experiences with certain models and brands. Another user may see your message and post a response, telling you that her office bought a Brand X Model 2000 and has had a lot of problems with paper jams. After seeing both your original question and the response, a second user may post a comment that he bought a Brand Y Model 4200, which has similar features, and has been very happy with it. You can view both responses, as can both other users and everyone else in the newsgroup.

Some newsgroups are monitored by a moderator who reads the postings and removes materials, either because the materials are not relevant to the subject matter or they are otherwise unduly offensive, obscene, etc. Other newsgroups post any message entered by any user. Usenet users, however, are not tolerant of postings that are off the subject. If a newsgroup is designed for discussion of scientific issues, a user that posts a message about a political candidate is likely to be *flamed* by a substantial number of newsgroup participants. A flame is an angry, even offensive, message directed at the offending user.

Advertising on the Usenet is even more offensive to users than off-subject messages. Although low-key, informative promotion, in moderation, is sometimes acceptable, advertising on anything other than a newsgroup that specifically authorizes it is a guaranteed way to turn users against a product. It is also a very good way to fill the advertiser's mailbox with flames from disgruntled users.

THE CHANGES AND CHALLENGES AHEAD

Without question, the technology associated with the Internet has almost limitless potential. But where will this potential take us? Over the coming decade, expect bandwidth to expand, dramatically allowing transmission of new forms of data almost instantaneously to the average home computer. As this occurs, the audio and video available on the Web will approach and exceed commercial television as we now know it. Instead of 100-plus channels now offered by your cable television provider or 500 channels from satellite television and music services, consumers might have access to millions of channels of information from every country of the world as well as outer space. Direct, high-resolution digital delivery of radio, television, motion pictures, music videos, distance learning, and who knows what else will all be possible, thanks to the Internet.

About the only thing we know for sure is that the Internet will continue to evolve in ways no one can foresee. Even as it exists now, the Internet poses some unique challenges that we are only beginning to uncover. It is quite apparent that many of the old rules don't fit comfortably with new technology. For instance, the concept of copyright licensing, which is clearly defined in the real world, is difficult to follow on the Internet due to the many different functions that the Internet serves. As the technology develops, more challenges are sure to follow.

Despite the certain changes to come, now is the time to become familiar with this technology and its many uses. It is also time to develop an awareness of the many issues that will certainly impact all of our lives.

CHAPTER 3

Making the Internet Your Window to the World: Internet Applications

There are not many things you cannot do on the Internet. Given the overwhelming number of web sites and information, the real trick is knowing what is out there. This is where a good imagination comes in handy. The Internet is, in effect, a giant interconnected mirror of the world. If you can imagine it, there is probably a web site that provides it.

When it comes to navigating the Internet, we have found it helpful to use the analogy of a race car. Both the Internet and a race car are powerful vehicles driven by high-performance engines that allow a driver to cover a great deal of ground in a short period of time. Instead of the conventional internal combustion engine which propels a race car around an asphalt oval many times in a matter of a few hours, a cyber driver at the keyboard of a computer can circle the globe many times in a matter of seconds, thanks to one of many Internet search engines. As discussed in Chapter 2, a search engine takes the search terms you enter and provides you with an almost instantaneous list of sites located in every corner of the globe that match your request. From that customized listing of resources, the Internet "driver" can take numerous split-second trips to the far corners of the world with a simple series of points and clicks.

There are many types of applications for you to explore on the Internet. Although we can't cover them all, what follows is a summary of the basic categories of applications you will find on your cyber trips.

ENTERTAINMENT

Perhaps some of the easiest things to find on the web are ways to amuse yourself. A wide variety of entertainment is available, including music, interactive programming, jokes, cartoons, and games.

Of all entertainment forms, music is probably the most pervasive thanks to the advent of MP3 technology. This technological breakthrough is great for music lovers, but it has also created serious copyright concerns (addressed in Chapter 7). However, setting aside the legal issues for now, finding music is as simple as typing "MP3" into any search engine.

Aside from a blind search, MP3.com is the most obvious place to begin. In addition to free music downloads, MP3.com provides a service using two controversial products known as "Instant Listening Service™" and "Beam-It™." These services allow you to "beam" your compact discs to MP3.com's web site for storage. If you later wish to listen to the music on that compact disc, all you have to do is log in from any computer and call up the files. MP3.com then transfers the music to your computer.

In addition to MP3.com, other web sites, such as CDNow and buysongs.com, provide MP3 files for download either for free or for a small fee per song. In general, you may listen to a short sound clip before deciding whether to make the purchase. CDNow also allows you to create custom compact discs.

You may create your own MP3 files as well. Software such as MUSIC-MATCH Jukebox, available on the Internet at no cost, can be used to convert music contained on any compact disc to MP3 format. You simply insert the compact disc into the CD-ROM drive and select the songs to be converted. The software converts the files and stores them on the computer. This software also allows you to organize your music library, create a play list, and play the music on your computer.

One of the most attractive features of this digital music format is complete portability of files. You can transfer your files to a portable MP3 player, a device about the size of an audiocassette, plug in your headphones, and take the music wherever you want to go. These devices provide the digital quality of compact discs without the inconvenience of skipping. Additionally, because these devices have no moving parts, they do not drain batteries as quickly as a compact disc player.

There are a number of sites that provide streaming audio in addition to audio downloads. These sites are essentially Internet "radio stations." RealPlayer.com, windowsmedia.com, and NetRadio.com offer a number of different stations for listeners, including both music and talk format.

Interactive programming is similar to television on the web. Sites such as digital entertainment network (den.net), itv.net, the sync (thesync.com), and windowsmedia.com provide television-like programming. Some of these programs are weekly serials developed by the web-site owners. Previous episodes are archived for users who wish to view them after the new episodes have been released. Other programs include *webcasts,* Internet broadcasts, of popular movies. Other sites provide video or cartoon "shorts" covering a wide variety of subjects.

There are a number of web sites devoted to jokes. Sites such as Joke-of-the-Day, The Jokes Barn (located at pnx.com/chomp/jokes.html), and z.com (located at dailydose.z.com) and comedy.com provide new jokes daily, plus archives arranged by subject. You may register with the site to have items e-mailed to you.

Games on the web include everything from cards played with other users to web versions of television game shows such as Wheel of Fortune and Who Wants to be a Millionaire. Several ISPs provide game areas where you can interact and play games such as spades or poker together, some for a fee and others at no charge. Other choices include crossword puzzles, casino-style games, and role-playing games. Fantasy baseball, basketball, football, and hockey are other applications that are played by millions of sports fans.

FINANCE

Although some individuals have concerns about the security of online transactions, the popularity of finance-related resources online is steadily growing. Among other tasks, you may now conduct your banking, check your credit account balance, pay your taxes, and trade stocks online.

Many banks allow customers to conduct their business with a computer, either by a dedicated line or over the Internet. Standard banking programs allow you to access account balances, transfer money between accounts, engage in the direct payment of bills, and obtain recent bank statements. In addition, many banking programs are compatible with personal finance programs such as Quicken or Microsoft Money, allowing you easily to transfer information from one program to another and to maintain computerized records of all transactions.

Similarly, most personal-finance programs are compatible with tax programs such as Turbo Tax or Tax Saver. This allows you to electronically transfer information to a tax program, saving a great deal of time and effort. Furthermore, most tax programs provide you with the ability to file your returns online, for a small fee, and receive refunds within two to three weeks. Some banks provide free online access to tax programs, allowing customers to complete and file tax returns from the bank's web site.

Many credit card and finance companies also allow customers to access their accounts online. Common features of these sites include access to amount of pay-off or total balance due, date and amount of next payment, available credit, and ability to change customer information. Some credit card companies also allow customers to view statements and recent transactions.

Another service that is growing in popularity is online stock trading. Providers such as E★Trade™ and Ameritrade℠ allow you to buy and sell stocks and other commodities for anywhere from $7.00 to $15.00 per trade. Generally, these companies provide historical data, company news, and other relevant data so that you can research your stocks. They also provide portfolio management features, which show you your gains or losses since the close of the last business day, the value of your portfolio and other accounts, and a history of your stock sales and purchases. These companies generally provide a range of other services. Some provide online banking and bill paying services. Most provide up-to-the-minute market information on the web site and will e-mail information that meets certain criteria set by you to your e-mail address.

INFORMATION

The Web is, in reality, nothing but an endless electronic stream of information. Therefore, it is good place to start when looking for types of information that you may normally seek elsewhere.

News, sports, and weather are available at a number of locations. The more traditional resources for such information, such as newspapers and television, have a significant presence on the Internet. Most local broadcasting stations have a web site where you can view national and local news items, sports, weather, programming information, editorials, community events, and other items of interest. Newspaper web sites commonly carry local and national headline stories, classified ads, real estate listings, and job listings.

In addition to the local media, most national networks maintain web sites where they provide coverage of a wide range of topics. CNN.com, for instance, covers many different news topics, including world, national, and local news, politics, and entertainment. This site also provides video clips, polling on issues of national importance, message boards, and chat rooms. Furthermore, CNN provides access to this site in nine different languages.

More specialized in nature is The Weather Channel®. The Weather Channel® (weather.com) provides detailed weather information, including radar, weather maps, and storm tracking, in addition to providing forecasts by zip code.

Not surprisingly, however, there are other, less traditional methods of getting the information you seek. America Online®, Yahoo!®, and Excite℠, to name a few, provide links to information in a wide variety of categories from their home page. These sites, and other similar sites, allow you to create a customized page that contains information that is of particular interest to you.

For instance, if you register with Yahoo!®, you would click the "My Yahoo!" link on the web site's home page to access your personal home page. The registration process commonly includes entry of your zip code so that your home page can be customized to your locality. You may be interested in items such as movies and music, local weather and horoscopes, but not in headlines or stock prices. Therefore, after you register and customize your page, when the page appears, it may contain the latest album releases, movie news, a weather forecast, and your horoscope, but no business news or sports scores.

Another way to obtain more traditional information online is through online education. Several universities, such as Jones International University, University of California, University of Phoenix, and New York University, offer programs of study that can be obtained entirely through Internet course work. A good example of a comprehensive degree program offering is the University of Phoenix, which offers degrees at the associate's, bachelor's, master's, and even doctorate levels.

Although some online courses include more sophisticated methods, online classrooms typically operate through the combined use of e-mail, message boards, and chat rooms. You complete assignments and turn them in via e-mail. Instructors post assignments and lectures on message boards. This provides a flexible program of study that you can access and complete any time of day. Using chat rooms for discussions is a common method of simulating classroom group participation, but requires the students to keep standard hours, which can be problematic when students are taking the course over different time zones. Therefore, some online courses limit class discussions to message board postings.

Aside from the more "formal" education provided by the virtual classroom, anyone can conduct informal research in a number of ways. In addition to a search through a search engine, many specialized databases provide detailed information in certain areas.

Genealogy is a popular research topic on the Internet. General web sites such as Ancestry.com provide a comprehensive body of materials including census records, social security records, marriage records, and periodicals providing research tips. Another example is The Genealogy Home Page (one of many, located at genhomepage.com), which provides links to maps, societies, software, and other useful sites. There are also numerous web pages that are geared toward specific surnames.

History is another subject that can be researched at length on the web. The Library of Congress home page (lcweb.loc.gov) is a great place to start any history research project. The Library of Congress web site has a multimedia history section that provides pictures, video, maps, and other materials for subjects including everything from the Civil War period to baseball cards.

There are many ways to obtain forms and documents online as well. The federal government maintains many sites where you can obtain commonly used forms. The IRS, the U.S. Copyright Office, and the U. S. Patent and Trademark Office are three such examples. These sites provide blank forms with instructions that can printed out from the site. Many forms provided by the U.S. Copyright office can be filled out online for printing and mailing via regular mail. Trademark applications from the U.S. Patent and Trademark Office can be filled out and filed online.

Several other government offices provide access to public records. These include court opinions and dockets, such as provided by the Fifth Circuit Court of Appeals (ca5/uscourts.gov); SEC filings, provided by the Securities and Exchange Commission's EDGAR Archives (sec.gov/cgi-bin/srch-edgar); and land records, provided by numerous county offices, including Rankin County, Mississippi (rankincounty.org/TA/index.htm), Essex County, Massachusetts (salemdeeds.com/index.asp), San Bernardino County, California (co.san-bernardino.ca.us/ACR/or/recsearch.asp), and Pierce County, Washington (co.pierce.wa.us/CFApps/atr/TIMSNet/index.htm). The availability of such records varies widely depending upon the office involved.

SHOPPING

The Internet is the only store around that never closes, delivers right to your doorstep, and has a nearly limitless array of goods. Online shopping sites include businesses with physical locations, such as JCPenney®, Barnes & Noble, and Wal Mart®; businesses that are exclusively mail-order, such as Fingerhut and Columbia House; and businesses that didn't exist before they opened on the Web, such as Amazon® and CDNow. Most of these businesses' online operations are similar.

Some online businesses accept orders online while others simply display products and allow you to print out an order form and fax or mail it to them. When ordering products online, you often find that the products are less expensive than their storefront counterparts. However, keep in mind that shipping charges are added to your purchase, although many companies provide free shipping for orders over a certain amount. This can, in some instances, result in your purchases costing as much or more than they do at the store down the street. Depending on the price of the product you are considering, though, it may be worth checking into.

Online ordering is a relatively simple process. Typically, you can search the site for a particular type of product, select the desired product from a list of results, view a product description and a photograph, then select the product for purchase. As discussed in Chapter 2, the use of cookies allows the site to keep track of all products selected until you are ready to check out. Most sites allow you to view their "shopping cart" and make additions and deletions before finalizing an order. Such a review includes a listing of the items and quantity and a total price before shipping charges are added.

Once you are finished selecting items, most sites send you to a "secure site" in order to complete the transaction. A secure site is one that uses encryption to mask the information, thereby making it more difficult for outsiders to access the information. Completing the transaction usually involves entering a shipping and billing address and establishing a payment method.

Once these items are entered, some sites allow you the option of registering the shipping, billing, and/or payment information. This means that the business stores the information so that you do not have to enter it every time you make a purchase. Because this is sensitive information, most sites remove it from the server and store it on a stand-alone system (that is, a system not connected to the Internet). The site then assigns you a log-in identification and password for future purchases. When you make a subsequent purchase, you enter the log-in identification and password, indicating that your information is on file. The business then accepts your order and retrieves your information from its database.

An interesting twist on Internet shopping is the online auction. There are countless auction sites that allow you to bid on anything from computers and accessories to autographed baseballs. Some of these auction sites, such as uBid™ and compusaauctions.com, offer products through their own business. Auctions typically use a log-in procedure similar to those offered by most other businesses. You select an item, log-in, and place a bid. When you are outbid by another user, the site usually notifies you by e-mail, allowing you another opportunity to place a bid. You may also monitor the bidding as it takes place by remaining at the site and clicking the "refresh" icon on the browser. When you end up with the winning bid, the merchandise is shipped to whatever address you have entered into your account.

Other sites, such as eBay.com, Yahoo! Auctions, and auctions.cnet.com, offer products for sale by other individuals, where payment arrangements are made amongst the parties. This would seem to be risky for both the buyer and seller. However, there are safety features that are designed to combat these risks. Such features include a business practices history of all users, if any, an insurance policy to cover low-cost purchases where the merchandise is never received, and escrow services.

In addition to physical goods, you can purchase items over the Web that can be downloaded directly to your computer. Such items include music downloads, as discussed earlier, and software. This can be especially appealing if you do not have the patience to await the arrival of the postman.

As noted previously, security is a major concern of many Internet users and businesses. Because it is such a concern, a security system has been developed to assist online shoppers. Secure electronic transaction (SET) protocol, a concerted effort between major credit card companies and technology leaders, is a set of uniform encryption and security measures designed to heighten the security of online transactions. This protocol, among other things, is designed to help protect consumers from false merchants and from interception of credit card numbers.

A simple precaution is to maintain a low-limit credit card for the purposes of online transactions. This allows the convenience of credit cards with reduced exposure. Furthermore, several major credit card companies have a zero-liability policy for unauthorized online purchases.

TRAVEL

Planning a trip has never been easier. You can get assistance with planning or booking several different methods of travel, including road trips, airline and train travel, and cruises.

As an initial matter, you can use the Web to decide where you wish to go. Many vacation spots, cities, states, and even countries maintain web sites with information and photographs. Some of these sites also provide travel packages and assistance making reservations. For examples, see australia.com, disney.go.com, and state.tn.us/vacat.html (Tennessee's official web site, with tourist information).

Some sites, such as digitalcity.com and epinions.com/trvl, specialize in providing facts for travelers and ratings of vacation places. Digital City furnishes such information for cities around the United States. At Digital City, you can find dining spots, sports and recreation information, local news, and reservation assistance. Epinions™ provides summaries and ratings, written by travelers, for attractions all over the world.

In addition to regular maps, you can obtain driving directions using map programs, available at sites such as Expedia™, Yahoo!®, and Map Quest™, by simply entering a starting and ending point. The directions can be displayed either in text form or as a map with the roads highlighted.

If you want more detailed information, Map Quest™ and Expedia™ provide complete travel services, including hotel and restaurant services, car rentals, traffic reports, and tourist sites. Sites such as this also allow you to search for and book flights and cruises. In addition to the full-service sites, many hotel chains and airlines allow booking directly from their home page.

...AND PRACTICALLY
ANYTHING ELSE YOU CAN THINK OF

There are so many other ways that businesses have used the Internet to make their services more appealing to customers. For instance, some drug stores, such as Walgreens, offer you the ability to enter prescription refills online, then designate a place for pick-up. FedEx® allows you to track packages online. At some educational institutions you can check your grades online. You can also access telephone and e-mail directories online. The possibilities are endless. The key to using the Internet to your advantage is to remember that, no matter what you do, there is probably a way to do it online. Once you have trained yourself to see the world from that perspective, the sky is the limit.

Of course, if you want to try all of this without investing in a computer system, there is the cybercafe. Cybercafes are local businesses that provide you, for an hourly fee, with a terminal, Internet access, and other services such as copies, printing, color scanning, design services, research services, and Internet classes. All of this, along with real-live human assistance, a cup of coffee, and dessert, makes the cybercafe an interesting alternative to hiding in your office with the shades drawn.

CHAPTER 4

Building a Better Web Site

It seems like everyone these days has a web site. Businesses, individuals, professional and amateur sports teams, charitable organizations, government offices, and just about anyone else you can think of have web sites. These sites range from elaborate and expensive corporate showcases to a single page containing pictures of the family dog and the new grandchild.

Whatever your reasons for wanting a web site, as the old saying goes, if it's worth doing, it's worth doing right. Some of what follows will be of greater assistance to organizations than to individuals. However, many of these suggestions will help you with your design no matter what your reasons for launching yourself onto the Web.

A successful web site begins with a great concept and well-written content. All or most of this phase should be completed before you call a web designer or undertake to design your site it yourself. Throughout the conceptualization process, two questions should be kept in mind. What will bring visitors to your site? What will keep them there? Only you can know the answers to these questions. Assuming you have done the creative heavy lifting in this respect, what are the basic considerations that separate a hot site from just another forgettable home page?

As with so many other creative endeavors, there is no right or wrong approach. But there are some tips that, when combined with a little know-how, a few good contacts, and a healthy dose of common sense, pay big dividends without the need of investing small fortunes. Please note that our focus here is on the basics of web site construction. Advertising and marketing considerations, which will be covered in Chapter 16, are another matter. For now, let's focus on some basic things you can do to improve the look and appeal of your site.

USING COMMON SENSE IN BUILDING YOUR SITE

The starting place for building a high-traffic site is the observance and application of basic common sense. Although some of the topics covered here may appear to be overly simplistic, a brief scan of the Web will show you that many people fail to take these principles into account. The price for ignoring the basics is a less appealing and less credible web site. Anyone who has surfed on the margins of the Web knows what we are talking about.

Run Spell Check

Some web sites (we won't name any names) have a great presentation, a lot of style, and a painful number of misspelled words. Such a needless oversight can make an otherwise impressive site appear unprofessional. It also makes visitors less likely to consider your site a trustworthy source for anything. Operating such a site is akin to a job seeker with great credentials and a terrific personality who transmits his résumé to prospective employers via a cover letter with multiple misspellings. It is highly doubtful that the applicant will ever be invited for an interview. Those few misspelled words have the effect of neutralizing years of education and experience just because the applicant failed to take a few minutes to double check his letter. So it is with your web site.

Remember, too, that spell check doesn't catch everything. Common examples of actual words used incorrectly include: *there, their,* and *they're* and *your* and *you're.* Although you have a spell checker and are diligent in using it, it never hurts to have someone else proof your work.

Colors Can Make All the Difference

Amazingly enough, we have it on good authority that someone, somewhere, actually believes that orange text on a red background is appealing. Once again—no names. This is about as close as we will come to laying down a hard and fast rule. If you absolutely cannot live with black text on white backgrounds, then at least avoid screaming contrasts, dark on dark (such as a black background with maroon text), or light on light (such as a white background with yellow text). Also, be aware that, although flashing text or blinking lights may grab the user's attention when they arrive at the site, these types of things quickly become annoying. If you wish to incorporate them into your design, use them by way of an introduction and then turn them off.

The lesson here is to honor basic principles of color, layout, and design. Put yourself in the place of the cyber stranger who happens to access your site. Is this a place that is visibly appealing, graphically compelling, and easy to read and understand? And if you think you are too wedded to your own ideas, don't hesitate to ask business associates, friends, or family for their opinion. A consensus answer of no is your signal to go back to the drawing board.

Consider Multiple Languages

The Internet is global. If your market expands beyond the United States, and it may, even if that is not your intent as some web site owners have discovered to their surprise, then you might want to consider making the site available in different languages (see, for example, cnn.com). However, if you do, make sure that you have someone who speaks the language proof your work! A Spanish, French, or Japanese language option can contain misspelled words and grammatical errors, too. Loss of credibility is a universal concept.

Make Your Site User Friendly

Make sure that the information or product that the user is looking for is easy to find. This is another way of saying don't cram too much information on one page or make users go through ten hyperlinks to find the information for which they are searching. Most users just won't do it. A site map and/or a search feature in addition to a table of contents on your home page can make your site easier to navigate. And be sure to provide a link to your home page on every page on the site so that users can always start over if necessary.

Leverage Other People's Work

Don't duplicate effort. You can reduce your work and make your site more authoritative by linking to other sites that have information that your users might want. In addition, although linking is generally a protected practice, duplication may not be, depending upon how it is done. Programs such as *bots*, software that searches the Web for data and compiles it for easy use, may be helpful in gathering information from other sites. However, be aware that some sites automatically block bots.

You Can Never Go Wrong with Free Stuff

The key consideration here is to be creative with the things that you show, share, or give away. Free material can be music and video clips, information, jokes, discounts, even recognition . . . the list is limited only by your imagination. If you can, give away something different every day to entice users to keep coming back. This is certainly more labor intensive but it can be well worth the effort.

Frequent Updates Keep Visitors Coming Back

If none of your visitors ever have a reason to return to your site, traffic eventually slows to a crawl. In addition, even if you have new features and giveaways on a regular basis, keep in mind that old news is no news at all. Keep your information fresh, update your site, and add new features frequently. This adds to the popularity and credibility of your site. More importantly, it creates priceless word-of-mouth advertising.

Users Like to Have Something to Do

An interactive web site is much more appealing to the typical user than one that is nothing more than a cyber-billboard. At the very least, you should include your contact information, preferably an e-mail address, since most Internet users prefer e-mail to "snail mail."

One popular way to make a web site interactive is to use surveys and opinion polls. Amazon.com allows users to rate books they have read. Epinions.com has created a successful web site based solely on the practice of allowing users to rate anything from travel spots to automobiles. Newspaper and sports sites commonly have short opinion polls for their users, and they post the results on a regular basis.

Other features to consider are mailing lists and simple games. Again, be creative, and keep in mind that features calculated to attract and keep online visitors don't necessarily have to have anything to do with the subject matter of your site. One site you should look at that combines several of these devices is amused.com. It provides links to a wide range of video games developed by other sites, and includes a mailing list, chat rooms, a "humor test," a guest book, newsletters, and an opinion poll that is mostly unrelated to the site. This site also illustrates some of our previous common-sense advice by incorporating features such as frequent updates and leveraging of others' work, as well as free graphics and software.

Tell the User Something about You
Whether you are a company or an individual, it is always helpful to include a page with a short profile outlining who you are. This helps a user to assess the credibility of your web site. For instance, if your site sells goods, the user may want to know that you are a company that has been around a while so that she can feel comfortable trusting you with her money. If you are an individual whose site contains analysis, opinions, or other factual information concerning any subject, the user wants to know if this is your hobby or your profession, and why they should listen to what you have to say.

TENDING TO TECHNICAL MATTERS
Beyond basic principles of organization, layout, and design, there are many simple yet important technical matters to consider when creating a site, whether for your business or for your personal home page.

Be Careful with Large Files
People with dial-up modems do not have the patience to wait for large files to open. Try to avoid intense graphics or sound files if at all possible. If you find a picture or clip that you just cannot live without, try giving the user the option of skipping the graphics. Some excellent examples of how the graphic option is best used can be seen by visiting millsapsfootball.com (Millsaps College Football team) or umusic.com (Universal Music Group). Another approach to maximizing speed of access without sacrificing graphics is to provide a thumbnail or very small picture that users can select if they wish to view the whole file.

Make Sure the Important Things Appear First
Larger files and graphics take longer to load than text. Note the way that your site appears when it is loaded. You want the most important items to appear before the less important ones. And you should give your user something to

read while waiting for the rest of the information to appear on the screen. A user with something to do while waiting is less likely to move on.

Consider Browser Compatibility

Each browser on the market has superior features that make a web site look really great. The problem is, not everyone uses the same browser. If you design a site that has to be viewed with a specific browser to be effective, then you are cutting out users who don't have access to that browser. Fortunately, there is a simple solution to this problem. If you have your pages designed with standard hypertext markup language, which is the typical Internet programming language, your site will look good no matter what.

Make Your Site Safe and Secure

Be sure to use secure areas if users are entering any information. This is particularly true where financial data is concerned. You should also take security measures to protect your own information from hackers and crackers. We'll discuss security issues in more depth in Chapter 11. For now, make sure that your site is as secure as you can feasibly make it.

Track Use Whenever Possible

There are many methods of tracking users without invading their privacy. Use of cookies that do not collect personally identifying information or use of hit counters are some examples. This is a very effective way of deciding what areas of your site are the most useful or appealing and which parts should be revised or deleted. Gathering information about site usage is also crucially important if you are trying to attract advertisers to your site.

Design for the Most Common Resolution

Design your site for the most common monitor settings that people use. The screen settings may be adjusted to fit more or less information on a user's screen, depending upon how small the user wishes for the information to appear. The default setting is 800 x 600, which we'll call average in order to avoid confusion. People with bad eyesight or who like large images on their screen may set the resolution lower, and people who like to have as much information on the screen as possible will set the resolution higher. Think of this like a camera lens. Zoom (the lower setting) gives you a larger image and cuts out the surrounding area. Wide angle (the higher setting) gives you the big picture, but all of the images are a lot smaller.

Your site should be designed for the average setting. Many site owners are tempted to design for the higher setting because they can put a lot of information on one screen. However, those with lower settings will have to scroll down and across to be able to view the page's contents. Using our camera analogy, this is like setting up a perfect photograph through a wide angle lens, then switching to zoom—instead of being able to see the entire shot through the zoom lens, you have to move the camera back and forth to be able to see all of the images in front of you. Most users do not like to scroll unless it is absolutely necessary. In addition, since the images have to fill more space, the files are larger and take longer to download. Both of these violate the basic rule of viewing web sites: make it fast and easy for the viewer. Period.

Make Your Site Search-Engine Friendly

There are several methods that search engines use to look through your site and see if it matches the user's search term. You may want to use meta-tags to summarize your site's focus. Get your domain name as close to the name you are using as possible. Also, take care with the use of so-called "frames" (that is, separate sections of your page which are, technically, each a separate page) on your home page because search engines may have trouble indexing them. Be sure to include a description on your site that describes what you want users to know about you—search engines search that, too. There are other ways to improve your standing with search engines that we'll discuss in Chapter 16.

CONSIDERING BASIC LEGAL COMPONENTS

While perhaps not as much a concern for personal web sites, there are some basic legal components that every business site should include.

Copyright Notice

Every web site should have a visible copyright notice. A copyright notice is a simple statement of ownership. In accordance with the United States Copyright Act, a proper copyright notice consists of three components: (1) the symbol © or the word "Copyright" or the abbreviation "Copr."; (2) the year of first publication of the work; and (3) the name of the owner of copyright in the work. Other terms such as "all rights reserved," "unauthorized use prohibited," or other such language, while not being a statutory requirement, certainly can add gravity and substance when giving the world notice as to your ownership of the intellectual property embodied on your web site. The only caution here is to not overload your notice so much that you will scare the living daylights out of people who visit your site. For an apt example of copyright notice overload, look at the copyright notice at the front of videos you rent at the video rental store. The beginning of every movie we have ever seen mentions the words "felony" and "FBI." This is probably over the top for your purposes. An example of a correct copyright notice is: "Copyright 2000, ABC Corporation." You may place a copyright notice at the bottom of every page in your site, regardless of whether you have filed for a copyright registration or not.

Trademark Notice

If your web site includes any trademarks or service marks owned by you, you should designate them as such. A *trademark* is a word, name, symbol, device, or other designation that is distinctive of a person's goods and that is used to identify those goods and distinguish them from the goods of others. A *service mark* serves the same purpose when applied to services rather than goods. A trademark that has not been federally registered is designated with the TM symbol; a service mark that has not been federally registered is designated with the SM symbol; and a federally registered mark is designated with the ® symbol. More about trademark use and infringement in Chapter 9.

Terms and Conditions

The Terms and Conditions of Use should state clearly that use of your site is governed by your terms. Therefore, you should include that statement both in the link to the Terms and Conditions page and on the page itself. Your site should have your copyright and trademark policy, a choice of law provision, a choice of venue provision, a privacy policy, and a statement disclaiming liability for any content found on sites that you may provide links to. Depending on your preference and your type of business, you may also wish to include an arbitration clause, a risk of loss provision, a disclaimer of implied warranty provision, and a limitation of liability provision. These are discussed in more detail in Chapter 14.

Privacy Policy

If your site collects any type of personal information, it should contain a privacy policy outlining what information is being taken and how it is being used. Privacy is discussed in Chapter 11.

Although the Terms and Conditions of Use and Privacy Policy generally need only be contained on the home page, if you have any concerns with any other site deep linking within your site (that is, skipping your home page and linking directly to one of your inner pages), you may wish to place the notice on every page.

A FINAL WORD OF ADVICE

A good web designer knows a lot of the tricks, so if you can afford one, they are well worth the money. We'll talk about what to look for in a web designer in Chapter 14. For now, you should simply be aware that web designers are capable of coping with most of the issues that we've covered. You should also be aware that most web designers are not equipped to address legal issues in any depth, so don't rely on your designer to supply your Privacy Policy or Terms and Conditions.

PART THREE

Law and the Internet

CHAPTER 5

Copyright Basics: What You Can Use, What You Can't, and What Can Happen to You

While everybody seems to know something about copyright, few people fully understand it and its many ramifications. This is especially true when it comes to the interplay between copyright law and Internet use. While many younger web surfers take the position that the term Internet is nothing more than a synonym for the word "Free," let us assure you that nothing could be further from the truth. If you don't believe us, just ask the founders of Napster.com, MP3.com, or any of the other high-profile civil defendants who have championed the proposition that new technology trumps traditional notions of copyright law. To date, every one of them have come up losers with little to show for their novel legal arguments other than hefty legal bills and out-of-court accommodations to the owners of copyrighted material they sought to use without paying for the right to do so. What has become abundantly clear over the past few years is that copyright remains alive and well in the brave new world of cyberspace.

Contrary to popular misconception—much of which, ironically, is fostered by Internet chat rooms and bulletin boards—the Copyright Act of 1976, as amended, does not give copyright owners a carte blanche, no-exceptions monopoly over their work. A close reading of the law and supporting cases indicates a much more user-friendly approach. While it is true that copyright owners are given significant rights that we will review in this chapter, the law also provides for many instances of legitimate free access to certain types of copyrighted material depending on the purpose and character of its use. A primary objective of this chapter is to better educate technology-savvy Internet users who may have limited knowledge of copyright law. This will not only help you with the do's and don'ts of copyright law, but will also help you develop an appreciation of the underlying rationale of why these rules have developed as they have. A thorough working knowledge of copyright law based on what you can and cannot do, and why, can guide you through the sometimes confusing and dangerous waters of potential copyright infringement liability. It can also help you to develop, protect, and license your own intellectual property for online use by you and by others.

THE CONSTITUTIONAL COPYRIGHT BARGAIN

Article I, Section 8 of the United States Constitution provides that:

"The Congress shall have Power...to Promote the Progress of Science and useful Arts by securing for limited Times to Authors, and Inventors the exclusive Right to their respective Writings and Discoveries."

This is popularly known as the Copyright and Patent Clause of the Constitution, on which all copyright and patent legislation is based. This clause grants to authors and inventors certain limited ownership rights in their creations. Additionally, this clause makes it clear that all law pertaining to copyrights and patents shall be federal in nature. As a result, the states are powerless to pass any legislation which would conflict with federal law. It also means that the federal courts have exclusive or "original" jurisdiction over this subject matter.

In drafting the copyright and patent clause of the Constitution, the founding fathers had a very pragmatic bargain in mind, calculated not only to reward innovation, but to benefit the public interest as well. Unlike European countries, which have always viewed copyright as a manifestation and extension of natural law, America's constitutional architects viewed the copyright and patent clause as being essentially a business deal between creators and the public brokered by the government. They recognized that economic and cultural vitality was dependent on innovation. They also realized that innovators needed incentive to ensure that they produced works and inventions that would benefit and enrich society. As a result, the framers authorized Congress in Article I, Section 8, to grant to would-be authors and inventors qualified monopolies for limited times, which would thereafter fall into the public domain for the unrestricted use of everyone in society without need for permission or compensation.

We need only look around at the cultural and technological advances of the last century to realize how visionary those handful of colonists were back in 1790. While in the short run it would be more convenient and inexpensive to view the Internet as a grand exception to this wildly successful scheme of incentive-driven innovation, it is clear that without it, America would cease to be the leader of global economic and artistic growth that has made it the envy of the world.

A BRIEF HISTORY OF COPYRIGHT

Despite the need to provide incentive to authors and inventors, the copyright monopoly authorized by Article I, Section 8 of the U.S. Constitution is limited not only by term, which is currently the life of the author plus a period of 70 years, but by scope as well. This is another way of saying that copyright law embodies a series of unfolding compromises and accommodations designed to balance private property rights against legitimate claims to public access by the public.

This process of compromise and accommodation dates back to the very first copyright statute, the English Statute of Anne, enacted by the British Parliament in 1710 in response to perpetual monopolies that had been granted since the sixteenth century by the English Crown. Previously, the Crown granted unlimited copyright to powerful publishers in response to the technological breakthrough of the printing press and the need to check the spread of alleged heresy during the time of the Protestant Reformation. The Statute of Anne was the first copyright law that sought to balance private ownership rights in creative works against the cry for public access. This balancing process, which was adopted in the U.S. Constitution and all subsequent copyright legislation, has weathered many new technological developments since then. These developments include photographs, piano rolls, motion pictures, radio, television, photocopy machines, and computers, to name only a few. The Internet is just the latest technological innovation. Without doubt, it has and will continue to be the catalyst for new compromises and accommodations in copyright law. Nevertheless, whether you are an owner or a user of copyrighted material, one thing is for certain—copyright is here to stay.

For those who argue that the Internet is so unique that it makes copyright obsolete, we must point out that the very same arguments accompanied the invention of the printing press, the tape recorder, and the photocopy machine. In each instance, copyright law has been adjusted to accommodate these technological advances. Because copyright in the age of the Internet is unfolding even as these words are being written, we can only report on the law as it is today and will likely be tomorrow. It will be the function of future editions to keep you abreast of the changes to come. But, in the meantime, you would do well to master the basics of copyright law, which are unlikely to change anytime soon.

A CRASH COURSE IN COPYRIGHT LAW

As in other areas, it is impossible to tell you everything there is to know about copyright law in this brief narrative. However, in order to demonstrate how copyright applies to the Internet, we must first give you a basic understanding of how it works in the non-digital world.

Copyrightable Works

By federal statute (Title 17 of the United States Code Annotated), copyright protection exists only in original works of authorship fixed in any tangible medium of expression from which they can be perceived, reproduced, or otherwise communicated, either directly or with the aid of a machine or device. The law covers mediums that are known or that are developed in the future. Section 102 of the Copyright Act specifies eight categories of copyrightable works: (1) literary works; (2) musical works, including accompanying words; (3) dramatic works, including any accompanying music; (4) pantomimes and choreographic works; (5) pictorial, graphic, and sculptural works; (6) motion pictures and other audiovisual works; (7) sound recordings; and (8) architectural works.

Works Not Eligible For Copyright Protection

Section 102 goes on to specify certain classifications of works which can never be copyrighted. They include any idea, procedure, process, system, method of operation, concept, principle, or discovery, regardless of how these things are described, illustrated, or embodied in a work. In short, it is only the expression of an idea, concept, or principle that is eligible for copyright protection, not the idea itself, provided it meets the test of being an original work of authorship fixed in a tangible medium of expression which falls within one of the preceding eight categories. The idea, concept, or principle itself is, by statutory definition, in the public domain, free for anyone to use to the same extent as a formerly protected copyrighted work whose term has expired, thus casting it into the public domain. As you can see, this leaves a lot of room for Internet users to come up with their own original expression.

Patents and Trade Secrets

Utility patent law addresses any process, system, or method of operation that is new, useful, and non-obvious. The term of a utility patent begins on the date the patent is issued and ends 20 years from the date of the application. Anything falling short of this exacting standard can be protected under the state law doctrine of trade secrets provided that steps are taken to keep such proprietary information secret. Otherwise, the process, system, method of operation, or proprietary information falls into the public domain just as any expired copyright or other unprotectable idea, concept, or principle. This leaves even more room for Internet users to maneuver, notwithstanding the Copyright or Patent Acts or state trade secret laws.

Exclusive Rights In Copyrighted Works

The owner of a copyrighted work enjoys several important exclusive rights. These are traditionally known as the "bundle of rights." To more fully understand the bundle of rights concept, imagine six sticks, with each stick representing a specific exclusive right. Under Section 106 of the Copyright Law, each stick corresponds to an exclusive right to do or to authorize any of the following:

1. To reproduce the copyrighted work in copies or phonorecords (such as cassettes, compact discs, etc.);
2. To prepare derivative works based on the copyrighted work;
3. To distribute copies or phonorecords of the copyrighted work to the public by sale or other transfer of ownership, or by rental, lease, or lending;
4. To perform the copyrighted work publicly, in the case of literary, musical, dramatic, and choreographic works, as well as pantomimes, motion pictures, and other audio visual works;
5. To display the work publicly, in the case of literary, musical, dramatic, and choreographic work, pantomimes and pictorial works, and graphic or sculptural works, including the individual images of a motion picture or other audiovisual work; and
6. To perform the copyrighted work publicly by means of a digital audio transmission, in the case of sound recordings.

Copyright Assignments and Licensing

As the previous section suggests, a copyright owner or proprietor doesn't just own a copyright, but rather owns a bundle of exclusive rights which are embodied by the copyright. Under the concept of copyright divisibility, a copyright owner may retain all rights or may sell some or all of his or her right, title, and interest in and to each of the exclusive rights, or may authorize others to exercise some or all of these rights through copyright licensing. In effect, each of the sticks comprising the bundle of rights can be subdivided and licensed by time, geography, and purpose. The only practical limitation on licensing is one's imagination.

A Case Study in Copyright Licensing

To illustrate the concepts discussed so far, consider world-famous author John Grisham's bestselling novel *The Client*. As the author of *The Client*, Grisham is the copyright owner of the manuscript. However, to maximize the potential of his compelling story of a little boy who witnesses a crime, Grisham needed the help of a major publisher with the necessary editing, marketing, and distribution resources to convert the manuscript with great potential into a bestseller. So, let's assume that he assigns the copyright in *The Client* to his publisher, Doubleday, in return for a contractual commitment to publish it in hardback form and to pay a specified author's royalty on each book sold along with a substantial cash advance recoupable from future hardback sales. This would make Doubleday the legal owner of the copyright and Grisham the beneficiary entitled to receive income, subject to the provisions of the contract making the assignment.

The customary book publishing deal also allows for a split of income from other subsidiary rights that the publisher licenses to others in the future by time, geography, and purpose. Because of Grisham's stature, he might well be able to command better terms than the standard deal. However, for our purposes, let's assume a 50-50 split of subsidiary rights. The publisher as the proprietor of the copyright now proceeds to negotiate licenses for various rights with users around the world. Subsidiary rights for a novel such as *The Client* will often include North American paperback rights, paperback rights for other countries, first North American periodical serialization rights, foreign hardback and paperback rights, book club rights, tape book rights, rights to electronic distribution over the Internet, movie rights, television series rights, etc.

Of course, the publisher seeks to maximize its income from *The Client* by first creating demand for the book. This is done by making it a hardback best-seller through intensive sales and marketing efforts. Once demand is created, the next step is to license the various sticks making up the bundle of rights. For instance, the publisher may issue a five-year license for European Book Club Rights. Note that the licensee may exercise the right to make and sell copies, for a limited time, in a specified territory for a restricted purpose.

When a famous author like John Grisham writes a new bestseller, it becomes abundantly clear just how valuable each of those little sticks can become. Besides income from licensing book rights, there is the second stick labeled as the right to create derivative works. Derivative works are new copyright creations based on the underlying copyright—the novel. Two of the most popular and lucrative forms of derivative rights are the production and distribution of movies and television series for which the proprietor and author will collect fees and royalties. Usually a novel is made into one or the other. *The Client* was made into both.

And, of course, there are the other sticks dealing with distribution, public performance, and display. Some or all of these rights are involved in distribution of books, movies, and television shows, and exhibiting motion pictures in theaters and television shows on network, cable, and pay per view. Add to this videocassette, museum shows, public readings, and just about any other medium by which a copyright may be disseminated to the public, and you begin to comprehend the importance of the bundle of rights concept.

The bottom line is this—when a best-selling novel, a hit movie, Broadway musical, award-winning television production, multi-platinum CD, or even a must-have toy such as a Tickle Me Elmo or Sony Playstation is involved, it is big business. Very big business. This is precisely why copyright owners and proprietors are willing to go to any lengths to protect their valuable intellectual property. If you still harbor any doubts, recheck the copyright litigation score-card involving Internet defendants.

Balancing Private Ownership Interests against Need for Public Access

Under the exclusive rights granted by copyright, no one else besides the copyright owner, his assigns (those that he transfers his rights to), or licensees (those that he allows to borrow his rights) are permitted to exercise the bundle of exclusive rights that are provided for by the Copyright Act. The same is true in most developed countries of the world by virtue of foreign treaties such as the Berne Convention and the Universal Copyright Convention. These treaties give citizens of participating countries reciprocal rights in foreign countries. In effect, all copyright owners are placed on an equal footing when it comes to the protection and enforcement of their copyrights on a global basis.

However, this scheme of absolute exclusivity of ownership and use has some basic exceptions written into the Copyright Act to allow for various legitimate interests of the public. One of the most important of these provisions is Section 107, covering the doctrine of Fair Use. Fair Use allows for varying amounts of use for such laudable purposes including, but not necessarily limited to, criticism, comment, news reporting, teaching, scholarship, and research. We will deal with this important users' right at some length in Chapter 6.

Likewise, the exclusive rights of copyright are balanced against a myriad of competing public interests, which are both nonprofit and commercially motivated. They include the need of libraries to archive works and make photocopies to support scholarship and research. There is also the right of the Public Broadcasting System to deliver programs at reduced rates. Among competing commercial interests are the rights of cable television broadcasters to make secondary transmissions of certain types of copyrighted programming. There are also allowances for individuals to make copies of recorded music for limited personal use. Indeed, a full sixty-five pages of the federal copyright statute are devoted to balancing competing interests of copyright owners and copyright users.

With this said, anyone who has occasion to deal in the realm of copyrighted works of authorship, which today takes in just about everyone who isn't living on a remote desert island, should not underestimate the power of copyright. Despite the technology revolution of the last decade, the resolve of the federal court system to uphold and protect the rights of copyright owners remains stronger than ever. The exclusive rights of ownership which are vested in copyright owners and proprietors applies not just to would-be infringers, free riders, and pirates in a traditional sense—it applies to the casual as well as commercial Internet user as well. To be more specific, if you are an Internet User, the sanctions provided by the U.S. Copyright Act apply to you!

Copyright Notice

An added word of caution. As a result of amendments to the U.S Copyright Act in 1989 that qualified the United States for membership in the Berne Union, copyrighted material created after 1989 now enjoys the protection of copyright whether it is or is not registered in the U.S Copyright Office in the Library of Congress and whether the © symbol appears or does not appear with the work. While a copyright registration entitles domestic owners to certain legal remedies provided by the copyright act, such as monetary damages in an amount specified by statute, failure to register no longer means that the material is not protected.

COPYRIGHTABLE MATERIALS ON THE INTERNET

The best place to start when discussing copyright on the Internet is with a description of the specific types of material that are protected by copyright laws.

Photographs, sound clips, and video clips are obvious examples. Printed text and materials provided for download are also protected. Logos and business names can be protected, too, but those are trademark issues that will be discussed in Chapter 9. For now, you should be aware that any *type* of material that can be copied from a web site can be protected by law. Whether a certain piece of material is protected depends on the *content* of the material.

To distinguish the type of material from its content, it might be helpful to provide some examples. One *type* of copyrightable material is written text. Whether or not text is copyrightable depends on its specific content and context of use. A news article or the words to a song are protected materials. As we have seen, certain types of information are not protected by copyright laws—ideas, processes, procedures, and the like. Public documents and mere listings of information also are not eligible for copyright protection. For example, the Recording Industry Association of America (RIAA) maintains the text of several pending lawsuits on its web site. The text of the suit may be copied and distributed because the suits are public documents.

When information that is not copyrightable is compiled and presented in a unique way, that presentation is protected by copyright laws as a "compilation." What is protected is the selection and order of the component parts of the work even in cases where the component itself may be in the public domain. For instance, there are many web sites that do nothing but provide listings of other web sites. One of those sites is "the groove guide," which provides listings of other sites in several categories. One of the categories is record company links, which you can find at grooveguide.com/distributor. Although an artist manager may copy down a web address from that site and give it to any of the artists she represents (the address is public information), she may not reproduce the entire page and distribute it in a newsletter she has created. The style, order, and presentation of the listings themselves are protected.

Files available for download are protected in the same manner under the same guidelines. An MP3 file containing a song performed by a musical group is protected. A file containing the text of a federal law is not protected, although its style and presentation may be protected.

Therefore, anything available on the web is potentially protected and should be used with care. This is not to say that you can't download or copy anything from the Internet—that is, after all, one of the main purposes of surfing the web. It simply means that you should copy and/or download with caution. As has been demonstrated in a number of recent lawsuits, the fact that material is available for download is not a guarantee that the offering of the materials does not infringe someone's copyright.

Napster.com provides a prime example of the fight over Internet downloads. Software available at Napster has been the center of a heated dispute involving the rock group Metallica, rap artist Dr. Dre, the Recording Industry Association of America (RIAA), and others, all of whom have filed separate suits against Napster for copyright infringement. In essence, Napster's software allowed the user to log in to the site and swap MP3 files with other users. Napster made no attempt to verify whether or not the files are authorized for distribution.

One of the points of controversy is Napster's knowledge of the purpose for which the site was used. Napster claims that the user was responsible for ensuring that he or she had the authority to offer or receive the file. Therefore, the argument goes, if there is infringement, then it is the user that is infringing and not Napster. In fact, Napster disabled access to its site for over 300,000 users under this theory. However, RIAA, Metallica, and Dr. Dre all claim that Napster was aware of what its software was being used for and should be held responsible.

Given Napster's recently forged strategic alliance with Germany's Bertelsmann, and recent court orders, new policies will likely follow. However, regardless of how the issues are resolved, this illustrates the point that you should never assume a file available for download may be taken without consequence. You should also be aware that making a profit is not an element of copyright infringement. You may give the materials away at no cost and still infringe a copyright.

What You Can Use and What You Cannot

So where does this lead the cautious user? Here are some basic guidelines for use of materials on the Internet.

Shareware or demonstration copies are generally safe to download. Many
sites, such as passtheshareware.com and shareware.cnet.com, either offer so-called shareware or offer links to other sites that provide shareware. Shareware is computer software offered for free use and/or distribution. This does not mean, however, that the shareware is not copyrighted—it simply means that the software

developer is permitting others to copy and use the program (that is, your use would be licensed). An excellent example of this type of use can be found at Garfield.com. The site offers free screensavers, and other materials, for download by site visitors. However, your use is expressly limited by the site terms posted on the site. The site terms allow you to download no more than three images from the site, allows only personal, non-commercial use, and prohibits any attempt to remove the copyright notices that accompany the images.

Similarly, developers offer many multi-media programs for free download. Multi-media programs are necessary to download or use certain types of files that are commonly offered on the Internet. Real.com, for example, offers RealPlayer (a program used to listen to sound files and view video clips) for free download and offers upgrades to the program, with advanced features, for a fee.

Another type of freely downloadable material is the demonstration program, which is offered in order to show the features of that program. Nonetheless, its use is generally limited in some manner. Common limitations include time limits and use limits. Time-limited demonstration programs cease to function after the trial period, usually thirty days. If you wish to continue using the program after the initial trial period, you must register and pay for it. Use-limited demonstration programs display the program's features with sample data, but do not allow you to actually make use of those features.

Before you download any of these programs, you should attempt to verify that the programs are authorized by the developer for distribution, rather than simply posted by another user. Downloading the program directly from the source is the best practice.

Never offer materials for download unless you created them or have a license to offer them. A short definition of the word "created" may be useful at this point. Created means that authorship of the work is original to you. If your only contribution to a work is that you changed it from a piece of paper or sound recording into a computer file, then you did not create the work and should not offer the file to anyone else. This is a very serious matter. Three years in prison (six, for second-time offenders) is only one of the many possible consequences you may face, even if you offer the file at no charge. This and other remedies are discussed below.

Obtain a license for materials you do not own that you use on your own web site. The quickest and safest answer to any question concerning duplication of copyrighted material is: get a license. Licensed use is nearly always safe use. As we will see in Chapter 8, however, even this answer is not a simple one—sometimes more than one type of license is necessary, and finding the copyright owner and asking for a license may not be an easy task. For now, you should understand the basic rule—if you did not create the materials, you cannot use them (either for display or download) on your site unless an exception (such as Fair Use or public domain) applies.

You may copy or otherwise use materials, or portions of materials, for certain non-commercial purposes. Generally, you may make additional copies of works that you have legitimate copies of, but you may not distribute them and may only use them for personal and non-commercial purposes. This is the essence of the Audio Home Recording Act of 1992 and of certain other exceptions contained within the copyright laws. These exceptions apply to both sound recordings and computer software.

The Audio Home Recording Act of 1992 amended the Copyright Act to address home taping on a cassette player. We'll discuss this in depth in Chapter 7. For now, you should understand that the Audio Home Recording Act permits you to make cassette copies of your music, provided your original is an authorized copy. There is some debate over whether this exception could extend to making copies with a CD-ROM, or other computer device, instead of a cassette player.

However, assuming the exception applies, if you purchase a copy of a sound recording via download (or, for that matter, in a more traditional manner) you may make additional copies from the original, but not from the copies. Making copies from copies is called *serial copying* and is not permissible. Specifically, if you purchase a sound recording via download from the Internet, the original copy is authorized (assuming the source was licensed to offer the sound recording to you), and you may download it to compact discs or load it onto an MP3 player.

Similarly, as noted in other sections of the law, you may make archive copies of software purchased either by a download or in a store. You may not, though, give those copies to anyone else unless you give that person the original as well.

And What Can Happen to You. . .

Copyright infringement is serious business. The consequences range from injunctions to jail time, along with an array of fines and other sanctions such as payment of damages and the other party's attorney fees, as well as seizure and destruction of infringing articles.

Injunctions. A court may restrain you from whatever activity you are conducting, such as restraining you from offering a file or operating a web site, if it infringes on a copyright. A court may also restrain other activities that might lead you to conduct similar activities. For instance, courts have prohibited users from having Internet access and have restricted Internet access to academic purposes only.

Impounding/disposition of infringing articles. A court may impound allegedly infringing materials, including copies and masters, or other materials that allow you to make other copies. When the court makes a final ruling, it may order that all copies and other materials be destroyed.

Damages/costs. A court may (and probably will, if it finds that infringement has occurred) award damages to the owner of the copyright. Damages consist of actual money lost and additional profits or statutory damages.

Actual damages are just that—the actual damage that the copyright owner can show that he or she has suffered, such as lost revenue. If the infringer has made a profit off of those activities, the copyright owner is entitled to that as well. You should note that profit means *gross receipts,* although the infringer is allowed to deduct expenses from that figure if it can be proven that such expenses were incurred.

The copyright owner may choose to take statutory damages in lieu of actual damages and profits. Statutory damages cover all infringing actions, by all infringing parties involved in the suit, for a single work and range from $750 to $30,000. However, the court may increase the award to $150,000 if the infringement was willful, or may decrease the award to $200 if the court finds that the infringer had no reason to believe that her acts constituted infringement of a copyright.

The court may also allow the copyright owner to collect attorney's fees and other costs, such as filing fees.

Criminal prosecution. Perhaps the most daunting consequence of copyright infringement is the threat of jail time. Criminal infringement occurs when: (1) a person willfully infringes a copyright for "commercial advantage or private financial gain"; or (2) a person willfully reproduces or distributes copyrighted works with a retail value, in the aggregate, of over $1,000 in a 180-day period.

Criminal infringement can mean time in prison, in addition to all of the other possibilities discussed above. If the infringer has operated for commercial advantage or financial gain, the prison time can range from one to five years, depending on the number of copies and value of the copies involved. Second-time offenses carry a ten-year potential sentence. If the infringer has reproduced or distributed works with a value over $1,000, the prison time can range from one to three years, with a six-year potential sentence for second-time offenders.

A sobering example of these penalties is that of a college student, Jeffrey Levy, who in 1999 offered software, MP3 files, and movies on his personal web site. He, like so many others, assumed that because he was not selling the materials, there was no harm in his actions. But, because the value of the files was estimated at $70,000.00, he discovered the hard way that profit is not an element of infringement. Levy pled guilty to a felony count of criminal copyright infringement and received two years of probation and limited Internet access.

In addition to the aforementioned penalties, a person convicted of criminal infringement loses not only their copies, but also all equipment used to manufacture and distribute the copies.

Service providers. The penalties we've mentioned may not apply to service providers. Service providers get special protection from the law if they follow the proper procedures. In essence, the law provides that a service provider is not liable for copyright infringement merely because the material is transmitted or temporarily stored on its servers while moving from one user to another.

If the material is permanently stored by a user without the knowledge of the service provider, the service provider may still be eligible for protection. In order to insulate itself against liability, the service provider must designate an agent to receive notices of copyright infringement and must post the agents' contact information on its web site. A service provider must also post notification requirements and its copyright infringement policies to assist copyright owners. Because service providers must act "expeditiously" to remove infringing materials, a detailed policy helps copyright owners properly to notify the service provider of the location of the materials.

If the service provider meets the qualifications and follows the requirements in the law, it is not liable for monetary damages at all. In addition, a service provider's activities can be restrained only in a very limited manner. This is a small example of how the new technology has spawned new laws to govern its use.

A FINAL WORD OF ADVICE

In the next chapter, we will discuss doctrines such as Fair Use along with other aspects of new laws and recent amendments of the Copyright Act and how they affect Internet use. In the meantime, our advice is to treat copyright law as a serious matter. You can count on copyright owners to do the same. Choosing to ignore the Copyright Act can create unwanted legal headaches and put a serious dent in your wallet, not to mention your credibility.

The best approach to using and distributing materials is to know and understand the law so as to take maximum advantage of the many exceptions and compromises available to you. Two surefire strategies are to look to the public domain for material, or better yet, to create your own original works of authorship and enjoy the protection of federal law and global treaties. Nothing changes one's outlook on copyright faster than to view copyright from the standpoint of an owner rather than just a user. Either way, it's the law.

CHAPTER 6

A Web User's Three Best Friends: The Public Domain, the Copyright Fair Use Doctrine, and the First Amendment

The owner of a copyrighted work has the exclusive right to reproduce, distribute, publicly perform, display, and prepare derivative works of that work. Nonetheless, despite the wide-ranging protection accorded to original works of authorship by the Copyright Act, there are substantial amounts of free material available to any web user thanks to the user's three best friends: the public domain, the Fair Use Doctrine, and the First Amendment. Other than creating your own intellectual property, these three avenues are your best bets for finding content produced by others that is cost free and absolutely legal.

THE PUBLIC DOMAIN

When looking for free material, the first place to look is the public domain. Think of the public domain as a giant, worldwide library of intellectual property that is available for use by any and everyone without the necessity of permission from or payment to creators or copyright proprietors. Once a work of authorship or, for that matter, an invention, enters the public domain, it can never be restored to the status of private property, but is free to use by all comers without limitation in perpetuity.

There are two primary ways that material finds its way into the public domain. The first is copyrightable material that for whatever reason was either inadequately protected or not protected at all. The second relates to copyrighted works whose term of protection has expired. Let's take a closer look at each of these two categories.

Unprotected Works

Prior to 1989, to merit protection, all copyrightable works were required to carry a statutory notice consisting of either the © symbol, the word "Copyright," or the abbreviation "Copr"; the year of first publication of the work; and the name of the copyright owner. Publication without the copyright notice was subject to limited cure provisions provided in the Copyright Act which could cause an otherwise protectable work to fall into the public domain.

Prior to 1978, the formalities for securing copyright protection were even more stringent. In addition to strict enforcement of the notice provisions, the old 1909 Act, which was comprehensively overhauled in 1976, provided for an original 28-year term followed by a renewal term of an additional 28 years. If a copyright owner failed to file a renewal with the Copyright Office in the last year of the original term, the work fell into the public domain. To make matters more difficult for copyright owners, prior to 1976 the concept of publication also played a more significant role in the protection of intellectual property. Published works were previously required to meet the formalities of the old 1909 Copyright Act in order to merit protection. In contrast, unpublished works received perpetual common-law copyright protection. For this reason, publication became the touchstone of protection. Court decisions dealing with this narrow question yielded some bizarre rulings that at times stretched the limits of logic. For example, a song was considered published when sheet music was sold to very few people, yet the commercial recording and release of a record of the very same song was viewed in many federal judicial circuits as being unpublished. These kinds of technical formalities caused many valuable works to unwittingly fall into the public domain.

The good news for copyright owners is that all of this has been radically simplified. The 1976 Copyright Act, which went into effect on January 1, 1978, abandoned publication as the touchstone of protection. The new and current standard is "original creation" accompanied by "fixation in a tangible means of expression" (that is, putting your creation in a form that can be phys-ically passed on).

There is even more good news for authors with regard to the technical notice requirements of the 1909 Act, which were retained by the 1976 amend-ments. As a precondition to the United States' admittance to the Berne International Copyright Union, which is the most important international copyright treaty organization, all notice requirements have been lifted for all works created after March 1989. Notice provisions remain for works created before March 1989.

Today's approach to copyright protection is more in line with the European concept that copyright is an extension of natural law, which recognizes and enforces legal rights of ownership on behalf of authors and artists upon creation of their work. Under the Berne Amendments, copyright protection is granted automatically upon creation and physical manifestation of an original work of authorship. Consequently, in the event of an infringement, publication with-out notice may preclude a plaintiff from collecting damages, since the alleged infringement was unknowing. In such cases, the compensation given to the copyright holder is restricted to an injunction restraining the infringer from future use without paying for past losses or displaced sales. So, while it is almost always a good idea to include a copyright notice on works of authorship, unless, of course, there is concern of dating the material, failure to do so no longer results in the work falling into the public domain.

Expired Copyrights

With the relaxation of the strict requirements in 1976 and the abandonment of the mandatory notice requirement by the Berne Amendments in 1989, forfeiture of otherwise valid copyrights to the public domain has ceased to be the problem it formerly was. As a result, most protected works automatically fall into the public domain only upon the expiration of the statutory term of copyright, which is life of the author plus 70 years for works created after January 1, 1978. Different terms apply to pre-1978 works, depending upon whether the works were registered, when they were registered and, if not registered, whether the works were published. For anonymous and pseudonymous works and works made for hire, the term of copyright is 95 years from the year of its first publication, or a term of 120 years from the year of its creation, whichever expires first.

The constitutional principle of limited monopoly of copyright measured by life of the author plus 70 years provides a creative opportunity to any web user. It means that the collected works of past creative masters are available to be copied verbatim or, better yet, to be adapted to strike a more contemporary tone for your web site. The collected works of Shakespeare, Chaucer, and just about anyone else you can think of who died before 1930 are available to you. The same goes for the work of composers, photographers, fine artists, or whatever the line of creative endeavor that sparks your interest. Here, as with so many pursuits, your imagination in concert with the concept of the public domain makes available more content than you can ever imagine exists.

Works of Authorship Not Protectable under Copyright

By statute, copyright protection is unavailable for any work of the United States Government. This means that any official document, study, or other publication of the government is in the public domain and is fair game. To access this treasure trove of free content, all you have to do is go to www.gpo.gov. One caveat, however, is in order when it comes to government documents. While all official government documents are in the public domain, you should know that the U.S. Government may receive and hold copyrights transferred to it by assignment, bequest, or otherwise. In other words, although the government cannot hold copyrights by virtue of independent creation, it can nonetheless be a copyright proprietor of works created by other authors.

In addition to the government document exception to copyright, keep in mind that facts, ideas, concepts, and processes are not copyrightable. This is the case even where the facts or ideas used are contained within the body of copyrighted material. Put another way, just because a novel, non-fiction book, article, or other original work is copyrighted, it doesn't mean that every single word is protected. Obviously a work of fiction consists of more protected matter than a work of nonfiction. In a non-fiction book or fact-based article, the original expression of factual material is protected. For example, some eZines (that is, electronic magazines) publish short stories. If an eZine publishes a short story about World War II using fictional characters but mentioning actual dates, generals, battles, etc., it would be almost completely protected, with the exception of the factual material it includes, which would be in the public domain, free for others to use. However, if the eZine publishes a non-fiction article about World War II that describes the same factual information, it would contain less protectable matter than the short story, but substantially more protected expression than a World War II almanac, which simply provides a listing of dates, generals, battles, etc. This is why quoting verbatim from a nonfiction book may result in infringement even though its theme is factual in nature.

When it comes to an analysis of permissible use versus copyright infringement, there is no easy or mechanical test that can be applied. Each work stands on its own and must be considered on its own facts. But even assuming that you copy a combination of unprotected factual material and protected expression, that copying may still be allowed under the Copyright Act with no permission or penalty. This is where the Web user's second friend comes into play.

FAIR USE

The Fair Use Doctrine is the product of over a hundred years of judicial decisions, developed on a case-by-case basis. Fair Use balances the rights of copyright owners against the needs of the public to make legitimate, albeit limited, uses of copyrighted materials. It has often been described as a rule of reason based on this very basic question: Would the reasonable copyright owner object to the use in question had he or she been asked? Cases dating back to the nineteenth century examined the facts in a myriad of contexts and situations using that basic question as their guide.

In 1976, this common law or court-made doctrine of Fair Use was for the first time codified in the new Copyright Act as Section 107. In effect, it says that even if an alleged infringer has used the copyrighted material of others, no liability will result, provided the court finds that the use was a "fair use" allowed by the statute. This provides every user of copyrighted material with an affirmative defense to a charge of copyright infringement. An affirmative defense to copyright infringement is one that any accused infringer can raise, even if the infringer admits to the copying, to be given the chance to prove that the use in question was a fair use.

In essence, the Fair Use Doctrine allows you to exercise any or all of the protected bundle of rights with respect to someone else's copyrighted work without permission from the author, subject to a four-factor test based on the specific facts of the situation. By statute, certain types of uses are presumed fair. According to Section 107, presumptive fair use includes those made for the purpose of "criticism, comment, news reporting, teaching (including multiple copies for classroom use), scholarship or research." And even if your particular use fails to fall under the previously quoted language, you may still be able to assert the privilege, provided you can pass the four-factor test we are about to discuss.

Before we look at the four-factor fair use test, you should be aware that in order to claim fair use, you must have copied the material you seek to use from an authorized copy of the work to begin with. Let's assume your friend photocopied a book to avoid having to buy it, then loaned the copy to you to make copies of certain pages for your own benefit. In this situation, you cannot take advantage of the Fair Use Doctrine, even if your use would otherwise pass the test outlined below.

The Four-Factor Fair Use Test

In order to determine if your use of the copyrighted work in question is a fair one, there are four factors that must be considered: (1) the purpose and character or use; (2) the nature of the copyrighted work; (3) the amount and substantiality of the portion used in relation to the copyrighted work as a whole; and (4) the effect of use upon the potential market for or value of the copyrighted work.

Purpose and character of the use. If the use of copyrighted material is for educational and non-profit purposes, then it is more likely to be considered fair use than if the use is commercial. So, if you print out a page of an eZine, then use it to prepare a college book report, the reproduction is probably a fair use. If, however, you print several articles from eZines to put in a research file that you use to prepare reports for your employer (assuming that your employer is a for-profit entity), then the reproductions will probably not be considered fair use.

Nature of the copyrighted work. If the copyrighted work has never been published, then it is entitled to greater protection. This is because a copyright holder is entitled to keep his or her work out of the public eye. Allowing an infringer to claim fair use would interfere with the copyright holder's right to keep the work private. For instance, say you are a reporter who has gone under-cover to write an investigative report. After you begin writing the article, but before you publish it, someone else discovers your files and then posts a portion of the article on his Internet newspaper. This takes away your competitive edge by beating you to the public with your own article, and it interferes with your ability to complete the report because it endangers your ability to remain undercover. It is unlikely that the infringer could call this fair use.

Furthermore, compilations are not entitled to as much protection as original works. A compilation does not require as much creative expression as an orig-inal work, since it is merely a combination of works created by others.

The amount and substantiality of the portion used in relation to the copy-righted work as a whole. If you copy an entire copyrighted work, it is less likely to be fair use than if you only copy a sentence or two. However, even if you only copy portions of a work, you can still lose under this factor. If the portion of the work you copy would tend to undermine or diminish the commercial value of the copyrighted work, then that weighs against you. Even if you only copy a small part of the work, therefore, if that small part is the selling point of the work, then the use is probably not a fair one.

The effect of the use upon the potential market for or value of the copy-righted work. Think of the last time someone told you the entire plot of a movie before you had actually gone to see it. If you know what's going to happen, why bother buying a ticket? This factor operates under a similar principle. The idea is that if purchasing your product is just as good as buying the original, then you have taken something away from the owner of the original work.

Of all the factors, the courts seem to place the most importance on this one. In essence, if your use would have little economic impact on the demand for the copied work, it is difficult to see the harm represented by the unauthorized use. On the other hand, if the copying would displace sales, divert income, or erode the value of the original, there is a much greater reason for the court to intervene to prohibit the use. Put simply, a copyright carries value for the author that a fair use should not unfairly diminish.

FAIR USE ON THE INTERNET

As with other areas of the law we have discussed, fair use on the Internet poses some unique circumstances with which we are only beginning to learn to deal. Linking and framing are two aspects of Internet use that present issues that may be affected by the Fair Use Doctrine. Linking and framing also present trade-mark issues that will be discussed in Chapter 9.

Linking

As explained in Chapter 2, linking is the practice of posting an icon (a picture, a web address, etc.) that may be clicked to transport the user to another web site. Keep in mind that displaying a link almost necessarily directs a reproduction of the entire work, meaning that the third factor in the fair use test (amount and substantiality of the portion used) will weigh against the person posting the link. As discussed later, in Chapter 8, a computer's RAM stores a temporary copy of the files on the computer. Therefore, when accessing a web site, you are not simply viewing it—you are reproducing it.

There are several considerations, however, that must be taken into account before concluding that the posting of a link is not a fair use. Since a succession of links is the very backbone of the Internet, to say that the posting of a link, in and of itself, is not fair use would seriously disable the effectiveness of the Net. The United States Supreme Court has echoed this sentiment, stating that the web operates by open access to most web sites, and by limited access to those sites that do not wish for their sites to be viewed by the general public. This implies a fair use authorization to link to and view any site that is not designed to restrict access—an implied license to reproduce, if you will.

Furthermore, a hyperlink is a web address, either posted on the page or, in the case of a photograph or other icon used for this purpose, embedded in a web site's program. It can be argued that this is not protectable because the web address is a fact—like a telephone number or street address—or a process used to access the web site. This is especially true considering that there is really no creative expression in a stand-alone web address.

As discussed earlier, deep linking poses a different problem. You may recall that deep linking is linking to a subpage on a web site, rather than to the site's home page. Although simple linking has not been a hot issue to this point, deep linking has been explored by courts and has been generally held not to be an acceptable practice.

Framing

Recall that framing is the displaying of several pages on the screen at once. Framing can be more of an issue, depending upon how it is accomplished. Framing almost necessarily involves creating derivative works, because its very nature involves adding information to the already existing information on the framed web page (this is without taking issue with the reduced size of the material). For instance, suppose you have a web site whose purpose is to provide information to users. A user can enter a question and your site will go find a site that has the answer. The user types "define browser." Your web page goes out and finds another page that has a definition of the term "browser," then displays that page on the screen. However, around that page is your border, which contains the name and address of your web page, your advertising, and your menu to the left of the screen. You have thus reproduced another site's page and added your information to it. If your user looks in the bar at the top of the browser, your address will be seen as main address displayed.

This is a fairly common practice, and is only mildly controversial compared to other framing practices. Framing becomes more offensive to web site owners when the originating site substantially alters the materials on the framed page. Returning to our previous example, assume that when your web page pulls in pages from other sites, it directs the controlling server to cover the advertising on the new page with your advertising and remove any identifying information that the page may have, such as the name of the person or company who owns or maintains the web page. Therefore, it appears that the new page is actually part of your site, and you are taking credit for the content, rather than allowing the identifying information to display the true creator or owner. Obviously, this is a more invasive procedure. Even if the displayed page is not substantially altered, framing can be used in a manner similar to deep linking so that the framed page does not take the user through the secondary page's home page (with the advertising, menu items, etc.) that the secondary page's owner would like its users to see.

In any event, as of yet, law in this area is sparse. Framing has been addressed by courts in Scotland and in the Ninth Circuit Court of Appeals, and from these cases, the following general rules have emerged: framing that allows the secondary page to be displayed as intended, not counting deep linking issues, most likely is okay, but framing that alters the secondary page to the point that the user believes the page was created by and is part of the originating site probably is not. Everything in between is a gray area.

This leads back to the fair use factors discussed above. If you intend to frame a page from another site, decide where your use falls in reference to the four factors, and look at how any modifications would affect the commercial value of the secondary site. A good rule of thumb is to look at how others are doing it, and keep your use in line with standard practice. This may not completely absolve you of any liability but, if your use becomes a problem, the fact that your practices are comparable to the industry should prove to be a mitigating factor.

THE FIRST AMENDMENT

Even if you are not copying or repeating verbatim, there are still issues to consider when making statements on the Web, or anywhere else for that matter. The First Amendment, among other things, prevents Congress from enacting laws that would interfere with a person's right to free speech, with only very narrow exceptions. This limits the government's ability to control speech even indirectly, for example, by enacting laws that would require ISPs to restrict certain kinds of materials.

However, as with other rights, there are limits. No one may use their free speech rights to wrongfully injure others. That is the essence of the concept of defamation.

Defamation is an injury to a person's good name or reputation. Although there are two types of defamation, written *(libel)* and spoken *(slander)*, we will discuss libel, since most online communications are written. Keep in mind that with the advent of video conferencing over the Internet, spoken communication will become more and more common.

Basically, libel is the publication of a statement made to another that is false, defamatory, and unprivileged. Anyone who repeats the statement may also be liable to the person about whom the statement was made. Contrast this with a false or derogatory statement made directly to the person to whom it refers. While it might be insulting and/or untrue, it can never be defamatory since it would not affect the person's reputation in the eyes of others, which is the interest that is protected by the law of defamation.

There are some limitations on libel claims, however, due to First Amendment concerns. Public figures—for example, politicians, celebrities, and even those that are involuntarily thrust into the public eye due to a newsworthy event—must prove more than falsity; they must prove that the publication was made with "actual malice" toward them. Suppose you operate a web site for the purpose of posting pictures and information about your favorite movie star (setting aside the movie star's right of publicity concerns, which will be discussed in Chapter 10), and on your web site you repeat a rumor you heard about her. In order to charge you with libel, that person must show not only that the rumor was untrue, but that you either knew that it was untrue and repeated it anyway or that you acted with "reckless disregard" as to whether the statement was true or false.

As with any other potential area of liability, there are a number of defenses available to defeat a claim for libel. Truth, naturally, is the easiest defense, although some jurisdictions also require that you have some justifiable reason for repeating the statement. Privilege is another defense. Officials acting in the course of their duties are privileged, as are judicial proceedings, legislative proceedings, and official reports of either of those types of proceedings.

The laws vary from state to state, but most injured parties have the right to demand that a defamatory statement be corrected in the same or similar fashion that it was originally published. As a general rule, if a state law allows for corrections in this manner, the injured party must make this demand or else forfeit any claim for damages unless there is some specific proof that the damage has occurred.

In any event, you should be aware that posting untrue statements may have serious consequences. Libel claims are alive and well on the Internet, so if you must make derogatory statements, make sure you understand the distinction between fact and opinion, and choose your words carefully.

While we're on the subject of the First Amendment, let's also focus on censorship. Private individuals and entities that operate online systems have absolute control over the content that is posted and published. One of the hallmarks of the Internet is that all kinds of people can run systems tailored to their own tastes; they make the rules and users can either follow those rules or move on. Therefore, system operators can edit or delete any part of or all of any information posted by a user. They can endorse or suppress any type of speech. They can set their rules to give maximum or minimum power to their users and to set the terms of their own legal liability subject to certain limitations, such as individual privacy rights and jurisdictional issues. They can change the rules at any time. The system operator can bar a user from the system for any or no reason. In short, users have no legal First Amendment rights against system operators.

So how does the First Amendment protect users' free speech rights? The First Amendment provides that the *government* may not interfere with an individual's right to free speech. Where Internet use is controlled by a governmental entity, whether this means that the government runs a site or allows access to the Internet, their involvement is subject to the First Amendment. This does not necessarily mean that the government must allow unlimited speech and/or access. It simply means that, if it does, it must do so within the confines of the First Amendment. For instance, a public library does not have to allow Internet access. If it does, however, it may not restrict the sites that its patrons may access unless it can do so without interfering with its patrons' First Amendment rights.

The First Amendment also prohibits prior restraint. This means that the government cannot restrain speech before it occurs. An Internet application of this rule has had some uncomfortable effects for at least one business. In 1999, a Michigan District Court in *Ford Motor Co. v. Lane* refused to issue an injunction that would have prevented an individual from posting Ford Motor Company's confidential trade secrets on his web site. The court noted that the posting of the information would violate trade secret laws but that the First Amendment would not allow the court to issue an injunction restraining future attempts to post the information. The company's only recourse was to sue for damages after the information was posted; it could not restrain the posting before it occurred.

In addition, subtle methods of censorship, such as taxation of systems that allow certain types of speech, are limited by the First Amendment, as is the government's ability to prosecute someone for expressing their views online. This extends to more than just speech in the traditional sense. Legally, speech can be spoken or written words, silence (such as refusing to recite the pledge of allegiance), photographs, or actions. Speech on the Internet would generally be limited to words and photographs, but keep in mind that other things, such as music, video, and animation, could very well be interpreted as speech.

However, this does not mean that an individual's right to speak on the Internet is completely free from government interference. As with most other areas that we discuss, there are exceptions. For instance, speech that is legally obscene is not protected by the First Amendment and may be censored. Such speech may also form the basis for a conviction under federal law. This leads to the question: What is obscene? Anyone who has spent any time on the Internet knows that there are some rather racy materials available online. Although it is impossible to provide a clear definition of obscenity, the interpretation is fairly liberal and is based on a community standard, not an individual one. We will discuss the standards and the potential liability for obscenity in Chapter 12.

Speech that may harm children can also be limited. Child pornography is the most obvious example. The government has an absolute right to limit the creation, possession, and distribution of child pornography and to prosecute for it. Other legislation limits the right to allow access by children to certain information and to ask for certain information from children. For instance, indecent speech, otherwise protected by the First Amendment, cannot be distributed to children via television or radio. However, at this time, all attempts by the federal government to limit distribution of indecent speech to children via the Internet have been overturned by the United States Supreme Court. Although several reasons have been presented for overruling attempts at legislation in this area, the basic reasoning is that parents can control their children's access far more easily than content providers can control where the information goes.

All of this is compounded by the fact that states are trying to get in on the action as well. Several states, including Georgia, Virginia, and Michigan, have attempted to pass or amend laws to restrict Internet access to certain materials. Although the U.S. Constitution was not designed to govern the relationships between the states and its citizens, the Fourteenth Amendment makes state governments susceptible to federal First Amendment restrictions. Therefore, the states may not interfere with its citizens' First Amendment rights. Furthermore, applying state, or even federal law, to an international medium is proving more and more difficult. For now, just be aware that private individuals and companies don't have to let you say or see anything, but that the government, for the most part, has to leave you alone unless you injure someone else or practice speech that falls within certain prescribed categories.

A FINAL WORD OF ADVICE

Notwithstanding the law of copyright and defamation, there is plenty you can do or say over the Internet and still be immune from the reach of the law even if others object. By the same token, there are legal lines in cyberspace. Some are bright while some are so indistinct as to be invisible at first glance. The best way to protect yourself from unwanted legal problems is to know the difference and to tread carefully while taking full advantage of what the law allows you.

CHAPTER 7

The Ongoing MP3 Controversy

So why should *you* care about MP3, the compression technology that makes music files smaller and more manageable? Well, that depends on your perspective. Undoubtedly, the technology affects practically everyone who writes, records, produces, distributes, purchases, or listens to music. That takes in a pretty broad spectrum of the population. More importantly, because MP3 is likely to alter fundamentally commercial music distribution and use as we now know it, it is worth taking some time to develop a working knowledge of the technology and law of online music usage.

The terms MP3 and Napster, unknown just a few short years ago, have become cultural icons and universal symbols of the digital revolution. Prior to these two technological innovations, politics and religion were always sure-fire subjects for igniting heated debate. Today, one need only mention MP3 and Napster to spark an impassioned response.

On one side of the issue are young, technology-savvy music fans and computer users, who regularly voice outspoken defiance against the big media companies and other institutional owners of copyrighted music. On the other side of the issue are many established record companies and some high-profile artists and songwriters who own the copyrights to the MP3 files for which the users claim the royalty-free right to trade. The hard-rock group Metallica has taken a leading role in the fight over how copyrighted music should be protected and licensed in the online world. For the first time ever, artists are taking aim on their own fans. This is both unprecedented and unsettling in an industry that has always relied on a strong common bond between artists and fans to sell records. Since the birth of jazz early in the twentieth century, musicians and fans have always been members of a common counterculture which gave expression to new ways of thinking and acting that were often in direct opposition to tradition and authority. Artists like Elvis Presley, Bob Dylan, Jimi Hendrix, The Rolling Stones, and The Beatles were agents of change against the Establishment. Now, thanks to the MP3 and Napster debate, today's music industry stars are too often viewed along with their record companies as being part of the Establishment.

THE AGE OLD DEBATE: USERS VS. OWNERS

While almost everyone agrees that MP3 is a fast, convenient, and cost-effective way to distribute and obtain music with a high sound quality, consensus usually ends there. To high-tech music fans who complain about the inflated prices of commercial compact discs and the lack of choice in having to buy a whole album just to get one or two of their favorite cuts, this new technology is efficient, fair, and timely. These predominantly younger music users often characterize their use of MP3 as "file sharing," contending that their acts are no different from making a cassette tape to share with a friend. They tend to view copyright law as being either obsolete or inapplicable to their activities.

Conversely, copyright owners, led by the Recording Industry Association of America (RIAA), the leading industry trade organization, contend that systematic file sharing of copyrighted music violates the exclusive rights guaranteed by Section 106 of the United States Copyright Act, including the rights of reproduction, distribution, and, in some cases, public performance by means of digital audio transmission. According to the industry, the consequence of this wholesale infringement is both direct and substantial, measured by lost sales running into the millions and even billions of dollars. This level of lost revenue translates into less money allocated by record labels and music publishers to help develop new artists and songwriters. In short, the music industry considers file sharing to be nothing less than piracy and theft that will radically reduce the amount and quality of new music.

The divide is both deep and wide, with each camp believing that their actions are both justifiable and morally correct. And while the courts have thus far consistently sided with copyright owners, the hearts and minds of Napster users have yet to follow.

What is clear is that the MP3 technology, like the Internet itself, is here to stay. As we discuss MP3, it will become increasingly clear how the technology affects different aspects of the industry and why many industry professionals are resisting its advance by way of an increasing number of lawsuits revolving around the various uses made of that technology.

Regardless of the tensions that currently exist between music owners and MP3 users, technical reality combined with mounting precedent from court decisions has created tremendous pressure on everyone involved to develop new approaches to distribution and licensing. Ideally, these methods should preserve incentive for creators while also providing more diverse and affordable choices to consumers. As a result, however, traditional means and methods of doing business dating back to the early days of rock and roll in the 1950s and before are in imminent danger. For some, this spells opportunity with a capital O; to others it represents a threat and perhaps even impending extinction. The new paradigm that will eventually emerge is still under construction. In the meantime, the best we can do is monitor events as they unfold while trying to understand and use the technology as it refines itself even as these words are written.

MP3 TECHNOLOGY BASICS

MP3 stands for MPEG 1 Layer 3. This technology allows you to compress audio tracks down into smaller, more manageable files by removing the sounds that the human ear cannot hear very well anyway. The effect is, in essence, like turning a computer into a stereo system without the need for compact discs.

Before this technology emerged, you could play audio compact discs on your CD-ROM drive with the sound being directed to the computer speaker. Creating sound files on the computer was not so simple, though. Music could be reproduced as a "wave" (.wav) file, but some files were so large that the computer had to pause during replay in order to process the file, causing the music to skip. The size of the files made them difficult, if not impossible, to download or transmit via e-mail.

Now, with the proper software (known as "ripping" software), music can be compressed into smaller files, making them easier for a computer to manage. You simply insert the audio compact disc into the CD-ROM drive and select the track. The program compresses the file and stores it on the computer's hard drive.

A single track of about three minutes is compressed into a file that is approximately two megabytes, just slightly larger than the capacity of a regular floppy disk. This means that the files download faster and the computer can process the information faster as it reads the file during use. After you download or create the file, with the assistance of MP3 software, you can play it on your computer just like pressing the "play" button on a compact disc player.

Until recently, use of MP3 files was limited to play on a computer system. However, further advances in the technology have made these files portable. Now, you can purchase a device similar to a portable cassette or compact disc player for use with MP3 files. You download the MP3 files of your choice from your computer into the device. Then, just like a portable cassette or compact disc player, you can take your music with you wherever you go. The advantage over traditional portable music players is obvious—you only take the tracks you want to hear. The unit is completely self-contained and needs no switching of cassettes or compact discs, and the sound doesn't skip and requires fewer batteries because there are no moving parts.

THE PROS AND CONS OF MP3 USE

The impact of MP3 technology is enormous. With it, you can place a compact disc in your computer and convert the music into files. You can then transmit those files to other places or to other users. Obviously, though, this presents a problem with copyright infringement—specifically, with provisions that give the copyright owner or proprietor the exclusive right to reproduce the copyrighted work in copies or phonorecords. You might wonder why this is such a dilemma. For years now you've been able to record from a compact disc onto a cassette for either your use or to give copies to friends. What's the difference?

The Internet provides a much greater capability for abuse. You probably wouldn't put cassette copies of your favorite compact disc in the mail and send them off to friends. However, you can e-mail files without paying for postage and blank cassettes. Furthermore, a single e-mail can be copied to literally dozens of addresses at once, and it takes mere seconds to compose and send an e-mail. In the eyes of recording artists and songwriters, each one of those innocuous little e-mails represents one more deduction from their next artist royalty and/or music publishing mechanical royalty statement. For record executives, it means the direct loss of revenue it takes to keep their businesses on track.

All of this is not to suggest that there aren't numerous legitimate, legal uses for MP3 files. You can computerize your music collection for home use. You can create custom playlists of your favorite music. You can produce a back-up copy of recordings to guard against destruction of the original and you can organize and catalog your music for easier access. You can even offer your own compositions to others for swapping and purchase or otherwise acquire downloads from legitimate sources.

From the standpoint of the music industry, recording artists, songwriters, and record manufacturers or retailers can use this technology to distribute music in the form of downloads. Instant gratification is one of the hallmarks of our society. This is even more pronounced since the advent of computer technology. People want satisfaction *right now*. Thanks to the computer and the Internet, that need is increasingly met—instantly. Ordering products over the Internet is becoming more and more popular, despite the fact that driving to the local department store to make a purchase would take less time than the weeks sometimes required to ship a product ordered from the Web.

Shopping on the Web puts every kind of merchandise imaginable right at your fingertips. An entire day of walking from store to store would not provide near the variety that shopping on the Internet provides. This also makes comparison shopping a much easier task. In addition, the Internet never closes, and there is no time wasted fighting traffic or standing in lines.

While all of the foregoing is a strong draw to online shopping, the determinative factor relates to speed. Cyber-merchants who can deliver their products immediately have a distinct advantage over merchants who must take orders and ship merchandise. Not only is the need for shipping charges alleviated, but customers get the product instantly. Given a choice between paying shipping for a product that will arrive in three weeks or avoiding shipping costs and receiving the product right now, most consumers will opt for *now*. Many software companies, recognizing this advantage, offer software packages on the Internet that may be downloaded as soon as the purchase transaction is complete.

It follows that artists, record companies, and retailers offering MP3 down-loads are a step ahead of the game. They can offer their music faster than other merchants can, and without distribution and production costs.

However, as discussed earlier, lawsuits against Napster, MP3.com, and Diamond (makers of the Diamond Rio MP3 player) illustrate the fact that this technology has not yet been widely accepted by record companies, music publishers, and some recording artists. From their perspective, the potential for abuse appears to out-weigh the potential for profit. That is likely to change, however.

Music "Swapping"

Prior to its suspension of operations, Napster used software developed by its 19-year-old founder, Shawn Fanning, to allow large numbers of users to offer their MP3 files to other users. Napster users created or otherwise obtained MP3 files and stored them on their computers. Once you registered for Napster and downloaded the software, you could sign on to the service. As soon as you signed on, the Napster software scanned your hard drive and took inventory of all MP3 files there, allowing you to select any files that you did not wish to share. You could then use Napster's search engine to find out whether there was anyone currently logged in that was offering a specific song or songs by a particular artist. Once you located the file, you could download the file directly from the individual offering the file.

Napster's popularity was unprecedented prior to an adverse copyright infringe-ment ruling by the United States Court of Appeals for the Ninth Circuit. At the height of its popularity, Napster by its own count is said to have had over 60 million users and required over 150 servers to manage the traffic. Some universities had to ban students from using the site because widespread use caused their networks to crash. Obviously, if the MP3 files being traded in such large volumes were unauthorized, record companies and publishers had cause for concern. This is especially true if, as some commentators have alleged, users were downloading the music to compact discs (with the assistance of write-able CD-ROM drives) and selling them at auction sites such as eBay.

While much of the industry, including some major artists like Metallica and Dr. Dre, have taken on Napster and other similar services such as Scour in court, and others, including Ted Nugent and Don Henley, have voiced their criticisms, there is not solidarity. Some artists such as Limp Bizkit, Chuck D, and Prince have declared their support for Napster-like sites, reasoning that they provide an effective way to get their music to the fans. In fact, Prince announced plans to actively promote some of his new music on Napster. German media giant Bertelsmann (RCA, Arista) now has a working agreement with Napster to help the company make the transition to a subscription-based service modeled after premium cable television channels such as Home Box

Office or Showtime. This newfound industry support of Napster seems to signal a recognition that the technology is an excellent way to expand the audience for their music for a price that will surely be lower than the current suggested retail price for CDs.

In the face of adverse court rulings and initiatives modeled after the Bertelsmann-Napster agreement, many users see the writing on the wall and are willing to accept whatever new scheme that Napster and others may offer, including paid subscription services. Many other users say that they will download music without payment from Napster's more elusive clones. Some will make limited use of these services in order to decide whether they would like to own a copy of an album while others will hold fast to the notion that this is a new technology and the old rules should not apply. Still others believe that continued unlimited downloading of copyrighted music is justifiable in the face of music industry price-fixing and institutional greed, which they believe is evidenced by current industry practice in the ownership and distribution of music.

Regardless of the benefits of this type of service, and of the widely varying points of view, it is clear that if the music swapping is unauthorized, it is copyright infringement. Whether or not the law should or will evolve to accommodate this new use has not yet been determined. However, the prudent entertainer should not turn a blind eye to the popularity of this service. In fact, some record labels are considering subscription services that would be similar in style to the service offered by Napster.

While the RIAA has been working feverishly to guard the industry's rights in this regard, it appears that their problems are only beginning. As previously mentioned, the Ninth Circuit Court of Appeals in February of 2001 affirmed a lower federal court's finding that Napster was engaging in copyright infringement and should be prevented from continuing this practice. From a legal standpoint, this is a significant victory for the music industry. But, as a practical matter, other more elusive online applications are likely to make the Napster issues pale in comparison.

Music Swapping after Napster

File swapping applications fall into two categories: centralized and decentralized (also called *open-source applications*). Basically, the difference is a matter of control. Centralized applications are run through a single organization. Therefore, when something goes wrong, the injured party has a company to point a finger at— like Napster. Scour is a similar centralized file-swapping service and is likely to have similar legal problems.

Although perhaps more difficult to use, Gnutella and Freenet may be the best known file swapping alternatives presently known. Unlike Napster and

Scour, these programs are decentralized and can be used to swap any type of file. Basically, this means that there is no one really responsible for the activities of the users. This bolsters the argument that these are simply programs that a large group of individual users utilizes to share information. There is no main server, no location where users have to go to search for files, and no limitation on the type of information that can be shared. More importantly, there is no one entity or web site for the RIAA or other potential plaintiffs to haul into court.

MP3 Players

The RIAA has also taken issue with MP3 players. In 1998, the RIAA sued Diamond Multimedia Systems, Inc. concerning its Rio MP3 player. The dispute in the RIAA's suit against Diamond centered around whether the Audio Home Recording Act, which applies to "digital audio recording devices," encompassed portable MP3 players. The classification of the player is important because of the duties that the Act places on manufacturers of such devices.

The Act requires that manufacturers of digital audio recording devices collect a royalty (called a "DART" royalty) that is then distributed to various types of recording industry participants, such as record labels, artists, and songwriters. The Act also requires that the manufacturers include technology within the device that is designed to prevent serial copying.

The RIAA filed for an injunction to prevent Diamond from manufacturing and distributing the Rio. However, the Ninth Circuit Court of Appeals held that the Rio is not a digital audio recording device. Therefore Diamond did not have to pay royalties or include the technology to prevent serial copying, although Diamond later began including such technology in the software that is used with the Rio.

The lower court had held that the reason the Rio is not a digital audio recording device is mainly due to the fact that the Rio did not have output capability from which copying could be accomplished. Considering that MP3 players with output capabilities are on the horizon, this ruling would not have held up for long. But, the Ninth Circuit Court of Appeals held that the Rio was not a digital audio recording device because, in essence, it does not record from a digital music recording. The court decided that a computer hard drive does not count as a digital music recording due to the other types of applications that a computer normally contains.

Keep in mind, however, that this is the Ninth Circuit's interpretation of the law and the surrounding circumstances. Until there is a more definitive ruling by statute or by the U.S. Supreme Court, the Ninth Circuit's ruling, while highly influential, only has the force of legal precedent in the states of California, Oregon, Washington, Arizona, Montana, Idaho, Nevada, Alaska, and Hawaii. One of the problems with this holding is that the court decided that the recording was made from the computer hard drive, rather than from the original file itself. This different perception may or may not have changed the outcome. In other words, this is entirely a matter of interpretation that is left to each of the eleven regional circuit courts of appeal. In the absence of an amendment to the Copyright Act or an on-point ruling from the United States Supreme Court, this particular issue, along with many more, will continue to create uncertainty in the cyberworld. Consequently, this issue is far from resolved.

Since the RIAA is claiming, on several fronts, that the technology is causing its constituents to lose revenue, providing for similar royalty payments makes sense. The Audio Home Recording Act allowed royalty payments from the machinery that made digital cassette recording possible, thereby covering some of the revenue lost due to home taping. Whether the law surrounding MP3 technology will move in the same direction remains to be seen.

Music "Beaming"

In addition to other pending suits, the RIAA is suing MP3.com over Instant Listening Service™ and Beam-It™. As noted in Chapter 3, these services allow customers of the site to either purchase music and store it at the web site, or to send music of their own to the site for storage. MP3.com has currently suspended both services while settlements are being negotiated.

The RIAA's primary concern is that the music being stored is not actually "uploaded" to the site. According to the complaint filed in this suit, MP3.com loaded music from thousands of compact discs onto its server without authorization from the copyright holders. The site then allowed users access to the uploaded material after verifying that the user owned a copy of the work, accomplished by inserting the compact disc into the computer's CD-ROM drive or receipt of a copy of the work after an online purchase. Therefore, rather than allowing users to "make copies" onto the site of works that the users were authorized to copy (by the Audio Home Recording Act, theoretically), MP3.com was actually using its own copies for a commercial purpose. Commercial use is explicitly excluded from the provisions of the Audio Home Recording Act, which provides only for private, home use.

The court agreed with the RIAA and granted a partial summary judgment (that is, the court granted judgment in the RIAA's favor as a matter of law without a trial), stating that MP3.com had committed copyright infringement. As of this writing, the parties have been in settlement negotiations since the partial summary judgment was granted, and MP3.com contends that it will restore the services once the parties have negotiated a satisfactory compromise.

Other Uses of MP3

Some MP3 sites provide less controversial uses for these files. These uses are worth noting because they contradict allegations that there is no way to put restrictions on MP3 use. One such site is MyPlay, which allows you to upload files from your hard drive to your account, meaning that you can listen to the files from any computer. However, any sharing of files is limited to streaming audio, meaning that you cannot actually make copies of the file. In addition, the program limits your ability to download MP3 files from the Web to your account. The site purports to block Web downloads that are not from "legal" sites.

A FINAL WORD OF ADVICE

In Chapter 8, we will discuss copyright licensing and how recent legislation has changed the way music is used. As you will see, the licensing process can range from simple to complex, depending upon the nature of the use. In any event, we urge you to keep abreast of unfolding developments in this fast-moving area of law and technology. Considering the ongoing litigation and the high-profile congressional hearings in this area, it is likely that the law in this area will continue to evolve at a brisk pace. If your business is affected by these developments, you unfortunately have little choice in the matter.

CHAPTER 8

Copyright Licensing on the Web

Copyright licensing is founded on the specific rights given to the copyright owner or proprietor under Section 106 of the Copyright Act. The holder of a copyright is authorized and given the exclusive right to: reproduce, prepare derivative works, distribute, perform publicly, and/or display the copyrighted work. If anyone else wishes to do one or more of these things with a copyrighted work, they must obtain authorization in the form of a license from the copyright holder before doing so. The most common licensed Internet usages of copyrighted materials include the use of photographs, images and other graphics, text, sound and video clips, and software programs.

When it comes to using copyrighted material on the Internet, recall from Chapter 5 that the safest way to protect yourself from potential liability for infringement is to seek a license from the copyright owner. This, of course, assumes that the work you seek to use is indeed protected by copyright. Since facts, concepts, ideas, and the like are not copyrightable, you are always free to use this type of material without fear of liability. Furthermore, obtaining a license is not necessary if the work you seek to use is already in the public domain. (The best example of a public-domain work is a copyrighted work whose term has expired.) If you are unsure as to the status of a copyright's term, asking the right questions or doing a little research will tell you whether a license is necessary. Finally, you will want to ensure that the work you seek to license is not available to you under some of the specific exceptions provided in the Copyright Act, such as the Fair Use Doctrine and the First Amendment. In the event that all of these avenues lead to a conclusion that the usage you wish to make would be restricted by the law of copyright, you will want to consider taking a license from the copyright owner.

THE BASICS OF LICENSING

A *license* is simply permission from the copyright owner or proprietor to use the protected work. Ownership of the copyright remains with the creator or proprietor, who is merely granting you limited permission to use that work on terms provided in the license. A simple example of this is your purchase of a compact disc, either as a download or in physical form. Although you are authorized to listen to the materials in your home, the separate bundle of rights embodied in the copyright, such as the right to play the materials in public and to reproduce and distribute them, remain with the owner. This permission, which can be exclusive or nonexclusive, is usually granted in exchange for some form of consideration or payment, but not always. When payment is required, it may be an up-front cash amount, a percentage of revenue, an in-kind exchange of goods or services, or a combination of all of these.

While there is often an exchange involved, there are also many instances of gratis or free licenses given by copyright owners. These free licenses may be motivated by an owner's desire for exposure of his or her material or it might represent an individual's support for a particular project in which you are involved. Usually, the only requirement in cases of gratis licensing is attribution of ownership to the licensor. The rule as to no-fee licenses is very simply this—*it never hurts to ask,* especially if the request is reasonable in light of the purpose.

Regardless of whether a fee is involved, your license will almost surely be limited by time, geography, and purpose, with the copyright owner retaining all remaining rights. Obviously, the greater the latitude of use, the more extensive the territory, and the longer the term, the greater the fee. Your task, then, is to negotiate for the right to use the copyrighted material only to the extent necessary and no more.

While ownership of the copyrighted work remains with the creator or proprietor, in the case of an exclusive license, you are being granted limited rights. Consequently, it is important to be very clear about how you intend to use the material, where, and for how long. There is no sense in paying for rights you have no intention of using. Since a license is nothing more or less than a contract, the limit of a licensing arrangement is your imagination.

THE STARTING POINT

Assuming you want to include copyrighted materials of others on your web site, where do you start? The first step is to determine who the copyright owner is and then to contact them, their agent, or representative to request a license. The copyright holder will want detailed information on exactly what you propose to do and to what degree the usage will result in financial return to determine whether to grant the license and to calculate the fee, if any, to be charged. For example, granting exclusive, worldwide, derivative motion picture rights to a John Grisham novel is a far cry from allowing the use of several lines of copyrighted song lyrics for inclusion on a college music department's web site. Context and character of the intended use together with exclusivity, term, and territory are always the determining factors. For this reason, you need to be prepared to provide specific details of the usage to the copyright holder.

To ensure that you are granted the most favorable terms, it is best to consider as many alternatives as possible should there be reluctance on the part of the copyright holder, or should the asking price be too high. It is important to communicate the fact that you have numerous alternatives early in the negotiating process; a copyright holder is more likely to give you a better deal if he or she is afraid that you might take a license from someone else. It is a basic rule of negotiation that the more uncertainty you can project, the more concessions you will gain. From a more positive standpoint, the more long-term benefits you can offer the copyright holder, the better your chances of success at affordable prices.

Assuming you are successful in obtaining a license, the copyright owner will undoubtedly want to restrict the permission granted to the specific use you propose while retaining all other rights which may later be licensed to others or withheld as the copyright owner sees fit to do. For instance, if you wish to use a copyrighted photograph on your web site, the terms of your license may allow you to do that, but may not allow you to sell or give copies of the work to others. The license will most likely not allow you the right to sublicense or authorize others to use the photograph on their web sites and usually will reserve the authority to grant licenses to other people for similar uses. Of course all this is based on your specific goals and your ability to negotiate accordingly.

Multiple Usage Licensing

One of the more difficult aspects of licensing is understanding that a single copyrighted work may have the potential for multiple uses, all of which must be separately licensed. For instance, consider all of the uses for John Grisham's novel, *The Client,* we discussed in Chapter 5. In addition to being used as a book, it was used for a screenplay and a television series. Furthermore, there can be several layers of rights within one work. For instance, if a web site has a clip of a motion picture with the soundtrack playing underneath, the layers of rights would include: the motion picture, the sound recording, and the underlying musical composition, all of which would require a license.

Categories of Licensed Works

Copyrighted works of authorship include a wide range of material, including literary works; pictorial, graphic, and sculptural works; and motion pictures and audiovisual works. Music is one of the leading categories of works for which licenses are sought both on and off the web. It is also the most complex. Music is protected in a number of ways. The composer may hold a copyright in the underlying music and lyrics. That same person, or another person or entity, may also hold a copyright in the inclusion of the music and lyrics into a sound recording. There are separate rights in the performance of the music to the public. Recent changes to the copyright law added a digital performance right for use on the Internet.

Compulsory Licensing

Generally, the copyright holder is not obligated to give you a license if that individual does not wish to do so. Consequently, if the copyright owner says no, you have no choice but to look elsewhere. This is why we advise you to be as flexible as possible by developing as many workable alternatives as you can. Better yet, it might be more cost effective in the long run to develop your own copyrighted material for which you will have to pay no fee and which you can use as you see fit.

While the copyright statute generally gives the copyright owner sole discretion as to whether to grant licenses for use of copyrighted material, there are certain statutory exceptions called *compulsory licenses*. Compulsory licenses are exactly that—licenses that the copyright owner is required to give at pre-set rates. If, for instance, you wanted to create your own recording of "Hey Jude" to play on your web site, you would request a license from the publisher and the publisher would be required to give you one, provided you agree to pay the rates set by statute and follow all of the rules. We'll discuss those rules below.

Compulsory licenses are an example of the balance of public and private rights. They protect private ownership in order to provide incentive for creativity and innovation, and they protect the legitimate interests of the public to use copyrighted works of authorship in certain circumstances, provided that a proper royalty is paid to the copyright owner for the use.

LICENSING MUSIC AND SOUND RECORDINGS

There are several different types of licenses that address the above-noted rights, including mechanical licenses, master use licenses, name and likeness licenses, and photographic copyright licenses. In the sections that follow, we will describe the rights that the licenses are meant to convey and the obligations that they place on the person requesting the right to use music and sound recordings.

Mechanical Licenses

A *mechanical license,* which gives an artist or record label the right to record a copyrighted composition ("mechanically reproduce"—hence the name "mechanical license") and then to distribute the recording to the public, is one of the two compulsory licenses that are addressed in the copyright statute. A songwriter may write a composition (music and lyrics), then assign the copyright to a publisher, who will be responsible for handling the administration of the composition. As part of the assignment of legal ownership to the music publisher, the publisher binds itself contractually to pay roughly half of the proceeds generated by the musical composition to the songwriter. When a recording artist wishes to make a recording of the composition, their record company must request a mechanical license in order to use the material.

Provided the composition has been previously recorded and distributed to the public, the artist or record company may take advantage of the compulsory mechanical licensing provisions of the Copyright Act. Copyright owners retain the important right to authorize or refuse an initial recording of the musical composition. By providing proper notification to either the copyright holder or by filing the notice with the copyright office if the holder cannot be found, the licensee can obtain the right to record and distribute the work, as long as the notice is filed within thirty days after making the recording and before the work is distributed. Thereafter, the artist's record company is obligated to pay a statutory royalty to the music publisher, which would later be split between the publisher and writer, subject to the previously mentioned contractual commitment.

To facilitate and streamline the process of compulsory mechanical licensing, most active music publishers utilize the services of the Harry Fox Agency in New York City to issue mechanical licenses and collect royalties on their behalf in exchange for a fee based on a small percentage of income collected. Users are encouraged to contact the Harry Fox Agency as a starting point in the compulsory licensing process. Another benefit of taking a Harry Fox license relates to terms superior to the Copyright Act. While there is no break on the amount of royalty paid, other items such as accounting requirements and exemption of royalty payments for records returned by a retailer will prove to be far superior to the statutory requirements.

The statutory royalty rate, which is periodically raised by special panels convened by the Copyright Office to keep pace with inflation, is currently 7.55 cents or 1.45 cents per minute of playing time or fraction thereof, whichever is greater, per record sold. The statutory mechanical rate is due to escalate to 8.0 cents or 1.55 cents per minute of playing time or fraction thereof, whichever is greater, on January 1, 2002. Thereafter, it will rise to 8.5 cents or 1.65 cents per minute, whichever is greater, on January 1, 2004, and to 9.1 cents or 1.75 cents per minute, whichever is greater, on January 1, 2006.

To illustrate how mechanical licensing works in the real world, let's assume that a band (we'll call them Chocolate Covered Gas Station) records their version of the previously recorded and released "Yesterday" by Lennon and McCartney, which happens to be the most recorded song in musical history. This new recording of the old Beatles standard is known as a *cover* in the music industry. Now let's assume that the new recording of "Yesterday" is posted on the Official Chocolate Covered Gas Station web site for their fans and other users to download. This particular type of usage would constitute the recording and distribution of a copyrighted musical composition written by Lennon and

McCartney and published by Sony/ATV Tunes, LLC, the legal owner of the Beatles catalog, and would thus require a mechanical license. Assuming that Chocolate Covered Gas Station followed all of the requirements set out in the copyright laws, the copyright owner could not deny them the license no matter how much they disliked the band, its name, the particular recording, or all of the above. This new measure of choice and freedom sums up the value of compulsory licensing to artists who would otherwise run the risk that copyright owners could either play favorites or withdraw valuable elements of our popular musical culture altogether.

Mechanical licensing allows the marketplace, rather than the copyright owner, to determine the value of the cover version of a previously recorded and released composition. As musical history indicates, many cover recordings have gone on to eclipse the original composition both artistically and financially. Just ask any Marvin Gaye fan which version of "I Heard It Through The Grapevine" they prefer, the original by Gladys Knight or the cover by Marvin Gaye. In the end, popular culture is the real winner.

Master Use Licenses

A master use license is a license to use a specific, pre-recorded version of a composition. For purposes of illustration, return to our example of "Yesterday," originally recorded by the Beatles and subsequently covered by Chocolate Covered Gas Station. Let's now assume that Chocolate Covered Gas Station's cover recording begins getting airplay, which generates sales. And let's assume, as is increasingly the case, that a regional promotion man for Capitol Records, which also happens to be the Beatles' record company, learns about the buzz being caused by the record. Based on the record's potential, the promotion man takes this news back to Capitol Records. As a result, assume the label wants to make a deal with the band to purchase the band's original recording and release it nationally. As we noted in our previous example, Chocolate Covered Gas Station has already taken a valid mechanical license from the Beatles music publishing company to record and distribute the Lennon and McCartney song.

So, let's assume the group sees Capitol's offer to distribute their song as their big break and decides to sign with the label, their first release being their cover version of "Yesterday." As part of the recording contract, Capitol requires the group to assign (that is, to completely relinquish the band's rights to the label) the copyright in their recording of the song in exchange for a royalty agreement. While the band agrees to this provision, obviously, the copyright owner of the Lennon and McCartney song remains the original music publisher, who is bound to pay a contractual writer's share to Paul McCartney and the Estate of John Lennon. Assume the record is released and experiences moderate success. Royalties are paid by the record company to both the music publisher and the artist.

Now let's further assume that, a year later, Direct Market Corporation (DMC), a company devoted to record distribution for special products that markets via cable television and satellite advertising, wishes to reproduce the Chocolate Covered Gas Station version of "Yesterday" as part of its *Salute To The Beatles* CD. This proposed tribute album will contain 20 Beatles hits previously recorded and released by various artists and will be sold by direct marketing on cable and satellite television. Before they can produce, market, and sell the tribute album, DRC would have to contact the Capitol Records business affairs department to seek a master use license for the Chocolate Covered Gas Station version of "Yesterday." Unlike the compulsory mechanical license, which permitted Chocolate Covered Gas Station to record "Yesterday" in the first place, the new copyright proprietor of the sound recording, Capitol Records, could refuse DMC's request, reasoning that they may want to do their own special products tribute album in the future. In this instance, DMC would then be unable to use the Gas Station version of the song.

In most instances, once a record has been released, most record labels view such special products requests as representing an opportunity to create new income streams from catalog material that would otherwise not exist. This is why you see so many repackaged cassette tape and CD offers on television. It is simply a cost-effective way for everyone concerned (new label, old label, artists, and writers) to realize more income. In the usual deal, DMC would pay an upfront advance against a recoupable share of the income generated by the new tribute album.

Name and Likeness Licenses

With both a compulsory mechanical license and master use license in place, you would think that DMC is now ready to press CDs and begin buying cheap cable and satellite time in the wee hours of the morning. But, not so fast. Let's assume that DMC wants to use the name Chocolate Covered Gas Station in its promotional material beyond a mere factual listing of the group's name of the record. Let's suppose that DMC also wants to include a picture of the group on its liner note insert material and on the television ads they will be running as part of their marketing campaign. Consequently, it will be necessary to get the permission of the group to use its name, likeness, and photograph.

It is important to note that this right stems from a state law doctrine known as the Right of Publicity and not from the federal law of Copyright. The Right of Publicity effectively gives celebrities the right to control and profit from the commercial exploitation of incidents of their identity including their name, likeness, and photograph.

The good news here is that name and likeness licenses are usually a standard feature of the recording contract between the band and the record company that would then allow Capitol Records to authorize these uses in connection with the sale and marketing of the tribute album. This specific permission is usually included in the master use license. However, a word of caution is in order. Don't assume this is done as a matter of course. Always ask.

Photographic Copyright Licenses

Finally, just because the record company and group grant DMC permission to use the band's name and likeness, that doesn't necessarily mean that DMC owns or controls copyrighted photographs of the group either as an assignee of a freelance photographer or on a work for hire basis. Although this is often the case, to cite the first rule of law school—*Never Assume Anything!* In this instance, it just so happens that a famous independent photographer specializing in rock groups took the photos of the band. These photos are the subject of copyright which the photographer retained while giving the band a non-exclusive license to use to promote and market themselves. In exchange for a reduced fee, the band gave the photographer a name and likeness license. Because of his fame in the rock music industry, the photographer had the bargaining power to strike the deal. Consequently, DMC would either have to make a deal with the photographer to use his photos or find and license other images of Chocolate Covered Gas Station.

But let's assume that DMC is inclined to do neither. Determined to avoid dealing with the photographer while still getting the benefit of the exact pose that the company feels would play a major role in the commercial success of the proposed tribute album, DMC hires its own photographer. With the cooperation of the band members, who are excited by the prospect of what the tribute CD could do for their career, DMC dresses and poses the band to get an almost verbatim substitute of the famous photographer's photograph. While admittedly clever from a marketing standpoint, the legal consequence of DMC's substitute photo shoot would be liability for copyright infringement based on unauthorized copying. This just goes to show that copying can be done in a variety of ways. Copying is still copying, no matter how cleverly done. If DMC wants to do it right, they need to create a photograph that is unique.

MUSIC USE AND LICENSING ON THE INTERNET

The use of music on the Internet is not nearly as clear as our more traditional previous example. Although, seemingly, the posting of a song for download would have the same effect as the reproduction and distribution of the song, it is not that simple. As the following discussion indicates, a download is *both* a performance *and* a reproduction as well as a distribution. Whether a master use license is necessary for Internet use is legally unclear.

Synchronization/Videogram Licenses

A *synchronization license* is a license to use a musical composition in conjunction with video. If you wish to combine a copyrighted musical composition with video for broadcast on your web site, then a synchronization license is necessary. A *videogram license* is a license that allows the synchronized work itself to be copied and distributed to the public. When you have only a synchronization license, you can neither reproduce nor distribute the song without the video for which the license is granted. Returning to our example, then, in order to post their video of their cover version of "Yesterday," Chocolate Covered Gas Station would need both a synchronization license and a videogram license.

Print Licenses

Let's now assume that you are a big fan of Chocolate Covered Gas Station, and that you would like your web site to post music and lyrics from one of their songs in printed form. To do so, you would first need to obtain a print license, which would need to include both the right to reproduce and the right to display the printed music. A print license covers the right to reproduce printed copies of music and lyrics (such as sheet music).

Performance and Digital Performance Licenses

In addition to other rights reserved by a songwriter, there exists a right to publicly perform his or her composition. This includes not only live performances, but also the playing of the composition on the radio, on television, and in restaurants, nightclubs, and the like. Therefore, any entity that chooses to play music in its establishment must obtain a license from every composer (or the music publisher) of every song it plays. Needless to add, this would be an impossibly cumbersome process for both the establishment and the composer, who would have to individually license literally thousands of such establishments and broadcasters. The transactional costs of user-to-owner licensing would effectively take the profit out of the music business. What was needed to facilitate this process was a mechanism to serve as a clearinghouse for music performance licensing.

This practical problem is why the so-called performance rights societies were created. The three best-known are the American Society of Composers, Artists and Publishers (ASCAP), Broadcast Music, Inc. (BMI), and the Society of European Stage Authors and Composers (SESAC). Songwriters and publishers assign the performance rights to their songs to these societies so that the society may issue licenses and collect royalties on their behalf. The societies, in turn, license all entities that play music in each society's catalog and charge those entities blanket fees for the performance of those songs.

Every television network, radio and television station, concert hall, college and university, and other commercial entity that uses music on their telephone "hold" system must obtain licenses from one or more (often all three) of the performing rights societies in exchange for a nominal percentage of the music-user's income. If, therefore, a radio station or a restaurant wants the right to play all music of any given genre, it would need a license from each performance society, since it would not be limiting its play to one particular society's catalog. Obviously, considering the ubiquitous role of music in the entertainment-driven world economy, it follows that performing income is substantial. To give you some idea of its importance to copyright owners and proprietors, the total domestic U.S. license fees paid to ASCAP, BMI, and SESAC top one billion dollars annually.

Once performances move onto the Internet, the licensing gets tricky. Until recently, if a web site wished to play music on its site, a license from the appropriate performance right society was sufficient—there was no exclusive performance right in the sound recordings. However, the Digital Performance Rights in Sound Recordings Act and the Digital Millennium Copyright Act created a "digital performance right" for copyright owners of sound recordings. The digital performance right encompasses *digital audio transmissions,* which are cable, satellite, or Internet transmissions. This right is specifically excluded when the transmission is part of an audio-visual product. Therefore, when transmitting video combined with an audio component, the copyright owner of the sound recording does not have a digital performance right.

Statutory licenses are licenses that the copyright holder—in this case, the record company or whoever produced the sound recording—is required to give. Statutory digital performance licenses are available to music providers that meet certain criteria, such as providers that do not use interactive services or that do not give advance notice of what music will be played. Otherwise, the licenses are completely at the discretion of the copyright owner of the sound recording.

To illustrate this problem, let's assume that Elevator Music Corporation (EMC), a music service division of DMC (who is not a music provider), commissioned an "easy listening" instrumental cover of "Yesterday" it intended to market to businesses and office buildings as background music via its web site on the Internet. In addition to a compulsory mechanical license for recording a new cover version of the song, and a performance license from the appropriate performance rights society, it would also need a digital performance license from the copyright proprietor of the new cover recording of "Yesterday."

Because this license is not statutory, EMC would have to negotiate with the copyright owner of the sound recording (although there are certain limitations even on negotiated licenses). As you can well imagine, this has the potential to create many problems. Unlike a performance license, which can be issued for an entire catalog of music by a performance rights society, a digital performance license requires separate negotiations for each song with each person holding the copyright for a sound recording. Although EMC would only have to negotiate one license, a record company would have to negotiate countless numbers of them. If EMC actually wanted to use a different song for each of the ten pages on its site, it also might have to negotiate ten separate licenses with ten different record labels.

Furthermore, because of the way that Internet technology works, a performance license is necessary whether the composition is transmitted via streaming audio or as a downloaded file. In order to understand why multiple types of licenses are necessary for Internet use, when they are not necessary for non-digital use, an explanation of the distinction between downloading and streaming should prove helpful.

Downloading involves taking a complete file, depositing it on the computer's hard drive, then stopping the transaction. When you play the file that has been downloaded, you can do so without the Internet connection. However, media files generally are very large and would take a great deal of time to download and a great deal of space to store. There is also the patience factor in that most users want to view the file quickly and move on, rather than storing and retrieving it.

Streaming audio, or video for that matter, is a real-time transmission. The computer processes and displays the file as the file is fed to the computer, and no permanent copy is made. In addition, since the computer is only processing parts of the file at a time, the size is not as much of an issue, however, most media files still use the compression discussed in Chapter 7 in order to reduce the size of the file.

Although there are notable differences, downloading can be compared to purchasing a compact disc, taking it home, then playing it, whereas streaming can be compared to a radio broadcast. The two most obvious questions, then, are: (1) why do songwriters and publishers get a performance right in downloads that they do not have for non-Internet sales/transfers; and (2) why do record companies get a digital performance right in streaming audio when they do not have one in regular broadcast transmissions?

Performance rights in downloaded materials. As noted above, downloads have elements of reproduction, distribution, and performance. A downloadable file exists on the sender's web site. In order for you to download the file, you usually click a hyperlink or icon, and the site transfers a copy of the file onto your computer. Therefore, it can be argued that a download is not a "performance" but a reproduction and distribution of copies to multiple private users for home use.

However, on the other hand, Internet transmissions are just that—transmissions defined by the Copyright Act as a communication by a process that allows images/sounds to be received beyond the place from which they are sent. According to the Copyright Act, a public performance has taken place whenever a transmission of a work occurs. Therefore, the answer lies in the delivery of the copyrighted work. If you go to the store and pick up a compact disc, no transmission has to occur for you to get your music. On the Internet, transmission is unavoidable.

Digital performance rights in streaming audio. In the same manner that downloads have elements of performances, streaming audio has elements of reproduction and distribution. When streaming media is transmitted to you, your computer makes a temporary copy of the file in its random access memory (RAM) in order to be able to process the file. Once the file is finished playing, the RAM disposes of it. The file has thus been reproduced, even if only briefly, and distributed to your computer.

The Digital Performance Right and the Right to Reproduce/Distribute

As noted above, it is not entirely clear whether the digital performance right is intended to complement or supersede the right of reproduction and distribution that would be addressed by a master use license. A reproduction and distribution occurs whenever audio files are streamed or downloaded to a user.

Since the new laws do not specifically revoke this right on the Internet, it would appear that a master use license would be required to use a sound recording on the Internet in addition to a digital performance license. However, requiring the master use license in addition to the digital performance license would effectively gut the obligatory provisions of the law—a record company that is required to grant digital performance rights could still prevent use on the Internet by simply denying the right to use its masters. As of yet, this has not proven to be a major problem. If, however, you find yourself on the wrong end of a license negotiation in this regard, a lawsuit to interpret the statute could be your only recourse.

Statutory Licenses for Digital Performance Rights

A brief listing of some aspects of the statutory licensing provisions may prove helpful. Statutory licenses are not available to web sites that:

* allow users to select which song they wish to hear (i.e., interactive services)
* cause the recipient to automatically switch between program channels (unless the recipient is a "business establishment")
* publish playlists or other advance notice of what music will be played
* do not provide certain identifying information (such as song title, artist, etc.)
* do not meet certain programming requirements (for instance, pre-produced programs cannot be less than 3 hours long and, if archived, cannot be less than 5 hours long)
* simultaneously transmit video that is likely to confuse the audience as to the association of the copyright holder or artist with the web site
* affirmatively cause recipients to copy the recording
* transmit recordings that have not previously been distributed to the public, or
* interfere with transmission of technical identification procedures.

In addition, there are term restrictions on exclusive licenses to interactive services under certain circumstances. However, these restrictions do not apply when a single holder of sound-recording copyrights has granted licenses to at least five different interactive services covering ten percent or more of the holder's sound recording copyrights (but no less than fifty recordings), or when a company that resells music licenses sound clips in order to promote sales of those same sound recordings. Finally, no statutory license, exclusive or non-exclusive, is effective unless a performance license has been obtained for the underlying composition.

This is only a very rough outline of the statutory licensing provisions for the digital performance of sound recordings. If there is any generalization that can be made in this area, it is that statutory licenses are largely for webcasters. If your site offers music for download, statutory licenses are not available and your terms may be limited in duration. The laws in this area are extremely complicated and are largely beyond the scope of this discussion. If you think that the statutory license provisions may apply to you and would like to take advantage of them, you should consult with an attorney who has knowledge of music licensing on the Internet.

Other Licenses

There are a few other licenses that are worth noting. If a web site is to post a movie clip, then it must have an exhibition license in order to show the clip. In addition, as discussed above, since the clip would be copied onto the user's computer, a reproduction license would also be necessary. If the movie clip contains recorded music, all of the licensing rules for music would apply.

If web site owners create their own videos, naturally, they do not have to license them from themselves. However, they need to obtain name and likeness releases from any individuals shown in the video or from the owners of distinct locations or objects that do not belong to them. Additionally, if the video shows copyrighted works within it, then licenses covering the use of those works are required.

LICENSES REQUIRED FOR COPYRIGHTED MATERIAL

Because it is essential that you understand what kinds of licenses may be necessary for Internet use of copyrighted materials, especially music, we have provided the list that follows. When reviewing this list, note that "song" refers to a musical composition that will be re-recorded by the web site owner and "recording" refers to a site's use of a prerecorded composition. Also note that due to the uncertainty surrounding the sound recording reproduction rights on the Internet, master use licenses may or may not be necessary when digital performance rights are involved, but are included for illustrative purposes.

Use of a song for background music on a web site:
* Mechanical license from composer/publisher
* Performance license from composer/publisher or performance right society

Use of recording for background music on a web site:
* Master use license from record company
* Performance license from composer/publisher or performance right society
* Digital performance license from record company

Use of a song in conjunction with a video:
* Video synchronization/videogram license from composer/publisher
* Performance license from composer/publisher or performance right society

Use of a recording in conjunction with a video:
* Video synchronization/videogram license from composer/publisher
* Master use license from record company
* Performance license from composer/publisher or performance right society

Offering a song for download:
* Mechanical license from composer/publisher
* Performance license from composer/publisher or performance right society

Offering a recording for download:
* ★ Master use license from record company
* ★ Performance license from composer/publisher or performance right society
* ★ Digital performance license from record company

Offering a song in conjunction with a video for download:
* ★ Video synchronization/videogram license from composer/publisher
* ★ Performance license from composer/publisher or performance right society

Offering a recording in conjunction with a video for download:
* ★ Video synchronization/videogram license from composer/publisher
* ★ Master use license from the recording company
* ★ Performance license from composer/publisher or performance right society

Webcasting:
* ★ Master use license from record company
* ★ Performance license from composer/publisher or performance right society
* ★ Digital performance license from record company

A FINAL WORD OF ADVICE

As the material in this chapter suggests, the legal and business considerations involved in copyright licensing are often complex, uncertain, and highly technical. Indeed, even lawyers who do not practice in the areas of intellectual property and the evolving specialty of Internet Law routinely defer to specialists when it comes to many of the issues and questions posed here. Our goal is not to make you an intellectual property law expert, but to instill in you an awareness of the basic issues and responsibilities faced by Internet users. In the best of all worlds you will be better able to handle routine licensing issues yourself while seeking out the advice of legal specialists when appropriate. At the very least you will know where to start, what to look for, and how to approach the legal side of your web-based business or usage with more confidence and sophistication. In the end, this material should help you be more proactive in your approach to the Internet. It should also help you to avoid traps and to dodge problems that plague those who choose to operate in the dark when it comes to issues related to copyright law. However, as we have stated before, a consultation with an Internet attorney would be well worth the time and money if you are considering uses in this area.

CHAPTER 9

Trademark and Unfair Competition Law: Navigating Trade Identity Issues on the Net

A *trademark* is any word, name, symbol, device, or other designation, or a combination of designations that identifies a person's goods or services and distinguishes them from the goods and services of others. Similarly, a *service mark,* also covered under trademark law, distinguishes services. As the definition indicates, the sole purpose of a trademark or service mark is to identify the source of those goods or services.

The essence of trademark law is the prevention of consumer confusion resulting in unfair competition. Trademarks, both registered and unregistered, have long been protected on the federal and state level by statutory as well as common law.

THE FUNCTIONS OF TRADEMARK LAW

In the classic trademark infringement scenario, a seller of goods or services (Company B) adopts and uses a name, logo, slogan, or even a product-packaging scheme or configuration of goods first used by a competitor (Company A). Due to the competing or related nature of the products or services combined with the confusingly similar appearance, sound, or meaning of the two marks, packaging scheme, or product configuration, an unwary consumer mistakenly buys Company B's product or service thinking it is Company A's. This is known as "passing off," which is the basic harm trademark and unfair competition law seeks to prevent. As this scenario clearly indicates, consumer confusion results not only in a displaced sale, but also, most likely, erosion of goodwill. Consumers' goodwill toward a company is affected by the dissatisfaction that follows from buying a product that is either inferior to or different from the original.

Trademark law performs two functions. First, to combat passing off, it provides private property rights to the first user of a distinctive mark, but only to the extent that the mark is actually used to sell specific goods or services. This differs from a copyright in that no absolute monopoly is granted to the first person to use a mark. Consequently, the same or similar trademarks can be owned by more than one entity provided that they operate in different product or geographic markets that would preclude consumer confusion. For instance, both Delta Airlines and Delta Faucets own trademark rights in the same mark—Delta. However, these trademark rights exist for non-competing, dissimilar products. Consequently, no reasonable person would think that an airline would also be engaged in the plumbing fixture-business.

The second function of trademark law is consumer protection. By giving first users priority over second comers to use the same or confusingly similar marks, trademark law helps minimize consumer confusion in the marketplace. As a result, consumers are allowed to select the products they want to buy based on quality and reputation rather than mistake and deception.

In addition to private property and consumer protection, trademarks also perform a valuable marketing function. For example, two of the best-known trademarks in the computer hardware industry are DELL and HEWLETT PACKARD. These respective product names let consumers know which company produced which product. Based on public association between the products and the trademark under which they are sold, the parent companies enjoy a substantial marketing advantage based on accumulated good will. Rather than having to go into laborious detail to explain the specific qualities and attributes of their product, a shorthand reference to DELL or HEWLETT PACKARD instantly tells the public not only what the product is, but also how well it will perform. Based on years of strong public association, these trade-marks act as an assurance of quality while also performing an advertising function that fosters brand loyalty. We all have preferences and expectations about the products we use. Because of these preferences, we depend on trademarks or product brands to guide us to the goods we want to buy. Consequently, a trademark literally becomes a vehicle that can capture and store all of this accu-mulated, albeit intangible, goodwill in a product.

The more advertising dollars spent on a product, the more sales and the greater the association between the product and the trademark or service mark. This success is measured in goodwill that is generated in the product. Contrary to the belief that advertising is wasted once the television or radio spot runs, every time an ad runs, the goodwill increases. This residual goodwill is captured and held in the trademark, making it a stronger more universally known brand each time it is exposed to the public. The more marketing succeeds, the stronger the mark gets and the more the law protects it. This is why Microsoft, IBM, Coke, and Pepsi are so well known.

THE VALUE OF A TRADEMARK

Like copyrights, trademarks can be extremely valuable business assets that companies will go to great lengths to protect. If there is any doubt as to the potential value of a trademark, we pose this simple question: How much do you think the Microsoft Corporation's mark MICROSOFT is worth? Put another way, what would the Washington-based software giant accept on the open market for a mark that is one of the most recognizable trademarks in the world? The respective answers are "priceless" and "they wouldn't accept anything under any circumstances." This suggests that the company would go to just about any lengths to protect its trademark. The same is true of other famous marks that have become worldwide icons of popular culture such as COCA-COLA, McDONALD'S, or NIKE. All of these companies have the resolve and the resources to protect what is arguably their most valuable corporate asset.

There is very little to suggest that the Internet is likely to change either the law or corporate resolve of the owners of the marks mentioned above. Consequently, you must know the law if you want to avoid unwanted trouble. And if you are a fledgling e-commerce entrepreneur, you need to know how to best select and develop a trademark or service mark that may one day be your single most valuable business asset.

THE BASICS OF TRADEMARK LAW

Although the Internet has put a new spin on an old concept, the basic rules of trademark law are still the same. They are especially important to anyone involved in e-commerce selling goods and services over the Net. As in the brick-and-mortar world, it is vital that cyber-merchants be able to effectively brand their goods and services by selecting marks and trade identities that are eligible for the greatest measure of protection possible.

Equally important is your ability to avoid liability for infringing trademarks belonging to others or engaging in other activities and uses prohibited by trademark law. While the Internet is an efficient and cost-effective way to reach a potential worldwide audience, it also increases the likelihood of problems related to the law of trademarks. For this reason, it is essential that you undertake a crash course in trademark law. Although this is an extremely complicated area of law largely dependent on the specific context and facts of a given situation, the basic rules are fairly simple. Please note that, while we seek to raise your awareness of the basics, the following information is not intended as a substitute for legal counsel from an attorney specializing in the law of trademarks and unfair competition.

Differentiating a Trademark from a Tradename

As defined earlier in this chapter, a trademark is any word, name, symbol, device, or other designation, or a combination of designations, that identifies a person's goods or services and distinguishes them from the goods and services of others. A *tradename,* on the other hand, is simply the name of the entity under which a business operates. Although often the source of confusion, it should be clear that tradenames and trademarks are not interchangeable terms. They serve distinctly different functions with tradenames receiving protection without regard to the advertising and sale of specific goods and services. Consequently, the fact that a corporation, limited liability company, partnership, or sole proprietorship bears a name confusingly similar to a specific product brand name does not necessarily mean that a trademark issue exists.

As an example of the difference between a tradename and a trademark, consider the McDonald's Corporation. McDonald's Corporation is the tradename of the international food services corporation headquartered in Oak Brook, Illinois. The tradename is registered with the Corporations Division of the Delaware Secretary of State. As a result, no other company can form a corporation under the law of Delaware under that name. The company owns a family of famous trademarks by which its specific products and overall services are advertised to the public. Some of the more famous marks include "Big Mac" for its popular sandwich, the Golden Arches logo, and the character Ronald McDonald who advertises the company's restaurant services.

While the word McDonald's comprises the tradename of the famous company, it simultaneously serves a service-mark function by which the company's overall restaurant services are advertised to the public. The service marks and trademarks form the basis of the corporation's franchising operations. A franchise is essentially nothing more than the license of a trademark, which instantly gives a franchisee the benefit of all the goodwill and brand identification a company has accumulated since it commenced business. Today, McDonald's Corporation operates or franchises some 28,000 restaurants in 120 countries, making it the largest food services company in the world, thanks in large part to its well-known tradename and family of famous trademarks and service marks. By going to www.McDonalds.com, you can see all of these famous marks on the web, which is increasingly the vehicle for worldwide marketing of products and services.

Contrast the McDonald's example with the Cincinnati-based consumer product giant Procter & Gamble. Proctor & Gamble is the tradename of the corporation. Its family of famous consumer product trademarks includes "Bounty" for paper towels, "Crest" for toothpaste; "Tide" for laundry detergent; "Crisco" for shortening; and "Head & Shoulders" for shampoo. Procter & Gamble offers no product under the trademark Procter & Gamble, rather relying upon its family of individual product marks. As a result, Procter & Gamble only functions as a tradename with no product specific trademark significance.

The Scope and Hierarchy of Trademark Protection

As we discussed in Chapter 5, a copyright gives the creator or proprietor world-wide exclusive rights to exercise, or even refrain from exercising, any of the rights provided by law. Trademark rights, on the other hand, coincide only with actual use. This means that the right to prevent others from using confusingly similar marks can only be enforced within the product and geographic market in which the business operates. McDonald's and Coca-Cola, by virtue of their worldwide marketing and distribution, can assert their trademarks not only in the United States but in most other nations of the world by virtue of treaties giving reciprocal rights to other signatory countries. On the other hand, a local mom-and-pop hamburger stand or local soft drink company can only assert rights to its marks in the particular city or region that the mark is used. As these local and regional businesses extend their reach, their trademark rights follow.

Use within Geographical and Product Markets

Prior to the arrival of the Internet, it was common to encounter businesses selling similar goods and services under the same or similar marks in local or regional geographic markets, usually without knowledge of other uses of that mark. Since there was an absence of likely confusion, these usages peacefully coexisted in their respective markets. Because the Internet has radically redefined the concept of "local," geographic markets are now increasingly national and even international. This has lessened the importance of the geographic market, especially in areas that are inherently local in nature such as restaurants, dry cleaners, real-estate brokers, and hundreds of other small businesses that now operate as franchises under a well-known national trademark or service mark.

However, the Internet has had little effect on product markets. As a result, trademark rights continue to be limited to specific product markets. This means that Delta Airlines and Delta Faucets can co-exist in a national market without any problem of consumer confusion. Both companies are said to be the owners of their trademarks even though they consist of the identical word or term.

Although product markets involving competing goods offer the clearest example of creating likely consumer confusion, it is difficult to tell businesses exactly how far their rights extend. For instance, it is clear that two companies selling floppy disks cannot do so under a confusingly similar mark. But what about one company that sells floppy disks and another that sells computer software? These are totally different products, but they are nonetheless related. It is quite likely that an appreciable number of consumers might simply think that the software seller had branched out into the blank disk business as well. As a result, the test of likelihood of confusion is extended to related products that while not competing can nevertheless result in some confusion.

Other examples where courts have found infringement in related product cases include locks and flashlights, high-fashion women's scarves and sportswear, and cosmetics and toiletries. On the other hand, it has been held that products such as men's golf jackets and women's coats, women's footwear and women's sportswear, and comb and brush cleaner for women and men and hairspray for men are not related.

Establishing Priority and Concurrent Uses

Trademark rights reach only as far as the product and geographical market they serve. While it is true that the registration of a trademark or service mark gives the registrant the exclusive right to use that mark, this does not necessarily mean that a mark owner can prevent someone else's use of the same or similar mark on the same goods or related goods in a separate geographic market. The reason is that infringement exists only where there is likelihood of consumer confusion. If goods or services are offered in a separate geographic market (keeping in mind the lack of geographic constraints on the Internet), no likelihood of confusion exists. However, once you expand your business into a geographic market occupied by a second comer, an injunction will usually be issued in your favor.

A common trademark issue relates to a first user who chooses not to register and a second user who is the first to register. Since the Lanham Act favors registration, the second user registrant receives exclusive nationwide rights to use the mark, except in the territory actually occupied by the first user. In effect, the first user is frozen into its existing area of usage, making expansion of his business impossible. These rules provide yet another compelling reason to adopt a mark that is "clean" in terms of other uses, followed quickly by registration.

However, consider the concept of "territory" as applied to the Internet. Traditionally, territory has been defined as the area in which the first user actually operated. If, for instance, the first user operated a store in Jacksonville, Florida, then he or she would be allowed to continue to operate in the original location, without interference from the second user, but could never expand the business by opening other locations. As we have noted, the Internet has no territorial boundaries. Therefore, it would appear that a first user on the Internet would be allowed to continue Internet operations without interference from a second user who held a registration for the mark. This would give the first user potentially unlimited territory, despite failure to register. Although this problem has yet to be addressed from a straight trademark standpoint, the problem has been resolved, sometimes unfairly, in favor of the second user in the area of trademarked domain names, as you will see in Chapter 10.

Not All Trademarks Are Created Equal

In addition to the concept that trademark rights only exist with use in a defined product and geographic market, you should be aware that the amount of protection a court will provide is in direct relation to the strength of your mark in the market place. Put another way, not all marks are accorded equal measures of protection. The more distinctive your mark is, the greater the protection to which you will be entitled. As a result, great care should be given to the mark you select. The more inherently distinctive it is, the sooner you will be able to register it in the Patent and Trademark Office. Of course, most marks can become distinctive through years of use and millions of dollars in marketing expenditures. But if you are a start-up e-commerce Internet-based company, do you have the time and resources to devote to this process? Back in the late '90s at the height of the dot-com public offering frenzy, plenty of would-be entrepreneurs could answer affirmatively to this question, but not any more.

In 1976 the Second Circuit Court of Appeals in *Abercrombie & Fitch v. Hunting World, Inc.* set forth a hierarchy of protection in ascending order from marks that are never accorded protection to the highest degree of trademark and service mark protection available.

Generically descriptive marks. A generically descriptive mark can never be protected as a trademark and should thus always be avoided. Our favorite example of a generically descriptive mark is a college luncheon spot known only for its sign that proclaimed, "Eat." Even though everybody knew of the greasy spoon café that sold hamburgers cheap, the owner could certainly not prevent other competitors from using the same term for a café or restaurant because of the unfair competitive disadvantage it would create. Other examples of unprotectable generic marks include "floppy" for a data storage disk, "automobile" for motor vehicles, or "ivory" when used to describe a product made from elephant tusks. In effect, the first competitor to adopt and use automobile as a trademark for motor vehicles would short-circuit competitors from accurately describing their products. Since generic marks are always in the public domain, free for use by anyone, a business would always want to steer clear of anything that could be construed as being generically descriptive. Conversely, you are always free to use a generically descriptive mark without fear of liability for trademark infringement. Unfortunately, unwary business owners violate this basic tenet of trademark every day by adopting generic names for their businesses. Just leaf through the yellow pages of any American city for a ready illustration. When it comes to choosing a name for your web-based business, we urge you not to make the same mistake.

Merely descriptive marks. A merely descriptive mark conveys an immediate idea of the ingredients, qualities, or characteristics of the trademarked product.

Here, the description falls short of being generic, yet is still not inherently distinctive. As a result, it is thus ineligible for trademark protection unless and until it develops a secondary meaning with consumers who use it. Secondary meaning or acquired distinctiveness occurs when the mark is used by a significant segment of consumers who through use and familiarity with the product come to uniquely associate the mark or term with the goods or services of the seller, notwithstanding its descriptive properties.

As an example, consider the retailer BEST BUY for electronic consumer goods. Without secondary meaning, the term advises consumers that this is a retail store that offers the best in price and quality. However, this is merely descriptive of the service. Through longstanding use and national advertising, most Americans would identify BEST BUY as a specific chain of retail stores. Consequently, the term has acquired distinctiveness and is eligible for trademark protection.

One of the benefits of using a merely descriptive mark is that it serves an informational function by telling potential buyers what the product does. The downside is that it is not protectable until it achieves secondary meaning. Since the process of achieving secondary meaning via the doctrine of acquired distinctiveness can be time consuming and expensive, you are best advised to avoid selecting a merely descriptive mark under which to market your goods and services.

It should be noted that in order to qualify for registration under the Lanham Act, marks that are primarily geographically descriptive (such as a mark for "Silicon Valley Software") or which are primarily merely a surname (such as McDonald) are treated the same as merely descriptive marks. This means that these types of marks must achieve secondary meaning before they will be registered. As far as other unregistered marks, they might still qualify for state law protection. However, given the significant benefits of a federal Lanham Act registration, we recommend adoption of a mark that will qualify for immediate registration.

Suggestive marks. For merchants who want the benefits that come from an informational mark, yet who also want a mark that is considered inherently distinctive by the Trademark Examiner and is thus immediately registrable without a showing of secondary meaning, a suggestive mark is the answer. A term is considered suggestive for trademark purposes if it requires imagination, thought, and perception to reach a conclusion as to the nature of the goods. An example would be "Windows Cleaner" for a program that erases unnecessary temporary files from your operating system. The product name would be considered merely descriptive if it was called "Temporary File Remover for Windows." In the second case, the name directly refers to a characteristic of the program. Since no imagination is needed, a trademark examiner would refuse the second slogan registration without secondary meaning.

Arbitrary marks. These are marks made up of familiar words or terms that bear no relation to the ingredients, qualities, or characteristics of the goods and services to which they are attached. Examples include AMAZON.COM for online retail sales or APPLE for computers. While the Amazon River is a well-known river in South America, the word has absolutely nothing to do with online retail sales. Similarly, apple is generic as applied to fruit, but has nothing to do with computers. Therefore, it is said that the use is arbitrary. Arbitrary marks are considered very strong and entitled to greater protection than other types of marks previously discussed. Other examples of arbitrary marks include CREST for toothpaste and BOUNTY for paper towels.

Fanciful marks. These marks are the strongest because they are in effect coined words that do not exist in conventional language and thus can have no relation to the specific goods or services offered to sale. Examples include EXXON, KODAK, and XEROX; all are now well-known trademarks, but initially meant nothing to any potential consumer.

The Requirement of Actual Use in Commerce

To qualify for federal registration of a trademark or service mark, a business must make actual, bona fide use of the mark in commerce. Although 1989 amendments to the Lanham Act, the federal statute first enacted in 1946 granting protection to distinctive marks, allow registration based on a bona fide intent to use a mark in commerce, actual use must follow within six months of approval by the Patent and Trademark Office. In other words, no trademark rights are provided to an individual or entity who merely adopts or develops a mark. Only one who actually uses the mark acquires legally protectable rights.

Abandonment: The Loss of Rights Through Non-Use

Abandonment of a mark is one of the primary ways trademark rights can be forfeited. Trademark law defines *abandonment* as non-use with the intent not to resume. Under the Lanham Act, three consecutive years of non-use creates a presumption of abandonment. This presumption can be rebutted in court upon a showing of actual use, or intent to resume in the foreseeable future, or other extenuating circumstances to explain the period of non-use.

Interestingly, the owner of an otherwise highly distinctive, well-known mark can run into trouble based on the trademark doctrine of genericism. As we just mentioned, non-use with the intent not to resume can constitute voluntary abandonment resulting in a loss of trademark rights. A form of involuntary abandonment of rights occurs when a mark that is considered very strong and successful becomes so well known in the marketplace that it becomes generic, causing it to lose its trademark significance and enter the public domain. Throughout history there have been numerous marks that were victims of their own success. Aspirin, Shredded Wheat, Linoleum, Trampoline, Dry Ice, Escalator, and Yo-Yo were all once valuable trademarks that became so popular they lost their distinctiveness by becoming generic.

Companies with very popular, well-known marks such as Xerox, Band-Aid, and Kleenex are acutely aware of the dangers inherent in their marking success and take great pains to police unauthorized uses by means of adding the word "brand" to their advertising or applying the mark to new products not normally associated with a generic name. The owners of these marks will also not hesitate to contact users, including those on Internet websites who use the word in any manner other than as a adjective.

If you are using a trademarked word or term as a verb ("I will Xerox a copy of the article") or as a noun ("please hand me a Kleenex, I think I have a cold") you are in for potential trouble. Major corporations guard their trademark rights jealously, knowing that if they acquiesce to incorrect usage by others, they run the risk of losing their rights by virtue of the mark becoming generically descriptive. Consequently, make sure you refer to the trademarks of others correctly.

Trademark Dilution

More recently, the Lanham Act has been augmented by adding protection for famous marks against dilution or loss of distinctiveness even though there is no competition or product relatedness. The latest amendments help trademark owners defend against abuses made possible by the Internet. Prior to 1996 about half of the states had passed trademark dilution statutes protecting the owners of well-known trademarks from uses by persons selling unrelated, non-competing goods and services. Since January 16, 1996, there has been, in addition to state claims, a federal cause of action under the Lanham Act for dilution. This provision extends only to "famous marks" as defined by the statute. The harm sought to be remedied does not stem from likelihood of consumer confusion, but rather from the erosion of selling power of the famous mark by virtue of a proliferation of non-competing uses (blurring) or by negative associations (tarnishment).

For an example of blurring, consider the world famous mark, IBM for computers and software. Now imagine other businesses selling IBM Paper Clips, IBM Disposable Diapers, IBM Coffee, IBM Hot Dogs, IBM Staples, and IBM Bird Feeders. Pretty soon, the mark made so famous by virtue of its reputation for quality and high-end marketing campaign would lose much of its cache through erosion in the market place. Instead of being special, it would become common.

The other type of harm in dilution cases stems from tarnishment. Here, the harm to one's famous mark comes from associations with unsavory goods and services, which result in negative reactions. In the 1989 case of *American Express Co. v. Vibra Approved Laboratories Corp.*, the federal district court in New York held that incorporation of the famous American Express slogan "Don't Leave Home Without It" on novelty boxes of condoms sold in sex shops diluted the plaintiff's trademark by means of tarnishment.

FEDERAL REGISTRATION OF TRADEMARKS

As mentioned at the start of this chapter, there is dual federal and state jurisdiction over trademarks. There are specific qualifications for federal protection and, while not all trademarks qualify for federal registration, there are also significant advantages accorded trademark and service mark owners whose marks are eligible for registration on the Principal Register of the Patent and Trademark Office (PTO).

Qualifications for Federal Protection

To qualify for federal protection under the Lanham Act, a mark must be used in commerce and be either inherently distinctive or have become distinctive by the doctrine of secondary meaning. As noted above, secondary meaning is an association, developed over time, by consumers between the product or service and the seller, despite the mark's descriptive properties. Additionally, it must not so resemble a mark already registered on the Principal Register so as to cause consumer confusion within the specified product class or classes for which registration of the mark is sought.

Notwithstanding the acquired distinctiveness through secondary meaning, no mark will ever be registered if it contains immoral, scandalous, or disparaging matter or if it is deceptive. The statutory definition of deceptive has in recent years been extended to any mark that is "primarily geographically misdescriptive" of goods or services. An example would be HAVANA for cigars that are in fact made in Tampa, Florida, from tobacco grown in North Carolina. Since Havana and Cuba are geographic locales known for quality cigars, the public would be potentially deceived by this mark even though longstanding use and the label saying "Made in USA" would tend to neutralize the harm.

Finally, no mark that is functional can ever be registered because of the competitive disadvantage it would represent to other competitors. Remember that a feature of a product or the product's packaging can be registered as a trademark. If you manufactured bicycles, you could not register the wheel as a trademarked feature. Other manufacturers could not produce bicycles without wheels. Since a wheel is an essential part of a bicycle's unique function, it can never serve as a trademark. However, a particular non-functional ornamental design of a wheel could serve as a trademark provided it served no practical function.

Advantages of Federal Registration

Assuming your mark qualifies for registration, a number of benefits are available to you under federal law.

Nationwide protection retroactive to the date of the application to register. Under Section 7(b) of the Lanham Act, registration on the Principal Register gives the registrant the exclusive right to use the registered mark in commerce on or in connection with the goods or services specified in the certificate of registration. Trademark rights are based on priority of adoption and use. However, actual rights accrue only upon registration. With the growing awareness of the importance of trademark rights, the wait between filing an application with the Patent and Trademark Office and receiving approval is growing longer with each passing year. The gap between application and registration is at least six months and in some cases eighteen months or more. To address this disparity, the Lanham Act provides that a registrant's rights relate back to the date of application, no matter how long the review process takes. Once received, the certificate of registration becomes proof of validity of the mark. This can be a valuable advantage in the event of litigation.

Use of the ® symbol or alternative phrases such as "Registered in U.S. Patent Office." This provides a warning to others not to use your mark. Likewise, a registered mark will show up on trademark searches, lowering the chances of an unintended infringement by others.

Governmental protection. Holders of registered marks, provided they are U.S. citizens, may seek the aid of Customs Officials to bar infringing imported goods. Any registrant will receive protection against trademark counterfeiting and in certain cases automatically qualifies for treble damage awards.

Incontestability. If a registered mark is used continuously for five consecutive years it may become incontestable. This means that most of the ordinary challenges that can be brought by those contesting the validity of your mark will be lost to them. Thereafter, your mark is largely immune from attack in perpetuity provided you file an affidavit of continuing use in the sixth year, renew your mark every ten years, and continue to use the mark in commerce in connection with the goods and services specified in your application.

TRADEMARK INFRINGEMENT AND DEFENSES

The test for trademark infringement is very simple in the abstract, but often more difficult in context. The single question courts ask, outside of the arena of famous marks entitled to protection from dilution, is: will the use of the same or similar marks on competing or related goods or services create a likelihood of consumer confusion in the relevant geographic and product market? To help with this analysis, courts have articulated eight factors that should be applied to every case of alleged infringement:

1. Strength of a company's mark
2. Degree of similarity between the company's mark and any infringer's mark
3. Proximity of the products or services
4. Likelihood that company owning the mark will expand into the product or service line offered by an infringer
5. Evidence of actual confusion
6. The infringer's good faith in adopting the mark
7. Quality of the infringer's product or service
8. Sophistication of the buyers

By the very nature of all the variables involved, questions of infringement must be determined on a case-by-case basis. To be certain, if you produced a word processor and called it "Microsoft Word Processor," attorneys would be paying you a visit. However, questions of trademark infringement are not usually that clear cut. If, for instance, you called your product "Mikrosoft," you would still have problems. Product and service associations go beyond more than just the spelling of a word. Pronunciation and meaning are also elements that are protected.

What if your product wasn't computer software? If you produced a magazine containing pornography and called it "Microsoft Magazine" would that be okay? Recall from our earlier discussion that when a trademark is famous, such as "Microsoft" or "Coke," and the products are neither competing nor related, the basis of protection shifts from infringement with its likelihood of confusion analysis to a dilution theory based on blurring or tarnishment. In our example "Microsoft Magazine" would draw a stern letter from Microsoft Corporation's attorney insisting you cease and desist based on a tarnishment theory. Clearly, Microsoft's top management would not want their customers to associate their product with pornography.

Moving these concepts onto the Internet does not change the test—it simply changes the medium. However, the medium is different enough that there are still problems, especially in the arena of unregistered marks (that is, marks that still deserve protection under state law, but that have not been registered with the United States Patent and Trademark Office). Whether protection stems from the Lanham Act or from the state law of unfair competition, you will want to take steps to avoid costly problems. A prime example of this is failure to obtain a federal registration for your domain name. We'll discuss the problems with this area in the next chapter.

Other problems include using a mark on the Internet that belongs to someone else. This is especially true considering the global use of the Internet. You can have a sign in your window at your small-town Alabama electronics repair shop, and if someone in California owns the rights to the name, chances are slim that they will ever discover your infringement. However, if your business is on the Internet, the California owner is much more likely to see your use. Many times, a simple trademark search will reveal that someone else owns the rights to the name, and that you should choose a different name to associate with your products or services.

While infringement actions have become increasingly prevalent as dilution gains in importance, there are defenses available to users. Recall that the First Amendment allows you the right to make a fair use of the protected materials of others. To illustrate, consider an Internet case on point, styled *Planned Parenthood Federation of America, Inc. v. Bucci* (42 U.S.P.Q. 2d (BNA) 1430 (S.D.N.Y. 1997), aff'd mem., 152 F.3d 920 (2d Cir. 1998).

Planned Parenthood Federation owned service mark registrations for the mark PLANNED PARENTHOOD and operated an informational web site at www.ppfa.org. Bucci, an anti-abortion activist, set up a "Planned Parenthood" web site at www.plannedparenthood.com, where he distributed anti-abortion information to the public. In addition to using the Planned Parenthood Federation's mark as his domain name and home page address, he welcomed Internet users to his home page with the message, "Welcome to the Planned Parenthood Home Page!" Planned Parenthood Federation sued for trademark infringement due to the related nature of the information being disseminated.

Bucci raised a First Amendment defense relying on a previous case holding, that of *Yankee Publishing v. News America Publishing, Inc. 809 F. Supp 267, 275* (S.D.N.Y. 1992). In that case, the court held that a defendant's use of another entity's trademark is entitled to First Amendment protection when the use of the mark is part of a communicative message, but not when it is used to identify the source of a product. Bucci argued that his use constituted part of the communicative message. This was, he argued, a fair use of a trademark even though it was done without the owner's permission. The *Planned Parenthood* Court disagreed, pointing out that the *Yankee Publishing* case draws a distinction between communicative messages and source identification. Since Bucci attempted to make users believe that he *was* Planned Parenthood, fair use did not apply. The opinion went on to point out that free speech does not extend to labeling or advertising products in a manner that conflicts with the trade-mark rights or others. As a result, it prevented Bucci's use of the Planned Parenthood mark.

At least one case has raised the issue of whether hyperlinking can constitute trademark infringement. Recall from Chapter 6 our discussion of linking and deep linking. As we noted, posting a link causes a reproduction of the entire site and, therefore, causes copyright concerns. Posting a link may cause trademark concerns as well. This was demonstrated in *TicketMaster Corp. v. Microsoft Corp.* Microsoft was deep linking to TicketMaster's web site by posting a link that took the user past TicketMaster's home page to specific information contained on sub-pages. TicketMaster claimed that this use infringed its trademark because, as owner of the trademark (and the domain name ticketmaster.com), it had the sole right to control how its information was presented to users. TicketMaster also complained that the posting of the link was deceptive because it indicated an endorsement by TicketMaster, or at least an affiliation between the two companies, and that Microsoft's use of the trademark to link the sites diluted TicketMaster's trademark. Although the case was settled before any deci-sion could be reached, it is worth discussing, simply because it highlights concerns that businesses have with the way other people and businesses use their trademarks. Therefore, when a link contains a trademark, it is a good idea for you to get permission before using it.

As our discussion of the *Planned Parenthood Federation of America, Inc. v. Bucci* indicated, had Bucci not been so blatant in his use of the Planned Parenthood mark, he might have made a claim of fair use that would not have been prevented. The lesson for all users on the web is clear. Trademark owners will not hesitate to seek protection of their valuable trademark rights. Similarly, courts will enforce those rights when the circumstances dictate. This is good news for e-merchants who use the Internet to reach an international market-place with their goods and services. Notwithstanding the extensive protection available to trademark owners, there is room for users to make appropriate and proper use of a name, symbol, device, or other designation that would other-wise be protected by trademark law.

SELECTING YOUR MARK

When it comes to selecting a word, name, symbol, device, or other designation to brand your goods and services, you need to have in mind what you are trying to accomplish. Will your mark serve as your domain name? Do you want a mark that plays an informational function? Will you use it to advertise in banner ads? While the obvious choice from a sales standpoint is that you want a mark that describes your goods or services as closely as possible, from a legal standpoint it is best to stay away from marks that will automatically tell your customers what goods and services are. The reason is simple. The more your mark describes your product, the weaker it is in the eyes of the law. Recall that some words, symbols, or devices are totally incapable of serving as trademarks, such as the generic words and terms we discussed earlier. Others, such as surnames (McDONALD'S) and descriptive marks (such as BEST BUY), while having initial limitations, can still become strong marks through continued use and recognition by the public. Whether you are seeking to adopt a mark for a new business, register an existing mark, or check for possible infringing uses, the best way to protect yourself is to conduct a trademark search. While we don't advise that you attempt to practice law without a license, you should at least run a preliminary screen to see if something directly on point has already been registered by someone else which would block your attempted registration or possibly subject you to an infringement suit. The Patent and Trademark Office offers its records online at www.uspto.gov.

For close calls and more reliable, up-to-the-minute searches, you are best advised to retain an attorney who specializes in trademark and unfair competition law. When it comes to trademark clearance issues, too many people create four-, five-, and six-figure problems by trying to save three-figure sums. We urge you to be smarter than that when it comes to trademark matters on the web.

A FINAL WORD OF ADVICE

As with so many other related issues drawing a line between permissible and impermissible uses of information on the Internet, there is no substitute for the knowledge necessary to secure your rights while avoiding the trouble that comes from infringing the rights of others. Your front-end investment in knowledge will pay big dividends measured in time, money, and peace of mind.

CHAPTER 10

Domain Names and the High-Tech Fight Against Cyberpiracy

Assuming you have given your web designer the go ahead to build your site, one of the first things you need to do is decide what you will name it. While this may seem elementary, let us assure you that it can be a difficult process. If you have ever done a domain name search, you already know that many of the more obvious identifiers are already taken. This is true despite recent moves to expand the number of new extensions. Furthermore, choosing a domain name is not just about registration. It is about making sure that no one else has trademark or service mark rights in the name. In addition, beyond choosing the right name, you must protect your marks against cyberpiracy by others.

DOMAIN NAME DEFINITION, SELECTION, AND REGISTRATION

Before we discuss cyberpiracy and other recurring problem areas related to domain names, let's start with the basics of what a domain name is and how you can get one. A domain name is a unique web address that denotes the location of your site. For example, www.blackberryrecords.com is the registered domain name for Blackberry Records, Inc. To provide your web site with an address that can be accessed around the world, you should choose a name that is appropriate for your site as well as to your specific purposes for using the site. In the case of Blackberry Records, it chose the name of its company, and the ".com" extension, to indicate that it is a commercial business.

You should know that there are several *top-level domain names* (TLDs), or web address extensions, in addition to a number of country code domains, such as .uk for the United Kingdom, .tv for Tuvalu, and .ws for Samoa. The most common TLDs are .com for commercial businesses, .org for non-profit organizations, .gov for government agencies, .mil for military organizations, .net for network organizations, and .edu for educational institutions. In an effort to meet the overwhelming demand for web addresses, additional TLD extensions have recently been added. They include .pro, for professionals, which will likely be reserved for licensed physicians, attorneys, and certified public accountants; .name, which will likely be reserved for a first and last name only; and .biz, and .info, which will be for general use.

Accordingly, when choosing your name, you want to select a TLD appropriate for the type of site you are operating. It should be noted that many people, after choosing their name, register it with multiple TLDs in order to curb cybersquatting, which will be discussed below.

The part of your domain name that precedes the TLD is just as important and is perhaps more problematic. Unlike the registration of trademarks, where actual use or bona fide intent to use must by established before a registration will be issued, it is possible to reserve domain names with no such use requirement. Consequently, with so many established web sites, and with so many people and companies "parking" domain names they have no intention of ever using, the challenge of coming up with a name that is not in use may be difficult. To complicate matters, you must take care not to choose a name that would be confusingly similar to someone else's trademark, thus creating potential exposure for trademark infringement. Anyone who has ever been through the process can attest to the difficulty in obtaining an appropriate name, especially in heavy traffic areas and industries such as computer hardware and software or other media- or entertainment-related sites.

Once you have selected a domain name, the next step is for you or your web designer to register your new name. In 1992, the federal government awarded a series of cooperative agreements to several companies to provide, among other things, registration services for domain names. The companies adopted the name InterNIC. Its subsidiary, Network Solutions, Inc., is responsible for administering the domain registration portion of services that InterNIC provides. You can either register directly with Network Solutions, Inc. at their web site (www.networksolutions.com) or with other accredited registrars, such as register.com or valuweb.com, many of whom provide web hosting services as well.

CYBERSQUATTING

One of the first problems to present itself with the rise of Internet use was *cybersquatting* or *cyberpiracy*. *Cybersquatting* can be practiced in a number of ways, but in its most basic form it involves someone with entrepreneurial spirit registering established tradenames and trademarks owned by others as domain names. The domain name registrant would then approach the tradename or trademark owner with an offer to sell the domain name in order to avoid confusion in the marketplace. A second form of cybersquatting involves the diversion of established customers away from the mark owner to the domain name owner by adopting a domain name that is confusingly similar to a registered trademark · or a well-known tradename. In 1999, Congress amended the Lanham Trademark Act by adding Section 43(d), which specifically prohibits the practice of cybersquatting.

Dennis Toeppen provides the most infamous example of cybersquatting. Toeppen registered more than 100 names, such as "Panavision" and "Eddie Bauer," then suggested to the mark owners that a payoff would be less expensive than a lawsuit. Even before the 1999 federal legislation on the subject, a federal appeals court had already warned Toeppen that this behavior was in violation of trademark law.

Similarly, Richard Bucci, as mentioned in Chapter 9, registered plannedparenthood.com, and used it to promote his anti-abortion views, thereby using the mark to divert consumers from the mark owner. A court prevented him from further using the name to cause consumer confusion.

Another type of cybersquatting, sometimes called typopiracy, involves registering the misspelling of a mark, such as "hewlittpackard.com" vs. "hewlettpackard.com." The idea is that a certain percentage of users will accidentally mistype the domain name and thus land on the squatter's site. The more well-known the mark is, the greater the number of misdirected users. Similarly, a cybersquatter may incorporate a mark into a domain name, such as "we_sell_microsoft.com."

In addition to marks associated with products, cybersquatting has arisen in relation to names of famous people. After Congress passed the cyberpiracy prevention measures discussed below, Brad Pitt filed suit to recover the domain names bradpitt.com and bradpitt.net. The .com domain owners attempted to sell the name to the actor, and the .net site posted photographs and operated a fan club from the site. However, because the federal statute ties liability to commercial gain, the use of a domain name for a fan club is probably not an infringement, depending upon how the fan club is operated.

The "Cyberpiracy Prevention" provisions of Section 43(d) of the Lanham Act provides for the protection of distinctive and famous marks against conflicting use by one who would register, traffic in, or use the mark as a domain name with "a bad faith intent to profit."

"Bad faith" is a subjective concept. The law sets forth some factors for a court to consider when deciding if the person who registered the domain name was acting in bad faith. In essence, if the domain name registrant intended to divert customers from the mark owner or to resell the name to the mark owner, then a court will most likely rule that there is bad faith. However, if the domain name registrant had a legitimate use for the name, or had a good reason to think he or she did, then there is probably no bad faith. For instance, consider Delta Airlines and Delta Faucets. Delta Faucets formerly had a web site at www. delta.com. Since Delta Faucets held a federal trademark registration for "Delta" for its faucets, it had a legitimate use for the name. When Delta Airlines wanted to create its own web site, it had to adopt the domain name www.delta-air. com, since there was no legal way to demand that Delta Faucets turn over their previously registered domain name. Incidentally, Delta Airlines now owns www.delta.com and runs its web site from that address.

One use that has arisen, much to the dismay of many mark owners, is the coupling of a mark with disparaging remarks concerning a product, company, or organization, such as "XYZCorpsucks.com" or "IhateXYZCorp.com." This practice is fairly common, and although a mark owner may consider this to be a bad faith use, the law does not agree. Even though this type of use is certainly intended to divert customers from the mark owner's site, the law still requires that the likelihood of confusion test discussed in Chapter 9 be met for trademark infringement to occur. There is little likelihood that a consumer would reasonably believe that XYZ Corporation is operating a site that is telling customers how bad the company is and why consumers should not buy its products. This may sound similar to the Planned Parenthood matter discussed in Chapter 9, but there is a difference. In the Planned Parenthood case, Mr. Bucci registered the exact name of the company, rather than the name coupled with something else. Users were drawn to the site believing that it was operated by Planned Parenthood. This initial confusion is enough to satisfy the test.

Perhaps the most frustrating experiences for mark owners who are the victims of this kind of consumer hate site is that sending cease and desist letters tends to make the problem worse. Consumers who operate hate sites generally take great delight in posting mail from the targeted company or organization, often accompanied by derisive comments of their own. However, some companies have actually taken advantage of these hate sites by contacting consumers who have posted negative comments on them and attempting to resolve the problems. Where the company may never have discovered that a customer had a problem, and was telling all of his or her friends about it, the hate sites provide a medium for expression to which the company has access.

The good news is that, to institute legal action under these provisions, the owner of the mark need not have registered the mark with the U. S. Patent and Trademark Office. As you will recall from Chapter 9, common law marks, that is, marks that are distinctive but have not been registered, are entitled to protection under the law, as are famous or distinctive personal names.

The bad news is that, if you are a potential defendant in the fight over a domain name, failure to register a mark for which you have established a valid use may cause you some problems. The Lanham Act provides protection for so-called famous marks against dilution. Dilution occurs when a famous mark is used in connection with a product that is unrelated to the mark's actual associated product, such as our Microsoft Magazine example in Chapter 9. The idea is that the mark is so well known that a consumer is likely to make an association with the famous mark owner even if the products are not the same, and consequently this association "dilutes" the mark's ability to cause consumers to associate the mark with the owner's actual product.

If you have a federally registered mark and someone charges you with dilution of their famous mark, the fact that you have the registration completely negates any liability. Based on your registration, you would be allowed to keep your domain name. If, however, you have registered the domain name for legitimate use with a non-competing product, such as our Delta Faucet/Airlines example, and you have not bothered to get a federal registration, you will have to prove your rights to the name.

Another method of disputing domain name ownership is through ICANN, located at www.icann.org. ICANN stands for Internet Corporation for Assigned Names and Numbers. ICANN has developed a relatively inexpensive and expedited dispute resolution policy, known as the Uniform Domain Name Dispute Resolution Policy, that a mark owner can use to attempt transfer of a domain name. The policy assists owners of marks that are registered, either federally or at the state level, or established by common law. The proof under this policy is similar to the statutory provisions discussed above, and it provides for a defense of "reverse domain name hijacking," which is an allegation that a complaint was filed for the sole purpose of depriving a lawful user of the right to use its name.

However, this policy was not intended to establish trademark or service mark rights, so if the mark owner wants money damages, a lawsuit is still the way to go. In addition, the mark owner has to remember that, if the domain name was registered by someone with a viable mark for a different category of goods (such as Delta Faucets compared to Delta Airlines), then the first person to register the domain name is going to be entitled to the domain name.

META TAGGING, KEYWORD PURCHASES, AND OTHER FORMS OF INVISIBLE INFRINGEMENT

Meta tagging, as discussed in Chapter 2, is the practice of placing certain words in a web site's source code so that a search engine displays a link to the web site when those words are entered by the user. Meta tags do not appear on the web page, so a mark's owner cannot tell by looking at the page that their mark is being infringed. A similar practice is creating text that is the same color as the background, so that even though the text appears on the page, it is invisible to the user.

A less than obvious method of infringing marks is by purchasing *keywords,* which are sometimes sold to advertisers by search engines. A keyword is a word that describes the type of site that the advertiser wishes to advertise. When the user enters the keyword that the web site has purchased, one of two things occurs, depending upon the type of use the buyer has purchased. The entry of the keyword either produces a list of links that includes the buyer's web site as the first site on the list that the search engine produces, or it produces a banner ad at the top of the page for the buyer's web site.

The uses of word placement mentioned above are designed to produce advertisements for the buyer's business or to move the web site closer to the top of the list that a search engine produces when certain topics are entered. The more instances that the engine finds, the higher confidence that the engine has that the site matches the user's criteria and the higher on the list the link goes. This is similar to naming a business "AAA" or "A-1" to ensure that it is first in the yellow page listings.

As an example, if XYZ Corporation sells widgets, and it knows that many people looking for widgets will type in the mark "Widgetware" when they run a search, they may put the name Widgetware in the meta tags, and in white text on the white background of the home page. They may also attempt to purchase the keyword "Widgetware" on one or two search engines. The keyword purchase only helps for the specific search engines for which XYZ purchases keywords, but the other two methods will raise XYZ's standing on any search engine for which XYZ is registered. Although, once they arrive, users are not likely to believe that XYZ is operated by Widgetware, XYZ is still infringing Widgetware's mark. XYZ is using the mark to divert customers from the mark owner to XYZ; chances are, if the competing companies sell similar products, the user is likely to purchase the product from the first web site that he or she visits.

The problem with this kind of trademark infringement relates to the lack of visibility of a particular use. For instance, if someone at Widgetware stumbles across XYZ's page, they will see nothing wrong. There are ways to combat this practice, provided the mark owner is aware that there is a problem. Generally speaking, if the web site widgetware.com is not the first hit on the page when the mark is entered, or if a competitor's ad appears when the mark is entered, it is worth investigating. There are other factors to consider as well, such as whether the sites listed above widgetware.com are authorized Widgetware dealers, or whether the sites contain news articles that evaluate Widgetware's products. If these possibilities are ruled out, Widgetware's CEO may wish to try to purchase the keyword to learn whether it is already taken, assuming that the search engine offers this service. It may also be helpful to visit the site and look at the source code by selecting View, then Source, from the menu bar of the browser, although some browsers may not operate precisely this way. Even if the programming is difficult to understand, a quick word search may reveal the mark in the text.

Jurisdiction and Venue In Cyberpiracy Lawsuits

In general, jurisdiction has to do with the power of a particular court to adjudicate a dispute, while venue dictates where an aggrieved party may sue the person or entity that is causing trouble. Usually a plaintiff must sue a defendant in the place where the injury occurs or in the defendant's home jurisdiction. Most often, the plaintiff will want to sue where the injury occurred, because that is easier than traveling to the defendant's home jurisdiction. However, there has to be more than just injury to bring suit in one's home jurisdiction; the plaintiff also has to show that the defendant purposefully directed activities into the forum or has other sufficient "minimum contacts" to make it fair for the defendant to have to appear in a jurisdiction that is not his own.

On the Internet, jurisdiction can be a fairly complex issue. Chapter 13 is devoted to a more comprehensive discussion of this subject. However, for purposes of domain name actions under the cyberpiracy provisions of the Lanham Act, jurisdictional problems prompted Congress to provide for "*in rem* civil actions." An *in rem* action is one that is brought against the *property*, in this case the actual domain name, rather than the *person*. These actions are reserved for instances where the plaintiff either cannot find the individual or entity that registered the domain name, as would be the case if the domain name was registered under a false name with false contact information, or cannot obtain jurisdiction over the registrant.

If you intend to use these procedures, you should be aware of several key points. Obviously, you must have trademark or service mark rights in the domain name. The law states that the owner of the mark must either have registered the mark with the U. S. Patent and Trademark Office, or the mark must be distinctive or famous. You also have to bring the action in the judicial district for the registrar that assigned the domain name; for instance, if the registrant registered the name with Network Solutions, Inc., you would have to bring the action in Virginia. Lastly, as with the ICANN dispute resolution policy, the only legal remedies available are forfeiture, cancellation, or transfer of the name. If you want damages, an *in rem* action is not the way to get them.

On a final note, similar to the protections provided for service providers in copyright infringement cases, domain registrars are protected from liability in both *in personam* civil actions (that is, actions against the person who registered the domain name) and *in rem* civil actions. If the action is against the person or entity that registered the name, then the only people that you can hold liable are the registrant and anyone that the registrant licenses to use the domain name. If the action is against the domain name itself, then the domain name registrar is specifically excluded from liability unless it has acted in bad faith or with "reckless disregard," which would include refusing to comply with any court order.

A FINAL WORD OF ADVICE

People often confuse trademarks and domain names. Indeed they both play similar roles of identifying businesses and their particular goods and services.

Another source of confusion stems from the 1999 amendment of the Lanham Act to prohibit cybersquatting of domain names. Add to this the fact that use of domain names, even in good faith, can create potential liability for trademark infringement or dilution. However, from the standpoint of registration of domain names, the law generally awards rights to the first to register, whereas trademark rights are based on priority of actual or constructive use (registration of a mark with bona fide intent to use). While it is perfectly permissible to "park" a domain name, the same is not true of trademarks. As we have seen, attempts to reserve a mark to keep it off the market will result in its cancellation. Since domain names and trademarks are potentially valuable assets to any company, take the time to distinguish between the two. We urge you to understand and appreciate that very different legal principles govern the proper use of these species of intellectual property. When in doubt, call your attorney. It is just part of doing business on the Internet.

CHAPTER 11

Privacy and Security Issues: Protecting Yourself in Cyberspace

Thanks largely to the Internet, the world continues to shrink as traditional barriers of time and distance evaporate. Over the past few years, anyone with access to a computer and an Internet Service Provider has experienced instant access to the world's storehouse of information. The result has been a degree of choice never before imagined, which has translated into unprecedented levels of efficiency, empowerment, and productivity in our daily lives. Unfortunately, these considerable positive consequences of the technological revolution are paralleled by heightened opportunities for abuse.

An unfortunate by-product of the online revolution is an increase in unscrupulous people who seek to profit illegally or unethically or otherwise exploit the interests of others. What makes this all the more unsettling is the fact that any Internet user can become an unwitting target of these electronic voyeurs within the seemingly safe and secure confines of one's own office or home. While none of us would consciously allow someone to install a hidden camera in our house or would leave our back doors unlocked at night, that is exactly what any Internet user is potentially doing simply by having an active online connection to a personal computer. What is worse is that we seldom if ever know whether we have been visited by an unwanted intruder. Consequently, we often don't discover that something is amiss until it is too late.

The Problem of Information Abuse

A concern just as real is what Internet companies do with information you voluntarily provide. Although the Internet community largely favors individual privacy and has taken significant steps toward self-regulation, you cannot assume that all with whom you deal online are so inclined. Given the ease of electronic surveillance and access to information we hold most dear, the question then becomes: what are our rights under the law of privacy and how can we best protect ourselves from the threat of these unseen abuses?

Privacy and security issues on the Internet are some of the foremost concerns of consumers and business people. From an e-commerce perspective, users want to be able to transmit personal data such as credit card and other personal information without risk of interception. They also want assurance that sensitive information about them will be used in an appropriate manner. Likewise, e-businesses want to protect their own sensitive proprietary data while also seeking to instill confidence in their customers to increase the likelihood that they will shift more of their business dealings and purchase transactions to the Internet.

While these are probably the most common concerns, there are a myriad of other privacy and security concerns that the average consumer gives little thought to, but which can have a profound effect on their lives. For instance, if a business wishes to sell the customer list it has developed from its web site, how may it do so without invading its customers' privacy? How much information can a web site gather from a visitor without informing him or her that the information is being compiled? If a consumer wishes to make an online purchase, how can that individual be sure that their credit card information will not be intercepted before it reaches the merchant? Once the business receives the information, how can it be stored for future use without risk of third parties breaking into their system and stealing or otherwise tampering it? How can a business accepting an order from a regular customer ensure that an order placed by e-mail actually came from that customer? How can anyone minimize the risk of viruses or other destructive programs?

These and other concerns have led to the development and continuing improvement of technology designed to help protect businesses and users from these types of problems. However, as long as there are seriously motivated hackers with computers, the problems will never be permanently solved. In addition, although the law is trying desperately to keep up with technology, technology is simply evolving too fast.

The good news for computer users is that the same technology that is creating the problems is also at work around the clock trying to combat problems related to privacy preservation and security assurance. And as with other issues of protecting our physical safety from would-be criminals and prying eyes, awareness is the first and often most effective step we can take. This chapter seeks to foster a higher sense of awareness by outlining the law of privacy as applied to cyberspace while suggesting some very basic, cost-effective measures designed to protect your identity and confidential information from the stealth-like abuses made possible by the Internet.

PRIVACY ISSUES ON THE NET

While so much is written and discussed about the law of privacy today, it is, ironically, a relatively recent concept in the development of our legal system. Prior to 1890 no legal scholar had even advanced or advocated the proposition that individuals were entitled to a right of privacy. Prompted by some unwanted newspaper publicity, Samuel Warren and Louis Brandeis wrote an article in the Harvard Law Review suggesting that the basic concept of personal freedom that had implicitly been a hallmark of the American experience included the right of all persons "to be let alone." While this idea of the right of privacy is universally accepted today, it was considered a daring assertion for the late nineteenth century.

So audacious was the concept of privacy, it was not until 1905 when the Georgia Supreme Court, in the case of *Pavesich v. New England Life Insurance Company,* wrote the privacy doctrine into the common law in connection with a case involving an insurance company that published an advertisement that featured a person's picture used without his permission. Thereafter, development of the doctrine was rather slow until the 1960s. The single factor contributing to the acceleration of the doctrine was the development of the mass media.

In 1960 William Prosser, former Dean of the University of California Law School, wrote a landmark article entitled *Privacy.* In it he outlined the basic interests served by the law of privacy. These categories continue to define the contours of the law of privacy today. They are:

* Intrusion upon a person's seclusion of solitude, or into his or her private affairs
* Public disclosure of embarrassing private facts about a person
* Publicity which places a person in a false light in the public eye
* Appropriation, for another's advantage, of a person's name or likeness.

The last of these interests has developed into a separate branch of the law known as the Right of Publicity. This branch of the law protects celebrities against the misappropriation of their celebrity identities for commercial purposes. The other three interests continue to form the basis of the Right of Privacy that we discuss in this chapter.

Prior to the development of the Internet, the law of privacy often revolved around unwanted media scrutiny and publicity targeted at a wide range of public figures, from movie stars to politicians. Separate considerations related to the First Amendment of the U.S. Constitution accorded lower protection to "public figures," since they voluntarily surrender much of their privacy for the rewards of living in the public spotlight. When it came to private individuals, the law of privacy was often asserted to gain relief from private investigators gathering information for purposes of litigation or to seek protection from stalkers. With the advent of the personal computer and the Internet for compiling, processing, and storing information for corporate, political, and charitable interests intent on targeting individuals for sales, votes, and donations, the privacy landscape changed radically.

Privacy and the Internet

Privacy on the Internet is a concern for individuals for several reasons: they want to know how information they give to web sites will be used, they want to know what type of information is being gathered about them automatically, and they want to be sure that their communications are not being intercepted.

Businesses may wish to compile the names and contact information of all of their customers and sell them to other businesses offering related goods or services—customer lists have a recognized commercial value. Or, a business may wish to use the information to contact the customer on later occasions about new products or services. The use of information that you voluntarily give a company on its web site should be governed by the web site's privacy policy. This is especially important if you are entering information of a personal or financial nature. In addition, many web sites include check boxes that require you to uncheck the box if you do not wish to receive future "e-mailings" from the company. This is especially important considering the "anti-spamming" legislation being considered by Congress.

Most users also want to know what kinds of information will be gathered about them automatically. This is where the use of cookies, and similar data collection methods, come into play.

Cookies and Automatic Data Collection

As discussed in Chapter 2, a cookie is a program that is forwarded by the web site to your browser. Your browser may then install the cookie, which gathers specific information that can then be accessed by the web site that originally stored the cookie on your computer. Browsers can be set to refuse cookies or to warn you when a cookie is about to be installed. However, many sites, such as those with "shopping carts," do not work without cookies, so the user that shuts them out cannot use the site effectively.

The kind of information collected through cookies depends upon the web site that sets it. Most often, cookies collect information such as so-called *clickstream* data, which is data collected concerning the activity of the user. For instance, you may enter the site at the home page, then click on a link to a sub-page called "products," then to another sub-page containing compact discs, then to another sub-page displaying a compact disc by your favorite artist. The program records the progress from the home page to the final page with the individual compact disc, but not necessarily any information about you specifically.

After the web site has collected and analyzed this data for a large number of visitors, the business has a picture of the parts of its web site that are most popular. The business can then reorganize the site, discarding seldom-used sections and expanding products about which users are most interested. The business can also sell ad space based on the number of visitors and the types of products that users view most often.

Clickstream data collection is relatively harmless because it allows users to remain anonymous. Some marketing companies have capitalized on this type of data collection, however, by compiling information about an individual user, usually from a search engine site. The company tracks the types of searches you conduct and the links that you follow from the page. As you visit the page more and more often, you will find that the banner ads at the top of the page are more specific to your interests. This type of data collection is a little less anonymous, and some believe more intrusive, because it focuses on a specific user.

Other information stored by cookies and similar technology includes selections made during online shopping sessions (by use of "shopping carts") and information storage (such as passwords, e-mail addresses, or user name), which keeps you from having to enter the information every time you visit a particular web site.

Many consumers are interested in knowing what type of information is being collected and how it will be used. This is why privacy policies are so important. TRUSTe is an independent, non-profit organization that assists in the development of privacy policies for business web sites. It grants its seal of approval to businesses with well-crafted privacy policies that inform consumers of all of the information collected from them (both through the consumer's actions and automatically) as well as what the business does with that information. TRUSTe's approach to privacy on the web is that if the industry regulates itself, two major benefits result: consumer confidence in e-commerce will increase, resulting in more money spent online; and the government will not be forced to step in and regulate in order to protect consumers' privacy rights.

There are other organizations that are attempting to address consumer privacy issues as well. The World Wide Web Consortium is working on a technology, called P3P, that will allow users to set the conditions of the provision of private information. Basically, P3P will provide for a system whereby a web site's privacy practices are stored in a standard format. You would be able to automate your decisions concerning the conditions under which you would release personal information, rather than having to read the privacy policy at every web site. Of course, this would be contingent on a web site actually following the privacy practices that it submits, but that is a concern regardless of whether or not the process is automated.

Lastly, the FBI's Carnivore program presents issues that many are likening to "big brother" watching everything done by an Internet user. Carnivore is an "e-mail sniffer" that peruses e-mails for certain keywords set by the program. For instance, the program can be set to search all e-mails for the address johndoe@abc.com in either the sending or receiving field or both. The program is run on a laptop or rack-mounted computer that monitors an ISP's network and scans all packets of information that flow through.

The problem that critics have with this type of program is that, unlike wire-taps which only record conversations that take place on the phones that are tapped, this program scans all e-mail, whether or not it originated from or is intended for the target of the investigation. The FBI counters with the assertion that this program can only be used with a court order and is actually less intrusive than wiretaps, since it can be used to screen out data that is irrelevant.

Some people consider corporate "e-mail snooping" to be a similar problem, although certainly not of the same magnitude. The fact is, with the expansion of technology, most businesses have the ability to monitor computer use, read employees' e-mail, and read employees' computer files from a central server. Although the thought of being scrutinized certainly bothers some, businesses are generally legally entitled to track employees' computer use.

Going Global

The difference between ordinary privacy concerns and Internet privacy concerns is also a matter of geography, or more precisely, lack of geography. Since the Internet is global, any business that deals in sensitive information cannot restrict its vision to U.S. laws and policies.

European privacy protections are more restrictive than those in the United States. Although a web site may collect information within certain parameters and use the data throughout the 15 countries that are members of the European Union, provided that the site complies with whatever right-to-privacy rules exist in the site's home state, such use does not allow export to other countries.

This specifically includes export to the United States, because U.S. privacy protections are not as strict. For instance, in the U.S., businesses are allowed to use consumer information unless the consumer specifically "opts out," that is, informs the business that he or she does not wish to have his or her informa-tion used in a specified manner of such use. In the European Union, businesses may not use consumer information unless the consumer "opts in" (that is, specifically approves a particular use of the information). Although the Euro-pean Union and the United States made significant strides in resolving these differences, the European Parliament overruled a compromise reached between the two.

Perhaps more of a problem for American businesses is what to do with infor-mation they receive directly from European Union consumers. France's *Loi Toubon* requires that materials directed at French users must be written in French. This is especially important when a web site contains terms and conditions of use with which it expects its users to comply. If the terms and conditions are not in French, French courts will rule the terms inapplicable. Therefore, if a web site contains a privacy policy in English, then collects information from a French consumer, the site owners could find themselves sued in a French court (even with a clause establishing jurisdiction elsewhere) for using information without properly obtaining the consumer's permission. This is even if the user accepts the privacy policy and other terms.

Another concern is simply the making available of certain information or products. As discussed below, the United States has relaxed its encryption export regulations, but some other countries have not relaxed their *import* regulations. Some countries will not allow their citizens to use strong encryption software for fear that the government will be unable to monitor speech that encryption software may hide.

Other global concerns are addressed in Chapter 13. For now, you should be aware that caution should be exercised when expanding your market to encompass citizens of other countries, especially if your site harvests information for use with third parties.

SECURITY ISSUES IN CYBERSPACE

Privacy is related to what is done with information once it is transmitted from one place to another. Security is related to ensuring that the information starts where it is alleged to start and arrives at its intended destination, without being stolen or otherwise tampered with while in transit. There are also security concerns with maintaining the integrity of systems that are connected to the Internet, so that information remains safe once it arrives at its destination.

Transmission Security

Many consumers are concerned about the safety of sending information, such as credit card numbers or financial information, over the Internet. The industry, realizing these concerns, is making constant efforts to stay ahead of those who make a game out of breaking encryption codes.

A rising concern is identity theft. This occurs when the thief pretends to be a person in order to gain access to, or create, accounts in that person's name. A recent incident of computer-assisted identity theft resulted in access to the accounts of over 200 wealthy Americans, including CNN founder Ted Turner, Disney CEO Michael Eisner, movie director Steven Spielberg, and talk show hostess Oprah Winfrey. With a little information about you, anyone can request or create credit cards in your name or access your accounts. You can imagine the havoc this can cause; some consumers have been surprised by credit card bills in the hundreds of thousands of dollars. Although federal law limits a consumer's liability for credit card fraud, that is only the tip of the iceberg. The resulting credit problems may take months or even years to untangle. In the meantime, getting credit for anything from mortgaging a house to buying a car may be nearly impossible. We will explore this problem in more detail in Chapter 12.

Although identity theft generally results when information is obtained from places other than the web, such as when a thief intercepts bills from your mailbox or from a purse or wallet, lax security on the web poses potential hazards in this regard as well. This is one reason why it is important to secure transactions on the web, which is where encryption comes in. *Encryption* is a way of coding messages so that, if a message is intercepted, the culprit cannot understand what it says unless he or she is able to break the code. Encryption can be simple, like the cryptoquote in the daily newspaper, or complex, like the algorithms used by most programs to encrypt messages.

The more characters used in the key, the tougher the code is to break. Therefore, a 40-bit (i.e. 40 character) key, which has more than a trillion possible combinations, is easier to crack than a 128-bit key. Although a trillion sounds like a lot, a computer can be programmed to try all combinations of a set of characters and break a 40-bit code rather quickly. Most programs, including most browsers, use 128-bit encryption which, at this point, has yet to be cracked.

There are basically two types of encryption: *public key* and *private key*. In order to better understand the difference between the two, an example might be helpful. Suppose you are a regular customer of Acme Corporation. You want to send an order for 1,000 skateboards to John Smith at Acme. You go to the web site, enter your name, shipping address, and customer account number, then submit the order for Acme to process. If your system uses the private key method, then your computer will have to transmit your message to John; it will also have to transmit the key to John so that his computer can descramble the message. Although this method is less cumbersome for a computer, it requires a secure method to transmit the key to the other person. If your system uses public key encryption, then you would have John's public key and John would have a private key. It really wouldn't matter who viewed your key, because only the private key held by John could be used to decrypt the message. Public key encryption is more secure, but it is slow, difficult to store, and difficult to transmit.

In addition, public key encryption cannot be used to authenticate a sender. Therefore, John may wish to confirm the order before preparing and shipping 1,000 units to you, only to have you tell him that he would have to take them back (and pay the shipping costs and restock the merchandise) because you didn't place the order. This is where digital certification comes in. A user or web site can get a digital certificate from a site such as VeriSign (www.verisign.com) that verifies that the person is who she says she is. For instance, if you go to a web site that claims to be operated by Acme, and the site has a digital certificate, it is easy for you to verify that Acme does, in fact, operate the web site. With no digital certificate, you cannot be entirely certain that this site is not a well-designed fraud run by Joe Crook who may take your order, fail to send your merchandise, then charge his one-way trip to Rio to your credit card.

Digital certification can also be used for e-mails. The certification is attached to the message in the form of a digital signature, which verifies that the sender is who she claims to be, and provides the receiver with a method of encoding a reply. Many states have enacted laws establishing rules concerning digital signatures. Under many of these rules, a digital signature is presumed to carry the same effect as a real one, unless the person contesting the signature can prove otherwise.

Incidentally, until recently, federal law placed strict limits on the export of stronger encryption technology, due to its historical use for military security. For example, before you could download a browser using the 128-bit encryption technology, you had to verify residence in the United States or Canada. However, due to the pervasive use of encryption on the Internet and in software programs, the government is in the process of relaxing the export controls. At this point, the requirements have shifted from a pre-export licensing requirement (that is, obtaining a license to export before being allowed to ship) to a post-export reporting requirement. Although still a very complex process, the vendor now reports all shipments after they are made, and more changes are in the works.

Network Security

Network security is another important aspect of Internet use. Any computer or system connected to the Internet is a potential target for hackers and crackers, individuals that break into computer systems. *Hackers* generally limit their damage to mischief making, since their only purpose in breaking in is to prove that they can do it. *Crackers*, on the other hand, are individuals that break into computer systems to cause serious damage or steal information. Therefore, it is vital that system security measures be taken to protect the information on your computer or network from intruders.

Computers with a permanent connection, such as cable access, are more at risk than those with a temporary connection (a dial-up modem). Every computer on the Internet has an Internet Protocol (IP) address that is nothing but a series of numbers. Servers use these IP addresses to determine where requests for information are coming from and where to return the information.

Generally speaking, a computer is assigned an IP address when it logs on. Therefore, a computer with a permanent connection retains the same IP address, and a computer with a dial-up connection receives a new IP address every time it connects (although some ISPs assign permanent IP addresses even to computers with dial-up connections).

Hackers and crackers surf the web looking for systems with weaknesses that allow them access. When they find a system with such a weakness, they return to the IP address to do their dirty work. Consequently, if a computer is constantly changing IP addresses, it is nearly impossible for a hacker/cracker to do any damage. It is also impossible for a hacker or cracker to access a system that is turned off, so powering down when not in use is always a good idea.

There are several ways that hackers/crackers can cause problems. They can steal information stored on the computer, such as passwords or credit card numbers. They can also disable programs, or the computer itself (called "crashing the system").

One type of problem of particular interest to web site owners is the denial of service attack. A denial of service attack occurs when the intruder is attempting to deny the service to other users. An interesting version of this attack is commonly used by a group calling themselves "Electrohippies," who have "sit-ins" at sites where they wish to deny service to other users. This can be done by tying up the system's resources or by destroying the system's configuration. Either way, the end result is to deny customers or visitors access to a site into which an individual has put a lot of time and money. This can range from a nuisance to a serious problem, depending upon the amount of revenue normally generated by the site and the amount of time that the system is down.

Common-Sense Security Measures

With the exception of powering down your computer or disconnecting it from the Internet, there is no completely reliable way of preventing unwanted intruders. However, the more and better measures taken, the slimmer the chances that someone will breach your system.

Some of the most common methods used by businesses to protect their servers are firewalls, proxy servers, and password protection measures. Password protection is probably the simplest measure to take, although it is also one of the easier measures to overcome. One way to make deciphering a password more difficult is not to use words or common names. A random combination of letters and numbers is the most difficult type of password to decipher.

Firewalls and proxy servers are a little more sophisticated. A firewall is a system that checks all incoming traffic before allowing it into your system. This is designed to enforce whatever access policy your network may have in place. Most firewalls are developed to protect against access from outside of the network, in order to keep intruders from logging onto computers on your network.

A proxy server is a computer that serves as a gatekeeper between a network and the Internet. Proxy servers check incoming traffic before allowing it on your network. The proxy accepts requests from inside the network and forwards them to the Internet. When the information returns to the network from the Internet, the proxy screens the information to ensure that it is of the type that you have requested. However, proxies are connected to the Internet and, accordingly, are still vulnerable to attack. Furthermore, most proxies are more concerned with information requested from the inside and not with requests originating from the Internet. The most effective proxy uses a firewall to assist in preventing attacks originating from the outside.

Another simple protective measure is offline storage. Some businesses maintain all sensitive information in a computer not connected to the Internet. Therefore, even if a web site collects sensitive information, it only remains on the system until it can be transferred to the offline unit. This minimizes the number of files at risk.

Security concerns apply to individuals as well as businesses. You should never believe you are not vulnerable to attack or that an attacker would not be interested in your meager computer. In truth, an intruder can use even a home computer as a point through which to accomplish a wide range of mischief, without you even being aware that anything is happening.

There are several programs on the Internet that will scan a computer to look for security weaknesses. ShieldsUP! (www.grc.com), HackerWhacker (www.hackerwhacker.com), and NetIQSecurityAnalyzer (www.webtrends.net) are examples of these programs. Each will search your computer's ports for weaknesses and give you an explanation of the results.

Viruses

Another concern of businesses and individuals are viruses, Trojan Horses, worms, and the like. A *virus* is a destructive computer program that is designed to reproduce and/or transmit itself to other computers. A *Trojan Horse* is a type of computer virus in the form of a destructive file that appears to be harmless. A *worm* is a virus that creates a large amount of useless information, with the goal of filling the computer's memory and crashing the computer. These types of programs are especially designed to damage a computer or network. The damage caused can range from innocuous, such as forcing documents to save without being prompted by the user or changing the names of certain types of files, to hazardous, such as stealing passwords or causing a system crash (both of which, incidentally, were features of the notorious "I Love You" virus). Most of these programs are embedded in e-mail attachments or downloadable files.

You should never download an e-mail attachment or other file from an unknown source. This is where digital signatures come in handy. Nevertheless, some viruses are able to attach themselves to e-mails from people who normally correspond with you. This was another feature of the "I Love You" virus—

it automatically mailed itself to everyone on the user's mailing list, thereby creating the impression that the attachment is from a friend or colleague. Therefore, you should have a virus protection program running in the background at all times. In addition, you should constantly update your virus protection, since hackers are constantly dreaming up new computerized nightmares to send out into cyberspace.

A FINAL WORD OF ADVICE

In the final analysis, awareness is your best friend when it comes to ensuring that your privacy is protected. While this isn't an invitation to become paranoid, it is indeed a challenge to be careful. Never underestimate the motives or ability of the hundreds of millions of computer users around the world to tap into your life via the Internet. Know the sites you visit and be aware of their online ethics and/or security capability before you make sensitive information available to them. In the end, no one can misuse information you choose not to make available.

CHAPTER 12

Criminal Liability on the Web

Crime is an unfortunate reality of the human experience that has been around as long as mankind itself. It is a serious and growing problem in the United States as well as in other industrialized countries of the world. Consider these statistics: the total U.S. prison population at the end of 1999 stood at a record high 1,366,721, or 476 incarcerations per 100,000 citizens. This figure is up dramatically in just a decade from 292 for every 100,000 in 1990. The breakdown by gender of individuals currently serving time in state or federal prisons in the United States is 1 in every 110 adult males and 1 in every 1,695 females. And while many of these inmates have been convicted of transgressions against person and property that could be classified as common street crime, a growing segment of the criminal population is turning to more sophisticated means to further their criminal design.

This is where the more sinister aspects of the Internet come into play. Just as the invention of the gun made it easier for criminals to ply their trade, so too has the technological revolution markedly increased the capability of those who seek to manifest their criminal intent in new and imaginative but equally damaging ways. Thanks to the personal computer and the Internet, many traditional crimes such as extortion, child pornography, drug smuggling, embezzlement, and larceny have been made easier to commit and harder to detect. Additionally, crimes unknown prior to the advent of the Internet, such as hacking, cracking, and unleashing viruses on governmental, corporate, and private interests, are becoming an unsettling and dangerous reality.

Criminal liability on the web encompasses a wide range of subject matter ranging from identity theft to obscenity; stock fraud to extortion; copyright piracy to cyber-stalking; and espionage to terrorism. What these crimes all have in common is a computer and Internet access. Computer-related crime is a daunting problem for law enforcement and potential victims alike for several reasons. First, unlike cases of armed robbery or burglary, there are substantially fewer preventative measures available. Dead-bolt locks and big dogs are no deterrent to a cyber criminal. And because every office and household with a computer and an ISP is potentially the online equivalent of an unlocked window, many of us depend upon our anonymity to escape being a target.

What's worse, in many computer crimes such as identity or credit card theft or unlawful surveillance, the perpetrator is invisible to the average and even sophisticated computer user. It is not unlike sitting in the living room of your own home while criminals are upstairs calmly taking inventory of your valuables, deciding what to keep and what to leave. And even where a victim and law enforcement authorities know a crime has been committed, the law is either sketchy or nonexistent due to the rapid evolution of technology in general and the Internet in particular.

While the problems are daunting, victims and law enforcement authorities are by no means at the mercy of computer criminals. Every state in the U.S. has laws on the books that are either directly applicable to Internet crimes, or which are being interpreted as applying to criminal acts committed on the Internet.

TRACKING THE CYBER CRIMINAL

Notwithstanding criminal statutes and initiatives, prosecution for Internet crimes has been minimal compared to the number of online crimes actually committed. As in the real world, there are many factors that account for this—failure to report, failure to locate the culprit, and, as we have indicated, failure to realize that a crime has even occurred. Anonymity and proof issues are probably the greatest hurdles to prosecution. However, the seeming ability of cyber criminals to commit crimes that will go undetected is in large part illusory. E-mail, hacking and cracking, and a host of Internet uses, regardless of the purpose and motivation, are traceable, provided the authorities and their computer experts have the requisite will to follow the electronic trail to its source.

Just as telephone records can establish when, where, and to whom calls were placed, the inner workings of a computer hard drive or network can be used to provide similar if not more detailed information. Of course, the more savvy the criminal, the more precautions he or she will undoubtedly take. However, as with traditional crimes, law enforcement's greatest edge lies in the fact that many, but certainly not all, criminals are not overly bright or particularly careful when it comes to covering their tracks. The manhunt for the author of the so-called "I Love You" virus, which caused millions of dollars of harm around the world in late 2000, shows that, given enough motivation (here, in the form of widespread economic damage), authorities take these actions very seriously and ultimately have the resources to pursue seemingly invisible or anonymous perpetrators.

If these crimes are so difficult to detect, how can criminals ever be caught? Although the more technical aspects of tracking cybercrimes is a more appropriate subject for a nuts-and-bolts technical manual, a simple answer is that computers can save information even when you intend to erase it. For instance, most people understand that deleting a file removes it to a "recycle bin" or "trash can," which is a staging area for files waiting to be deleted. From there, you can either restore the file or permanently delete it by "emptying" the bin. However, a recent case litigated by the authors on behalf of one of their clients illustrates that this is not the end of the matter.

In this case, a company whom we'll call DEF Corp. purchased a computer system from another company, whom we'll call The Computer Co. The computer system was never properly installed and networked, and after six months of tinkering with it, DEF's frustration led to a decision to delete the software. After another year of arguing with The Computer Co. over whether it was due a refund, DEF decided that it was time to take the matter to court. DEF realized that, if it were to receive a total refund for the system, it would have to return the hardware to The Computer Co. However, The Computer Co.'s subsidiary was a business that was in nearly direct competition with DEF. Since deleting the software package did not erase the customer data that DEF had entered in order to run the system, DEF Corp.'s Technology Director became concerned that The Computer Co. would be able to retrieve all of the data from the system by simply reinstalling the software package. The Computer Co. would then have access to DEF's entire customer list, giving its subsidiary a distinct competitive advantage. The Technology Director decided to wipe the computers completely clean of data by using a software program designed to remove all information from computer systems.

When the litigation commenced, The Computer Co. did exactly what DEF thought it would do—it demanded access to the hardware with the intention of trying to recover the software and/or customer data that had been on the computers. Due to the Technology Director's precautionary measures, however, The Computer Co. was unable to recover any customer data, or anything else, for that matter. You should note, however, that The Computer Co. accused DEF of destroying the data in order to hide the fact that the system was functional after all. Destroying evidence when litigation is imminent is never a good idea.

Although this case was settled before the court could decide whether the destruction of data was warranted, it does illustrate the point—deleting software or other files does not guarantee that the information is removed. Information deleted in this manner is not really deleted at all. In the case of deleted software, files containing the information that you input may remain intact, only there is no longer a program on the computer that knows how to read the files. A good example of this would be files created with an ordinary word processor. If you create a letter to a friend and save the letter as "MyLetter," when you delete the word processing program, the file "MyLetter" will remain on your computer.

In the case of deleted files, the computer removes the information that tells the computer what is located on that portion of its hard drive. Since the computer has no information about what is located in that area, the computer assumes that there is nothing there and that the area is free to store other material. As the above case illustrates, however, the information is still retrievable by people who know how unless you take the added measure of wiping the computer clean with a utility program that is designed for that purpose.

COMBATING HACKING, CRACKING, VIRUSES, AND OTHER COMPUTERIZED NIGHTMARES

As we discussed in Chapter 11, security issues related to hacking, cracking, viruses, worms, Trojan Horses, etc. can range from mildly annoying to financially serious. The most common crimes on the Internet are cyber-trespasses and vandalism of these sorts, with the number of breaches increasing by several hundred percent each year. Financial institutions, government and military agencies, and multi-national corporations have all proven vulnerable to these attacks.

There are a few new laws and several pre-existing laws that have been adapted to Internet crimes that can be used as a basis to prosecute violators for breaches of government security. Most relevant to the focus of this book is the Computer Fraud and Abuse Act ("CFAA"), which has a more general application. Although the sentencing is largely based on the amount of damage or loss suffered by the victim, some areas are applicable even if there is no tangible loss. Basically, the CFAA protects seven specific areas from abuses associated with computer crime.

Classified Information

The classified information section of the CFAA makes the intentional, unauthorized access of such information a felony. However, in order to make the access actionable, the person accessing the information must believe that the information can be used to injure the United States or assist foreign countries. This is, in essence, computer espionage.

Financial Information

Financial information copied, removed, or even simply viewed from a financial institution or credit reporting agency and information of any kind held by the government is protected under the financial information section of the CFAA. In addition, this section protects any private data viewed without authority through a computer system. For instance, some credit reporting agencies allow you to access and view your credit report online. When you attempt to access your credit report, the credit-reporting agency asks certain questions in order to verify that you are the person for whom you are requesting the report.

Under this statute, then, misrepresenting your identity to access someone else's report would appear to be a crime.

Trespass against Government Computers

The section regarding trespass against government computers protects computers used by the government, even if the use is on a part-time basis and even if no damage occurs and no information is stolen. Although the first item on this list protects government computers, it only protects classified information. This item protects information that is not classified, and again, creates liability even if the information is only viewed and not otherwise affected.

Trespass against Any "Protected Computer" to Take Property

The section concerning trespass against any protected computer to take property prohibits using a computer knowingly to take property valued at more than $5,000.00. A *protected computer* is any computer used, completely or partially, by the government, a financial institution, or used in interstate commerce or communications. On the Internet, this would seem to apply to just about every computer connected. It is difficult to imagine a computer located in one state and using an ISP and connecting to web sites only within that same state. Internet use is, almost by definition, interstate communication. The simplest example of taking property valued at more than $5,000 would be accessing a computer and transferring money from someone else's bank account.

Damage to "Protected Computers"

Deliberately or recklessly causing damage by dispatching worms, viruses, Trojan Horses, and other damaging programs is covered under damage to protected computers. This violation can be a felony if certain types of damages are caused, including monetary damages (in excess of $5,000), modification (even potential modification) to medical information, or threats to public health. Unintentional damage is a misdemeanor if the person accessing the system is an unauthorized user. Some laws appear to apply only to unauthorized users, meaning that an authorized user, such as an employee, who deliberately causes damage may not be liable. That is not the case with this statute.

It might be helpful to define the difference between "intentional" and "unintentional" damage. It is not necessarily essential that the individual intend to cause the damage, but only that he or she intends to access the computers. A case in point concerned a Cornell University student who created a worm for the purpose of illustrating security breaches. The student misconfigured the program, causing it to crash systems and to clog network routes all over the country. He was convicted under the CFAA even though he had not intended to design the worm to cause any damage at all. However, he did intend to spread the worm, and it cost him $10,500 in fines, 400 hours of community service, and three years probation nonetheless.

Distribution of Passwords Used to Access Computers

As we noted in Chapter 11, the distribution of passwords used to access computers was a feature of the "I Love You" virus and is, in fact, a common feature of many viruses. However, consider that other sections of the act are intended to cover viruses. The coverage here is more complete. Giving away passwords in any context, so long as the trading relates to government computers or occurs in interstate or foreign commerce, which is necessary to give the federal government jurisdiction, is actionable.

Extortion

Perhaps the best example of extortion under the CFAA would be that of a computer cracker who threatened to steal and divulge information from a system unless the system operators paid money. Consider the case of *Ford Motor Co. v. Lane* in Chapter 6, where someone took trade secrets from Ford Motor Company and posted them on his web site. Obviously, this information was important enough to Ford for them to go to court to preserve it. Suppose a cracker instead accessed the computer system and stole the information, then threatened to post it on his web site if Ford didn't agree to pay a large sum of money. This would be actionable under this section, and possibly others, of the CFAA.

As an aside, you should be aware that, although in many places the CFAA imposes liability even without damage, the sentencing is determined based on the amount of damage suffered. For instance, if a hacker gained access to a computer, looked at the information on the system, left a message that said "Ha, Ha, I was here," then left everything else exactly as he found it without copying or stealing anything, it is unlikely that a sentence would be very harsh. This takes some of the force out of the portions of the statute that apply to simply viewing information. However, imposing harsh sentences on those who don't intend any harm is a step that the law is not yet willing to take.

WIRE FRAUD, ELECTRONIC THEFT, AND COPYRIGHT INFRINGEMENT

In essence, a conviction for wire fraud requires the defendant's knowing and willful participation in a scheme to defraud someone using interstate wire communications. One issue in dispute in cases of wire fraud, to date, has been its applicability to the theft of intellectual property over the Internet. In 1994, a federal district court held that copyright prosecutions did not fall under the wire fraud statute because the statute applied only to tangible property, not intangible property, such as copyright interests.

Although this is the law with respect to wire fraud, the issue does not end there. The case that established that wire fraud does not support copyright prosecutions has been limited by the No Electronic Theft Act. As we discussed in Chapter 7, a prominent copyright issue on the Internet is "file sharing." Many people believed they could "share" copyrighted materials as long as they received no payment in return. In 1997, Congress made it clear this is not the case. The No Electronic Theft Act created criminal penalties for willful copyright infringement. Recall from Chapter 5 that criminal infringement occurs when a person reproduces and distributes copyrighted works with a retail value totaling over $1,000, even if there is no financial gain. Considering the large number of MP3 files offered by some Napster users, it would appear that the statute may technically apply to them. However, at this point, no one has indicated that prosecutions are in these users' near future. As with many other situations, this may be partially public policy, in addition to the difficulty that tracking each individual user would pose, since Napster took sketchy information on its users and did not attempt to verify any information collected. Whether file sharing is a violation of copyright laws has been a hot issue in the public forum and has been the subject of many congressional hearings. This debate has created a gray area where obtaining a conviction would be difficult until the law is clear on the subject.

OBSCENITY AND PORNOGRAPHY

Pornography, so long as it is not considered to be technically "obscene," is generally considered protected speech, and therefore is readily available on the Internet. As discussed in Chapter 6, speech that is legally considered to be obscene is not only unprotected by the First Amendment, but can subject the speaker to prosecution. Federal law prohibits interstate transportation of obscene materials. The ongoing problem that has always plagued courts in obscenity cases is the lack of some objective standard by which to define controversial works. One person's work of art is another's smut. This subjective element that pervades the law of obscenity prompted former Supreme Court Justice Potter Stewart to utter the famous aphorism regarding pornography "I know it when I see it."

The Supreme Court has attempted to bring some clarity to the problem of defining an obscene work by viewing it in the light of, among other things, an analysis of community standards. Generally speaking, the analysis directs the court to determine whether the local community would believe that the work appeals to "prurient interests."

When it comes to the Internet, the obvious question is posed. Just whose community sets the standard? In 1996, a married couple was charged in Tennessee with violation of the federal statute for transporting obscene materials by mail and via the telephone company. The couple resided in California where they operated their bulletin board service. It offered pornographic materials posted in California. However, a postal inspector accessed the service from Tennessee, downloaded files, then requested via telephone that items be mailed to him in Tennessee.

Although the service originated in California, the more conservative Tennessee "community standard" was used, resulting in a conviction. Several questions were raised on appeal, including the community standard issue, but the conviction was upheld. The court noted that the place of origination did not affect the ability of the materials to be viewed in Tennessee. The couple was subsequently convicted in Utah for similar offenses.

Even if a person's local community would not consider certain materials obscene, distribution of the materials on the Internet could subject the distributor to prosecution anywhere in the United States, or, for that matter, anywhere in the world where extradition could be obtained. Given the brave new borderless world of cyberspace and the increasing homogeneity of not only the United States but the world by virtue of mass media and communication capability, it becomes readily apparent that the idea of "local community" is quickly vanishing in the emerging global village. As a result, look for innovation in the area of legal definition of pornography, just as in other areas of the law that are surely being transformed by the Internet.

While reasonable minds can differ over the sometimes thin line that separates legitimate, albeit controversial, art from obscenity, few would disagree that child pornography is not merely just a controversial art form. Consequently, it is considered to be unprotected speech for purposes of the First Amendment. Federal law prohibits the production, distribution, and receipt of child pornography, in addition to the posting of advertisements offering to sell, buy, trade, produce, display, or distribute these types of materials. Intentionally possessing child pornography taken off the Internet is punishable by fines and/or imprisonment of up to five years for a first offense. The penalties for possessing with intent to sell range from up to 15 years for first offenses to up to 30 years for second offenses.

In fact, sentencing for Internet child pornography can be even more severe simply because a computer is involved. In at least one case, *United States v. Delmarle,* a man caught sending pornographic materials to a law enforcement officer posing as a 12-year-old boy had his sentence increased substantially, among other reasons, because he used the Internet to transmit the photographs. Although transmitting child pornography is a criminal act, which would have called for a normal sentence, the court reasoned that the increase was justified because the man was also intending to solicit a 12-year-old.

CYBERSTALKING

Cyberstalking, the use of e-mail or Internet communication to stalk another person, is one of the new breed of crimes made possible by the technological revolution. Due to the anonymity provided by the Internet, it can be prime ground for cyberstalkers. Online stalking may seem harmless if both users are anonymous and live across the country from each other. In such a case it may seem that the worst that can happen is a few startling e-mails. However, while the anonymous stalker could be on the other side of the world, there is no guarantee that he is not just around the corner. Cases of cyberstalking may take many forms, all of which can cause not only mental and emotional disturbance, but dire physical consequences as well. Documented cases of cyberstalking include multiple threatening e-mails sent daily for a period of over a year; the posting of the address and phone number of a victim, along with invitations to rape her; the posting of doctored photographs and false information; and blackmail. As noted by the Department of Justice in its study on cyberstalking, threatening e-mails can be a prelude to more serious behavior. A resourceful stalker can retrieve a lot of information about a person with the right questions and a little investigation. Once the information is gathered, a stalker is only a plane ticket or a short walk away.

As with other crimes against persons, such as assault, criminal trespass, and even homicide, stalking is largely a matter of state law. Where a state prohibits stalking, online stalking also may be actionable, depending upon the specific statute. There are currently 23 states that have enacted laws specifically designed to address this problem. California, the first state to enact such a law, prohibits stalking communicated by computers and other electronic devices. Connecticut's law criminalizes harassment through computer use. In Arkansas, the law prohibits frightening, intimidating, threatening, or abusing a person through e-mail communications. In Maryland, a person may not use e-mail with the intent to harass. The penalties for cyberstalking vary from state to state.

Cyberstalking originates with, or is exacerbated by, giving another user too much information. Many people trust other users with personal information, believing there is no harm in it. They also divulge bits and pieces of seemingly useless information that can be put together to form a startlingly complete profile. As we have stated before, when it comes to dealing with strangers, either in person or online, you can never be too careful.

SEARCHES AND SEIZURES ON THE WEB

Generally speaking, the same search and seizure rules apply to Internet devices as to anything else. This means that, with proper authorization (such as a properly obtained search warrant), authorities may seize computers and/ or computer files that have been used in a crime, or that contain evidence necessary for investigating a crime, or that may prove a crime. However, there are some special protections for electronic communications and publishing materials.

The Electronic Communications Privacy Act of 1986 ("ECPA") protects electronic mail from interception or disclosure by anyone except online operators in the performance of their duties. An exception is provided if an online operator happens to come across an e-mail that appears to contain evidence of a crime. Under these circumstances he or she may disclose the message to the proper authorities. Recall the discussion in Chapter 11 concerning privacy on the web. Of particular interest in this area are programs such as Carnivore, which is designed to intercept e-mail communications that contain certain information. The ECPA prohibits interception in this manner without a properly obtained search warrant.

Stored data is treated differently. E-mails are considered to be stored even if they have not yet been read by the recipient. Any unauthorized person who accesses stored communications, such as saved e-mail messages, or who discloses those messages, is subject to fines and imprisonment. Law enforcement agencies must first obtain a search warrant to seize the files, however, and must allow the system operator to make and keep a backup copy of all data, so that the data can still be used while it is in possession of authorities.

The Privacy Protection Act of 1980 provides further protection for publishers. These protections were designed to aid in investigative reporting and journalism supporting the Freedom of the Press provided in the First Amendment. If people know that information they send reporters can be confiscated, it may have the effect of "chilling" free press by discouraging people from participating in investigative reporting. These protections more than likely apply to those who use computers and the Internet for publishing activities, such as online newspapers and periodicals. Law enforcement authorities may not seize publishing materials unless the person in possession of the materials is suspected of a crime and the materials to be seized are related to that crime.

For instance, if you operate a retail business through your web site and someone sends you an e-mail that has evidence of a crime, such as an e-mail with a stolen credit card number that they want to use to buy goods, then authorities may seize that e-mail. However, suppose instead of a retail operation, you run an eZine (electronic magazine). If you are writing a story about credit card fraud on the web, and someone sends you an e-mail with a list of stolen credit card numbers and a description of how they got them, then authorities may not confiscate that e-mail because you are not involved in a crime. Let's take it a little further. Say your eZine makes a lot of money that you deliberately conceal from the IRS. Now you would be involved in a crime. However, authorities still can't have the e-mail, because the e-mail doesn't relate to the crime that has been committed.

A quick word about warrants, while we're on the subject. A law enforcement agency must be specific about what items they wish to seize before a magistrate may issue a search warrant. However, they do not have to provide the names of the particular files that contain evidence, nor provide specific information on what each file may contain. As long as they provide information concerning the type of file and the person to whom it is connected, such as e-mails to a person with a certain e-mail address, as well as examples of what the files they are looking for will contain (for example, if the e-mails with the criminal evidence have attachments with pornographic images of children), the information is sufficient. When a law enforcement agency approaches a service provider with a warrant for this type of information, it does not have to specify which of the e-mails to the recipient contain criminal evidence and which do not.

IDENTITY THEFT

As we discussed in Chapter 11, identity theft is a growing problem, both on and off the web. Celebrities and private citizens alike have felt the affects of cyber-criminals who have either accessed their accounts, or created new accounts in their names, sometimes with damages running into the hundreds of thousands of dollars. Where security, on the Internet or otherwise, doesn't protect you from becoming a victim, your liability is limited by current law to $50. The criminal is subject to criminal penalties for stealing credit cards or blank checks from a purse or wallet (these are largely a matter of state law), in addition to possible penalties under the CFAA. However, this doesn't help you repair the damage the theft causes. The damage to your credit and good name is not something your insurance can cover.

If you are the victim of this kind of fraud, you should contact the fraud divisions of all three major credit reporting companies (Equifax, Trans Union, and Experian), in addition to the fraud division of the credit card companies and banks where the accounts are tampered with. In fact, for a fee, some credit reporting companies offer an alert program that will notify you any time an entry meeting certain criteria is placed on your credit report. Fixing the damage may be a long, cumbersome process, so be prepared.

A FINAL WORD OF ADVICE

This chapter has been only a brief overview of crimes that can be committed on the Internet. Again, in addition to federal laws, state laws and international laws vary. Consistent with our advice in the areas of privacy and security, reasonable vigilance and common sense are the best ways to avoid becoming a victim. Know who you are dealing with and maintain a healthy sense of skepticism. As in all other walks of life, trust should be earned. Interacting with others online does not change that rule.

CHAPTER 13

Jurisdiction: Whose Law Applies in the Borderless World of Cyberspace?

One of the greatest advantages of the Net is its global reach. From the standpoint of web site operation, however, this can also be one of its biggest drawbacks. As we have mentioned several times, practices (such as the use of customer data) that may be perfectly acceptable in one place can get us in a lot of trouble somewhere else. For most of us, the prospect of being pulled into civil litigation or, worse yet, being subjected to criminal prosecution outside of our home state may seem remote. But, as some web site operators have learned, the prospect of having to face the music somewhere other than their own backyard is very much a reality due to both traditional and emerging rules of personal jurisdiction that are being applied to the new technological frontier of the Internet.

THE RULE OF LAW AND CIVIL PROCEDURE

To better understand the procedural rules related to jurisdiction discussed in this chapter, it is worthwhile to consider the "rule of law" on which contemporary notions of jurisdiction are grounded.

We have all heard the expression "the rule of law." In essence, this simply means that disputes are settled by a neutral judge or jury, using a uniformly administered set of laws. The aim is the objective resolution of problems based solely on notions of fairness and impartiality. The rule of law may well be the greatest achievement of the legal system. Just as the ability to logically reason makes a civilized society possible, the rule of law provides the certainty, stability, and predictability necessary for a free market economic system to prosper and a free society to flourish. Without exception, it is the centerpiece of every single economically prosperous nation in the world. Where the rule of law breaks down or is nonexistent, we see repeated patterns of corruption, economic uncertainty, lack of opportunity, low levels of investment and standards of living, and high levels of disease, illiteracy, and poverty. It is civilized society's single most important factor in economic development and personal well-being.

The rule of law requires a political system willing by and large to level the playing field for all economic comers. This means adoption of a uniform set of substantive laws and rules that apply to everyone in order to assure there is consistency and accountability regarding standards of business as well as personal conduct. There must also be a uniform set of procedural rules that provide assurance to everyone that they will be given a prompt and fair hearing when the inevitable disputes that punctuate modern life arise. This requires fairness, uniformity, and credibility coupled with a population that has a stake in the system. When any of these elements are missing, we see disputes being settled by force not reason, governments acting arbitrarily rather than systematically.

The concept and underlying rules of jurisdiction are founded upon the idea that fairness is guaranteed to every American citizen by the U.S. Constitution. In the context of jurisdiction, only certain courts in certain circumstances may require citizens to appear before them for a settlement of disputes or a determination of guilt or innocence in criminal matters. The courts are in effect referees charged with ruling on jurisdictional lines drawn by the legislative branch. Until now, these lines have always been based on territory. However, problems begin to arise when they are applied to the Internet because of its ability to transcend conventional territorial boundaries.

As with so many other areas of the law, the Internet has created questions which have never before been asked or answered. Nonetheless, if we are to preserve the rule of law in the Information Age, it is vital that we adapt it in such a way as to preserve the goals of legitimacy, fairness, predictability, certainty, and stability that it has served so effectively and efficiently in centuries past. From a more personal standpoint as an Internet user and a participant in e-commerce, you need to know when, where, and under what circumstances you can be held accountable should those inevitable disputes and disagreements involve you.

JURISDICTION BASICS

Jurisdiction is the power and authority of a court to hear and determine a judicial proceeding. Generally, there must exist jurisdiction over the subject matter as well as the particular parties to a dispute. Courts lacking in one or both of these essentials are powerless to decide legal issues or disputes.

Subject Matter Jurisdiction

The term *subject matter jurisdiction* refers to a court's authority to hear and determine cases in certain general categories. For example, issues relating to copyright validity and infringement are matters of exclusive federal subject matter jurisdiction. This means that the state courts are powerless to compel anyone to appear for a trial arising out of a dispute grounded in copyright law. Consequently, the federal court system has exclusive subject matter jurisdiction over copyright. On the other hand, let's assume that a dispute arises between two parties who have negotiated a license of one of the exclusive rights under the Copyright Act. Since the basic dispute in this case is contractual in nature, even though it deals with subject matter protected by copyright, the state law of contracts would apply.

Personal Jurisdiction

The term *personal jurisdiction* concerns the power of a court over a defendant (also known as *in personam* jurisdiction), in contrast to the jurisdiction of a court over a defendant's property (also known as *in rem* jurisdiction). In addition to subject matter jurisdiction, a court is also required to have personal jurisdiction over the person charged as the defendant. This means that the defendant charged must have some tie to the state to make him or her answerable to that state's courts. Assuming that a connection is found, personal jurisdiction is complete when the plaintiff serves a summons on the defendant, which is in effect actual notice of the complaint against him. The most common way this is done is personal delivery by a process server on a defendant who resides in the state where the dispute arose or where the court issuing the summons sits.

But suppose the defendant's whereabouts are unknown or the plaintiff is unsuccessful in personally delivering a summons because the defendant is a non-resident of the state in which the dispute arose or the lawsuit was filed. In certain circumstances, a plaintiff may serve a defendant through what is known as a *long-arm statute* or by publication. By statute, legislatures of various states allow personal jurisdiction over non-resident persons or businesses, such as corporations or limited liability companies, that are deemed to be doing business in that particular state, who commit a wrongful act in the state, or who own, use, or possesses property within the state. For instance, let's say you are driving through a state other than your own and have an accident. If the other driver sues, that state's court may take jurisdiction over you because you caused injury and property damage on your trip through. As you will see, this concept becomes a little fuzzier when applied to the Internet.

Venue

While we are defining terms, it is useful to distinguish another commonly used legal term that is often confused with jurisdiction. Assuming a court has proper subject matter and personal jurisdiction over a defendant, *venue* refers to the physical location where the court will hear the case. For example, let's say that your accident occurred in Dade County, Florida. Florida courts would have jurisdiction and venue would be in Dade County.

NATIONAL JURISDICTIONAL ISSUES

Jurisdiction within the United States, or for that matter, within the borders of any given country, are of primary concern to any web user. A few examples of situations that have actually arisen may provide a clearer picture of how jurisdictional problems can arise.

Consider the couple discussed in Chapter 12 that was prosecuted in Tennessee for the operation of their bulletin board service in California. As you will recall, the couple ran a subscription bulletin board service for pornography, available through downloadable files and by mail order, from their home in California. They were prosecuted and convicted in both Tennessee and Utah for violation of federal obscenity laws, based on the local standard for determining if a work is obscene.

In another Internet jurisdiction case, the Attorney General for the state of Minnesota prosecuted a Nevada corporation that was running a betting operation through a server in Belize. The court decided that, because the corporation actively solicited U.S. citizens and had received calls from within the state of Minnesota, it could take jurisdiction.

Although the standards for assuming jurisdiction in criminal matters are a little more lenient than those for civil matters, there have been many situations involving the Internet where a court has assumed jurisdiction over out-of-state defendants in civil cases. A Massachusetts court assumed jurisdiction in a case involving an Israeli corporation that negotiated a contract with a Massachusetts resident by e-mail. An Ohio court assumed jurisdiction in a case concerning a Texas man who used a network service based in Ohio, both for personal use and to advertise and sell his software on the Internet. And a Connecticut court assumed jurisdiction in a case regarding a Massachusetts corporation simply because the corporation had continuously advertised on the Internet.

There are several legal concerns at issue when one state attempts to assume jurisdiction over a citizen of another. Basically, whether you can be commanded to answer to a court in another state depends on two things: the U.S. Constitution and the individual state's *long-arm statute,* which sets out a state's guidelines for when it will allow its courts to attempt to assume jurisdiction over someone who lives in another state. While the examples given earlier in this chapter are typical of long-arm statutes, there is no substitute for a detailed reading of the particular state statute at issue.

The U.S. Constitution, and the law that has subsequently explained it, requires that certain conditions be met before you can be forced to answer to a court outside your own state. In essence, the Constitution requires that you have sufficient contact with the state involved and that expecting you to appear before that court would be fair. These may appear to be very vague guidelines. However, state courts have specific elements that they look for when analyzing these factors.

State courts consider whether you, as an out-of-state defendant, "purposely availed" yourself of that state—for instance, by soliciting business from that state. If you deliberately solicit business from a state, then you should have to answer for your actions there. The problem, however, lies with the word "deliberate." If, for example, you place an ad on the Internet that you know can be viewed by anyone in the world, can it be said that you deliberately solicited business from a particular state? Several courts have said yes, especially where sites have accepted inquiries or filled orders from the state in question.

Even if sufficient contact with the state exists, a court must still determine whether assuming jurisdiction is fair. There are a number of factors it must review before coming to a decision. The court must consider how difficult it would be for you to defend the case out of your own state, as well as the plaintiff's interest in the convenient settlement of his or her claims, plus a few other issues that have to do with the individual state's interests and the efficient operation of all of the states. Although these issues are important, if sufficient contacts exist, then jurisdiction in that state is generally considered fair. Only once has the U.S. Supreme Court found that jurisdiction would not be fair even though the contacts were there.

As we noted above, courts have reasoned that most aspects of Internet use create grounds for a court to assume jurisdiction. Generally speaking, users do not have the same jurisdiction problems as those operating web sites, although as you will remember from earlier in this chapter, two parties negotiating a contract through e-mail came across this issue.

There are basically two ways that a web site can operate: it can be passive, similar to a cyber-billboard, or it can be active, sending out promotional e-mails, requesting that users enter information, advertising through banner ads, or other activities. The owner of an active site is far more likely to find herself called into court in a state other than her own, due to the fact that the site is deliberately interacting with users.

A number of courts have noted that simply having a web site is not enough reason to assume jurisdiction over a non-resident, although a few have not taken that view. Many plaintiffs have attempted to persuade courts to assume jurisdiction based on the existence of a web site that the plaintiff never used. For example, let's assume you go to a hotel in New York and, while there, you slip on a wet floor in the lobby, resulting in a broken arm. Can you then go back to your home in Wyoming and sue the hotel there simply because the hotel maintains a web site? Probably not, especially if you did not even look at the web site before you made your visit.

On the other end of the spectrum are the cases where courts frequently find that assuming jurisdiction is constitutionally acceptable. For example, let's say you click a banner ad that takes you to a web site that sells products, then you enter your name, address, and credit card number to order the product through the site. If that product blows up and burns down your house, you probably will be able to sue in your home state. This is because the web site actively solicited your business, and therefore has sufficient contact with your state.

There is a large gray area between these two extremes. Returning to our hotel example, what if the Wyoming hotel erroneously reports to a credit-reporting agency that you failed to pay your bill? If the hotel has a web site that allowed you to enter your e-mail address for notification of special deals, can you sue them in your home state for your financial injuries? Maybe. The interactivity of the site is important, although it may depend on how many people in your state have actually interacted with the site. What if they also have a page on the site that lists your travel agent for booking arrangements? The answer then changes from maybe to probably. Including your travel agent on the site is even more likely to help you bring the hotel to your state, since that "localizes" the web site to some extent.

GLOBAL JURISDICTIONAL CONCERNS

One of the increasing problems related to issues of jurisdiction has to do with the phenomenon of borderless activities. Online casino gambling is a case in point. Casino gambling, once legal only in Nevada, has enjoyed tremendous expansion within the United States. Likewise, casino gaming, and sports betting on professional and collegiate sporting events, has enjoyed significant expansion throughout the world. This interest has spawned online gambling casinos that operate outside the jurisdiction of the United States in such places as Antigua or other islands in the Caribbean. The question is simply this, can a person in Utah, which bans all forms of gambling, go online and place a sports bet with an offshore casino without fear of being prosecuted by the State of Utah? More ominous for patrons of online casinos and sportsbooks is pending federal legislation to make this type of activity a federal crime. While it has yet to be signed into law, it has a great deal of support, not to mention funding, from the gaming lobby in Nevada and elsewhere.

An interesting example of international conflicts on the web is iToke.co.uk. iToke, a European site, aims to offer marijuana to its customers via a 30-minute bicycle delivery service. There is no indication that the site ever intends to ship orders. However, for the purposes of illustration, what if it did? For obvious reasons, U.S. sales from this site would be problematic, and the site disclaims liability for any illegal orders. Perhaps a more sobering example of this conflict is evident in a suit brought by the Paris International League against Racism and Anti-Semitism (LICRA) and the Union of French Jewish Students (UEJF) against Yahoo!® Although Yahoo!® maintains a French site that complies with French laws, Yahoo!'s United States site carries an auction which allowed users to offer Nazi paraphernalia for sale. Since the offering of these materials violated French law, Yahoo!® found itself ordered to block French users from its U.S. site—a logistical problem, to say the least.

Yahoo's problem raises concerns over whether a site should be required to restrict its use to a specific country, an idea which seems in direct conflict with the free flow of information that the Internet was designed to encourage. Furthermore, considering the makeup of the web, is such restriction even possible? Although Yahoo!® created a web site specifically for France, that did not make its U.S. site any less accessible to the French. Remember that the make-up of the Internet is a series of servers, linked to each other and to the users that access them. Therefore, any site is accessible by any person on the web, unless restrictions, such as those used by members-only sites, are in place.

If you are wondering how a government across the world can get to you, the fact is, they may not be able to. Companies that operate in other countries typically have holdings in that country that may be attached, especially if they file tax returns or the like. These companies may use foreign ISPs or other mechanisms that the government can take action upon. If you don't have property in another country, they probably will leave you alone unless they have a good reason for seeking extradition, although plantiffs may occasionally attempt to enforce a judgement in your country.

GLOBAL CONTRACTUAL CONCERNS

Another jurisdictional issue has to do with contractual relations among individuals or business entities residing in different countries. For instance, assume a U.S.-based company has, by virtue of a contract, the exclusive right to distribute a product in the United States, and a different company has the exclusive distribution rights in the United Kingdom. If the U.S. company places the product on its web site, does that violate the U.K. company's distribution rights since the site may be accessed and orders placed from anywhere in the world? What about a record company with a license to record and distribute a composition in the U.S. and Canada? Can it accept an online order from Australia?

Of course, the easiest response to questions such as these is to make sure that territories are delineated in your contracts. If you are licensed to distribute products on the Internet, you should make sure that the contract specifically states whether you may take orders worldwide or only from specified areas. The answers are not always that simple, however. If you have any doubts, you may refuse orders outside of a certain geographical area by noting "U.S. Orders Only" (there are other reasons for restricting orders in this manner as well, such as legal restrictions in the excluded areas).

If the territory is not spelled out in the contract, then in the situations outlined above there is a violation of the contract if the goods are sold outside of the territory. For instance, remembering that copyrights are actually a bundle of individual rights, if you obtain a license to sell compact discs in the United States, then you have acquired a "stick from the bundle" that allows you to use the material in a limited manner. If you then sell the CDs to someone in another country, you have violated the owner's copyright because you are selling goods in a manner for which you are not licensed.

This problem has arisen more often in the area of pre-recorded music than anywhere else because it is less expensive in the U.K. to purchase a CD online than to buy one in a store. The European Court of Justice (ECJ) has frequently held that importing products from outside of the European Economic Area without the consent of the owner of the intellectual property right is impermissible. However, the cases largely concern real-world, large-scale imports rather than individual Internet purchases. Although the ECJ would likely find that individual Internet purchases are impermissible, the purchases are obviously more difficult to track, especially when they are in the form of downloads rather than shipments. In addition, with the growth of the Internet, there is pressure to conform to the practices that are already in place on the web, especially considering the benefits that the consumer realizes from them.

TAX ISSUES

The old adage about nothing being certain but death and taxes compels us to at least mention tax issues—you're bound to come across them. A full discussion of tax laws is beyond the scope of this book. An in-depth discussion of the Internal Revenue Code alone could take up an entire volume. However, it bears mentioning that the same problems related to jurisdiction you encounter in other areas can certainly surface with regard to tax liability.

Just as there are federal statutes, state statutes, and local municipal ordinances, so too are there federal, state, and local income, sales, and excise taxes, not to mention international tax levies. This multiplicity of taxes raises a multiplicity of tax questions. For instance, if you operate a web site in Florida offering products for sale, are you obligated to collect state sales tax for residents of Maine who order from your site? If you conduct your web-based business from your home in Alabama, but use a web host based in Virginia, what state do you operate out of for income tax purposes?

There are additional tax issues related to the specific activities you conduct on your web site. For instance, let's say you allow your customers to download a software program. From the standpoint of sales tax liability, by giving permission and furnishing the means that allow customers to download the software, are you selling goods for which taxes should be collected or are you merely granting a license? Some companies operate on the web by providing purchasers services as well as goods. The classification of goods and services is important because the tax liability may be different, depending upon which you are offering.

Generally speaking, the answers to these and other questions depend on exactly how you run your web site. Because every web site owner has a different approach to conducting business over the Internet, we advise you to allocate a little time and money to consult a tax attorney who can tailor his or her advice to the specifics of your operation. As with medicine, an ounce of prevention is worth a pound of cure. Anybody who has ever received an unexpected bill from a tax authority knows what we are talking about.

SAFEGUARDS AGAINST JURISDICTIONAL DISPUTES

One bit of knowledge you should get from this chapter is that there are no concrete rules. However, there are a few specific ways to help limit your legal exposure in jurisdictional matters.

One of the simplest safeguards that a web site owner can take is to include terms and conditions on your Internet product offerings. Most web sites include this information, although the law is beginning to change how this must be done in order for it to be legally effective. For instance, a link on the home page entitled "Terms and Conditions" may not create legally effective terms. On the other hand, a link on the home page that says "Your use of this site is governed by our Terms and Conditions" is more likely to create terms that a court will enforce.

Assuming that your method of displaying terms and conditions makes them binding on your users, what terms should you include? A privacy policy, copyright and trademark policy, a disclaimer of liability for third-party sites, choice of venue, choice of law, and arbitration clause are fairly common. Some of these are discussed in more depth in Chapters 4, 11, and 14. However, to illustrate the concepts discussed in this chapter, we will discuss the venue, choice of law, and arbitration provisions in a little more depth.

A *venue provision* is a statement designating the geographic locale of any prospective litigation, if any, to which your user agrees as a condition of using your site. You must pick a location that is actually related to the transaction. If you live in Florida, and have a web host in Virginia, you cannot choose California law just because you like their rules. Most courts won't honor your choice. Generally, you should choose your home state or the state in which your server is located for both venue and law. This will help limit a user's ability to drag you into court halfway across the world. A *choice of law* provision is a statement indicating whose laws will apply to the transaction. An arbitration clause is a good idea as well. *Arbitration* is a binding, non-judicial method of solving disputes by presenting them to a neutral third party. It is generally faster, easier, and less expensive than full-blown litigation. You can also designate where arbitration is to be held which, again, limits your geographical exposure to the place where the arbitration is held.

A few words of caution, though. First of all, a choice of law, venue, or arbitration provision will not help you if the person does not actually use your web site. Remember that it is use of your site that indicates acceptance of your terms. For example, let's say that when you design your home page, you decide to use your favorite song as background music. If the owner of the copyright finds out about it, even though he hasn't used your site, he can attempt to sue you in his own jurisdiction.

Secondly, just because you have a venue provision doesn't mean that someone won't try to sue you somewhere else. Anyone can attempt to sue you anywhere for anything. You may still have to fight the jurisdiction battle—you just have a better chance of winning it.

Finally, keep in mind that there are no guarantees that a court will honor your choices. As we have demonstrated, there are a wide range of decisions in this area. Terms and conditions are simple and low cost. If a court honors them, then they are definitely worth the small amount of effort. If it doesn't, then you haven't lost anything by trying.

A FINAL WORD OF ADVICE

Like so much of the rest of the Internet's legal landscape, issues related to jurisdiction are in varying states of flux. Our coverage of jurisdictional problems and issues is illustrative of probable outcomes. However, always remember that in this country there are 50 states, each with separate statutes and rules relative to jurisdiction. Add to this the sprawling body of law applicable federal statutes and administrative regulations. The best advice is to analyze the specifics of how you run your e-business or otherwise use the web where issues of jurisdiction might arise.

There is simply no substitute for consulting an attorney to give you a definitive answer to your particular question. It is not our goal to turn you into an Internet lawyer, but rather to educate you on recurring issues that might be applicable to your particular circumstances. Because most lawyers charge by the hour to advise you on issues such as these, we want to help give you the necessary background to make your questions more highly focused while also helping you understand the answer your lawyer will likely give you. Being better informed and more savvy can help you keep your legal problems and bills to a minimum.

CHAPTER 14

The Law of Contracts: The Cornerstone of the Commercial World—Virtual and Otherwise

Just as contracts play a central role in the commercial life of the bricks and mortar world, so too are they a fundamental building block of e-commerce. Unlike other areas of the legal landscape we have surveyed, the law of contracts provides the means for entrepreneurs, businesses, and consumers to assert and retain control over every aspect of their economic lives. Whether a contract involves a purchase of goods, the rendering of services, a license of rights, or a recitation of terms and conditions pertaining to web site usage, it provides a vehicle for creating and protecting valuable rights that will, if necessary, be enforced by a court of law.

Even in cases where a dispute never arises, a contract provides a forum where potential problems and pitfalls can be identified and resolved in advance. It also provides the parties with a mutually accessible tool that allows them to document the terms of their agreement. In the best of all worlds, parties will make a deal, shake hands, reduce the agreement to writing, and file it away, using it only as a reference to clarify the specific terms of the deal that was made. Whether or not problems ever materialize, each party to the contract can proceed in an environment of security and certainty where surprises are replaced by predictability, and anxiety by peace of mind.

While there are an almost limitless number of contractual fine points that may confront you in your use of the Internet, we want to focus on some of the most frequent and recurring issues you are likely to encounter. These include contracts with your web designer or anyone else you might engage to create custom software packages, contracts formed over the Internet with other business people, Internet licensing agreements, and specific Terms and Conditions language you will include on your web site to create a contract with your users.

Each of these types of contracts has different implications. For instance, contracts with web designers may be negotiated in person, so your main concerns will relate to what rights to keep and what rights to allow the designer. On the other hand, contracts created over the Internet may not satisfy certain traditional legal requirements that are necessary to make a contract enforceable, so it's critical to ensure that your agreement will stand up in court should problems arise. Still other types of contractual relationships can require your attention in both of these areas.

CONTRACT LAW BASICS

A *contract* is an agreement between two or more persons that creates a legally enforceable obligation to do or refrain from doing a particular thing. So how exactly do electronic contracts differ from paper contracts? Before we can explain the differences, it is essential that you understand fundamental legal principles applicable to all contracts. While the traditional law school curriculum devotes two semesters to this essential subject, we have but a few pages. Nevertheless, that should be sufficient to give you the basics.

Prerequisites to a Legally Binding Agreement

Although a basic agreement between parties can be fairly simple, in order to request that a court help you enforce it, there are several conditions that must exist before the contract is made.

Competent parties. The first prerequisite to forming a legally binding agreement is having competent parties possessing the capacity to enter into a contract. Minors or people under the influence of alcohol, drugs, or other mental infirmity are said to lack the capacity to legally bind themselves. Consequently, these types of contracts are voidable at the option of the legally incompetent party at any time before they become competent or within a short period of time after they become competent. This means that if you contract with a person who is underage, they, or their legal guardian, can choose to either honor or avoid their obligation as they see fit. Conversely, entering into a legal agreement as a competent party, you are not afforded the same flexibility under the law. As a result, if you are about to enter into any substantial contractual relationship with someone who might be a minor, it is best to request some identification first.

Consideration. Assuming you negotiate the first hurdle, you must next determine which promises will rise to the level of enforceable contractual obligations and which ones are just promises that, while perhaps sincerely made at the time, will later prove to be unenforceable. This suggests that not all promises are enforceable by the legal system. Put another way, the fact that a person makes a promise to another person with a bona fide intent to be bound at the time does not necessarily mean a court of law will later enforce that promise. The ancient requirement that a contract be supported by consideration (that is, a benefit to each person involved in the contract) to be binding was developed for the sole purpose of distinguishing between promises that are legally enforceable in a court of law and those that are not. This somewhat technical and misunderstood requirement has survived the ensuing centuries and continues to be applied to every purported contract entered into by competent parties on the Internet or otherwise.

Three elements must coexist for consideration to be found:

* The promisee (the person to whom the promise is made) must suffer legal detriment. Legal detriment is defined as doing or promising to do something that you are not legally obligated to do; or conversely, not doing or promising not to do something you are legally permitted to do.
* The detriment must induce the promise. In other words, the person making the promise must have made the promise because he or she, at least in part, wishes to exchange the detriment for the promise.
* The promise must induce the detriment.

In essence, the test for consideration is that it must be bargained for and given in exchange for the reciprocal performance by the other party. Therefore, doing something or promising to do something you are already legally obligated to do does not satisfy the test.

An example may help. Suppose a father e-mails his daughter, saying, "You have always been such a good daughter. I will give you a car for your next birthday." This is not an enforceable contract, because the daughter gives nothing in return. On the other hand, if the father said, "I will give you a car if you will go to college and get a bachelor's degree," there is consideration for a contract. The father promises his daughter a car if she agrees to go to college and get a degree, which is something that she is not legally obligated to do.

For an Internet example of consideration, suppose the parent of a three-year-old child who resides in Southern California sets out to find a stuffed white tiger for her son. She boots up the computer and starts surfing. In short order it occurs to her that San Diego Zoo's online shop would be a great place to find a stuffed white tiger. She also reasons that by buying from the zoo, she can support their work to protect species of wild and exotic animals. Within seconds she brings up Sandiegozoo.org. After surveying the home page, she clicks on Shopzoo.com and then on animal categories, where she selects "Big Cats." As she browses the stuffed animals she sees "Lee the White Tiger" priced at $24.99. She clicks Add To Shopping Cart and then enters her credit card information. By doing so she has obligated her credit company to pay $24.99 for the stuffed tiger plus shipping. She has, in effect, promised to pay the card company for her online order. In turn the zoo has now become obligated to mail her the stuffed animal.

Even though part of the parent's motive is to support the work of the non-profit zoo, she has supplied sufficient consideration to support the zoo's promise to send her the tiger within a reasonable period of time. Had she pledged a $24.99 donation to the zoo as part of its e-mail fundraiser solicitation, her promise would be viewed as being gratuitous and not supported by consideration. Assuming she later changed her mind about the donation for the sole reason that she was close to her credit card limit, the zoo would have no recourse, even though part of her motive in making the pledge was identical to her motivation for buying her son the stuffed white tiger online.

Applicable law. Contracts are governed by state law. The particular state law that applies to a contract depends upon what state has jurisdiction. There are generally three possibilities when it comes to determining jurisdiction:

  * The state in which the contract was made or signed;
  * The state in which the contract was performed;
  * The state that the contract designates.

When parties in the same state enter into an agreement to be performed in that state where no jurisdictional clause exists, there is no question about applicable law. However, things are seldom this straightforward when it comes to the Internet.

When it comes to online transactions, it is important to read the terms and conditions. More often than not, you will come across a jurisdictional designation, which may be determinative in the event of a dispute. As you will see, whether it is binding depends largely upon how it is posted, what type of claim is made, and what state is chosen. We'll discuss this in a little more depth below.

Offer and acceptance. Assuming all of the aforementioned prerequisites have been met and we know which particular state's law will handle disputes, let's look specifically at how a contract comes into being. Contracts are formed by offer and acceptance. One party makes an offer and the other party accepts. Sounds simple enough, right? Well, there's a little more to it than that.

Let's say you tell your friend Bill you will pay him $1,500 to design a web site displaying pictures of your new puppy. Bill can do one of three things: he can simply design the site (accepting by performance); or he can say, "Okay, sounds good. I'll have you a disk with the site on it by next week" (accepting by return promise); or he can say, "Well, I don't think $1,500 would be enough, but I'll do it for $1700" (rejecting your offer and making a counter-offer).

Provided that you haven't revoked your offer before he shows up with the disk, any of the preceding methods of acceptance will create a binding contract where Bill will create your web site, and you will pay him $1,500. If he rejects your offer, then there is no contract unless you accept his counter-offer. This is called the *mirror image rule*—the acceptance must be a mirror image of the offer.

What if Bill accepts your offer by placing a post card in the mail, telling you that he will start on your web site next Tuesday? Is that a legally enforceable acceptance? Generally, Bill should accept in the same manner that you offered. So, if you made the offer over the telephone, he should accept over the telephone. If you offered him the work by sending him a letter, then he can accept with the post card.

The mailbox rule. Assuming your negotiations have been conducted by correspondence, it is a basic tenet of contract law that if you revoke your offer before Bill accepts, then no contract is ever formed. With this in mind, let's assume you change your mind and send Bill a note saying that you need the money to pay your taxes and thus you are revoking your offer. Let's further assume that Bill has already put his post card accepting your offer in the mail. Is there a contract? The answer is yes, thanks to something called the mailbox rule. The mailbox rule says that an acceptance creates a contract as soon as the acceptance is placed into a mailbox, but a revocation is not valid until Bill receives it.

The perfect tender rule. What if Bill accepts your offer, then designs a web site using pictures of your children, rather than the pictures of your puppy? Do you still have to pay him? The answer is no. The perfect tender rule says that when Bill designs your site, he has to use the pictures you told him to use. If he does not adhere to your request, then you do not have to pay him. However, there is also a doctrine called substantial performance, which applies to contracts that are substantially, but not totally, completed. This doctrine applies in some limited circumstances, such as with construction contracts. For instance, if you hire a company to build a house on your land and the builders finish the house but forget to put the lock on the front door, it is unlikely that you will be able to get away with refusing to pay the builders under the contract. The builder will, however, have to put the lock on or pay you to have someone else do it.

Contract Enforceability and the Statute of Frauds

A common contracts question for lawyers is: must a contract be in writing to be enforceable? As you might expect, the answer is, it depends. Many oral contracts are enforced every day in the court system. However, because of the doctrine of the Statute of Frauds, certain types of contracts must be in writing or at least must be in some written form and signed by the party against whom you are trying to enforce the contract.

The Statute of Frauds was initially enacted in England in the late 1600s and became effective in the English Colonies at the same time. The purpose of the statute was exactly as stated—to prevent fraud in contracts. Where the Statute of Frauds applies, a contract must be in writing to be enforced, unless one of the parties has begun to perform under the contract or has acted in reliance upon it. A "writing" does not have to be the formal written contract that most people think of when they consider contracts. It can be any document, or series of documents, that shows what terms were agreed to; terms not listed in the writing are not enforceable.

A writing has to be signed by the person that you want to enforce the contract against. Therefore, if you are the one trying to force someone else to live up to a bargain, your signature is not generally necessary, although some jurisdictions require both signatures. A signature doesn't have to be the traditional cursive writing of your own name. It may be stamped, typed, or preprinted, for example, on letterhead. In fact, a mark or symbol, such as your initials or your fingerprint, counts as a signature, too, as long as you intend for the marking to constitute your signature for the purpose of validating the contract. Your agent, such as your business partner or employee, can sign for you as well.

Although specifics may vary, there are a few general categories of agreements to which the Statute of Frauds applies. Where the Statute of Frauds applies, the agreement must be in writing or it is not enforceable. Therefore, an oral agreement to enter into a written agreement is not enforceable. Neither is an oral agreement to make a bequest in your will. If an agreement can't be performed in less than a year, a writing is required, although there are some very technical issues as to whether a contract can be performed within a year. An agreement to be responsible for someone else's debt must be in writing. Likewise, a contract for an interest in real property falls within the requirements of the Statute of Frauds.

In essence, although oral contracts are perfectly legal, the Statute of Frauds removes your ability to enforce these contracts, regardless of how many witnesses you may have. More realistically, regardless of how many written documents you may have, if there is no signature, you have no legal recourse unless you can show that you have begun to perform or have acted in reliance on the agreement.

Unconscionability. Sometimes a contractual obligation can be legally avoided where there are unconscionable (grossly unfair) terms. There are two kinds of unconscionability: procedural and substantive. Procedural unconscionability has to do with bargaining power. If the person who wants to avoid performance of the contract didn't have any real choice in the matter, there is procedural unconscionability. For instance, if the other party refuses to allow you to negotiate with them concerning terms and there is no other place you can go to get better terms for the same product, there may be procedural unconscionability. Sometimes, burying the terms in small print in an inconspicuous place can create procedural unconscionability.

Substantive unconscionability occurs when the terms are grossly one-sided. Most often, in order to avoid a contract for grounds of unconscionability, there must be both procedural and substantive unconscionability—the terms were one-sided in the other party's favor and you had no choice but to agree to them. Generally speaking, contracts between businesses are less likely to be held to be unconscionable, because business people are presumed to be dealing "at arms length." Theoretically, this means that the element of unfair advantage will not be present.

Mistake. There are certain circumstances under which a contract can be voided if there is a mistake. Usually, the mistake must be mutual. If the mistake is only unilateral, then the party that made the mistake will usually be held to have assumed the risk of unknown circumstances, rather than to have made a mistake. An illustration may be helpful. Let's say you agree to purchase a house from its owner and that both parties believe you may live in the house after the sale. However, neither of you realize that the area has been rezoned commercial, and although your friend could live in it as long as he liked, when he sells it, he must sell it as commercial property. This is a mutual mistake, and it is possible that you can avoid the contract on that ground.

However, let's say instead that the owner knows the property has been rezoned, but is unsure of the specifics of the new zoning ordinance. He thinks that the new ordinance allows multi-family housing (apartments) in addition to single-family homes, but he tells you he isn't sure. Therefore, he sells you the house "as is." If you purchase the house without checking on the ordinance, then you have assumed the risk that the rezoning may render you unable to live in the house. In this situation, the owner is not mistaken. He knows that the property has been re-zoned and he also knows that he isn't sure what the exact terms of the new zoning ordinance are.

Contract Subject Matter and the Uniform Commercial Code

Beyond the issue of the Statute of Frauds, the subject matter of contracts can be important for another significant reason. If the contract in question involves the sale of goods, the provisions of the Uniform Commercial Code (UCC) come into play. The UCC was originally promulgated by the American Law

Institute, an organization that exists to promote laws that are uniform from state to state. The legislative bodies in all 50 states, except Louisiana, have implemented the UCC. It should be noted that even Louisiana, whose law is based on the French Civil Law, has adopted portions of the UCC. It should also be noted that minor variations exist from state to state. Therefore, although not completely identical, there is a high degree of uniformity between the states when it comes to commercial transactions. Finally, since the UCC has no application to the rendition of services, common law contract principles that we have reviewed previously continue to apply to contracts for services and other subject matter that falls outside of the sale or leasing of goods.

There are many sections of the UCC, pertaining to such things as negotiable instruments, security agreements, and other matters. Relevant to our discussion in this chapter are Article 2 of the UCC, which governs contracts for the sale of goods, and Article 2A, which applies to the leasing of goods. Leasing of goods is similar in many respects to selling, so we will discuss only the sale of goods here. Many of the same rules apply to the sale of goods as apply to the provision of services. However, there are a few differences:

The Acceptance of an Offer under the UCC. Due to the commercial realities surrounding contracts for the sale of goods, the rules for acceptance are a little different. Suppose you own a company that sells widgets. ABC Corporation sends you a purchase order on its standard form ordering 500 widgets at your catalog price. You send a confirmation on your own standard form, which contains entirely different terms. You then ship the goods, which ABC accepts and distributes to its retailers. Even though your acceptance was not a mirror image, there is a contract in place.

Whose standard terms apply in this situation? Yours, because you were the last to send correspondence? Not necessarily—they never sent you a writing agreeing to your different terms. Their terms? No, you didn't agree to their terms. You proposed your own. There are some fairly complex rules that come into play here. However, the basic outcome is that the terms the offer and acceptance share become part of the contract, and the terms that are substantially different from the offer do not. Merchants and nonmerchants are treated differently, but most of the differences revolve around nonmaterial differences in terms.

What then happens to all of the different terms that are dropped? If a dispute arises and there are no terms left in the writings to address it, how is the dispute resolved? In addition to other terms that a court will use to supplement a contract, such as industry practice, the UCC provides terms, called *gap fillers,* that apply to every contract to which it applies, unless the parties' contract states otherwise. One of the most important gap fillers is the *implied warranty.* Implied warranties are just that—they are warranties that are added to the deal even though they are not expressly stated in the written contract. In a contract for the sale of goods governed by the UCC, certain implied warranties are made a part of the contract unless the terms of the contract expressly disclaim them. An example of this is the implied warranty of merchantability. In your contract with ABC, there is an implied warranty that the widgets will be suitable for the normal purposes for which widgets are used.

Assuming that your terms survive the so-called battle of the forms, you can disclaim all warranties, express or implied, and can limit your liability for damages and ABC's remedies against you should you breach your contract. However, some states regulate your ability to disclaim warranties and place restrictions on your attempts to limit your liability. For instance, some states allow you to restrict your exposure to the amount of money that you received for your performance under the contract unless someone is personally injured. You can then be liable beyond the amount of money you received. Other states limit the circumstances under which you can disclaim warranties on consumer products.

The Perfect Tender Rule. Although the perfect tender rule is effective under the UCC, its application is much more limited. For instance, let's assume you order 500 magazines for resale in your online store. If, after accepting your shipment, you discover that only 499 have been shipped, you can't force the supplier to take them all back because the loss of a single magazine does not "substantially impair the value" of the shipment. Even if you discover the deficiency before you accept the magazines, if there is still time for the supplier to deliver the last magazine before the agreed delivery date, you have to allow the supplier to cure the defect by delivering the last magazine.

The Statute of Frauds under the UCC. There are a few differences in the UCC's version of the Statute of Frauds. Under the UCC, the Statute of Frauds applies to contracts for the sale of goods over $500. In addition to requiring a writing sufficient to demonstrate that a contract has been made, signed by the party against whom it is to be enforced, the UCC also requires a stated quantity of goods to be specified in the contract. The UCC allows parties or courts to imply any term other than quantity into a contract in order to fill out the terms. For instance, if a price is not stated, a court could assume that the contract would call for a reasonable price based on then-prevailing industry standards or market conditions. It could also insert warranties, imply delivery within a reasonable time, etc. However, without something in writing that indicates quantity, either an exact number or a statement by which quantity can be determined (such as "all you produce"), there is no valid contract under the UCC.

ELECTRONIC CONTRACTS

Superimposing these contract rules onto the Internet, you can immediately see where there might be some problems. The most obvious challenge is to produce a signed written agreement in order to bring your contract into compliance with the Statute of Frauds. It is not at all difficult to bring a contract over the $500 minimum, which triggers the need for writing. As previously stated, anything you intend to use to authenticate the contract can be deemed your signature. Authentication of your intent on the Internet is a bit more problematic. Another challenge is in the area of agency. Remember that your employee or business partner may sign a contract on your behalf. What if your widget business is set up to take online orders? If your computer automatically accepts orders on your behalf, does that mean that you have accepted an offer to purchase? What if, as in our earlier example, ABC Corporation has an automatic ordering system that places its order as soon as its inventory decreases to 100 units? ABC's computer recognizes that its parameters have been reached and places the order, which is accepted by your computer—no human interaction ever occurs. Is there a contract?

Uniform Acts Affecting the Internet and Computer Industries

Several uniform laws have been developed to address these, and other, issues. Again, a uniform law is only a suggested model unless and until it is specifically adopted by the legislative body in the state in which your situation arises. And even where the uniform provision is adopted, each state's legislature is always free to make specific modifications. As a result, while we have an idea of where the law is headed, you must always check your state's statutes to determine what has been enacted into law as well as the specific provisions applicable to your specific circumstances. While many of these model provisions have been enacted into law by individual states, do not assume that all have.

The Uniform Computer Information Transactions Act. One of the most important model acts affecting the Internet and computer industries is the Uniform Computer Information Transactions Act ("UCITA"). The UCITA addresses contracts involving computer information, such as software. If computer information is only a portion of the entire contract's subject matter, the Act applies only to that portion. UCITA applies to electronic contracts for services delivered through electronic transfer, such as web design or marketing conducted and delivered over the Internet, and for services delivered in the more traditional sense, such as the development of a software package that is physically delivered and installed on your computer system.

The Uniform Electronic Transactions Act. Another model act worth noting is the Uniform Electronic Transactions Act ("UETA"). UETA is designed to ensure that electronic records or signatures are still legally valid even though they are electronic. However, the Act only applies if the parties expressly agree to conduct their transactions electronically and if they are able to retain the electronic documents in some form, whether it be printouts or on disk. In essence, UETA contains four provisions that accomplish this purpose:

1. Records and signatures cannot be declared legally ineffective simply because they are electronic.
2. Contracts formed with electronic records cannot be declared legally ineffective simply because they are electronic.
3. If a document must be in writing, then an electronic writing will suffice.
4. If a document must be signed, then an electronic signature will suffice.

UETA does not apply in situations where UCITA would apply; that is, it doesn't apply to computer information transactions where state law expressly overrides it; or to any provisions of the UCC other than Articles 2 and 2A (that is, those portions of the UCC that apply to the sale or leasing of goods, as discussed above), and a couple of other general provisions.

Offer, Acceptance, and Additional Terms

A primary portion of contracts affected by UCITA are so-called *shrink-wrap agreements.* These agreements are the licenses that come with software that dictate the terms of your use. Generally, these terms may include a copyright notice, a limitation on what you can use the software for (such as a limitation to noncommercial use), a limitation of the number of computers that you may install the software on, a limitation of the vendor's liability for damage if the software malfunctions, and a choice of law and/or venue provision.

Shrink-wrap agreements have been the subject of much controversy. Typical of these agreements is that you don't have a chance to view the license until after you have already bought the product. You purchase the software, take it home, open the box, and there, inside, is a shrink-wrapped computer disk with a piece of paper wrapped around it. How can the license be a part of your deal with the software vendor if you did not have an opportunity to read it and agree to it before you purchased it? Most of these licenses state that if you open the shrink-wrapped package, you have automatically agreed to the additional terms. Obviously, this is not quite fair, since you have already purchased the product. Are you then stuck with a product that you cannot or are unwilling to use if you don't like their additional terms? No. The software vendor must provide you with the opportunity to return the software if you don't agree with the terms of the offer endorsed in its packaging.

Click-wrap agreements are similar in nature. A click-wrap agreement is an online license that the software vendor displays for you when you purchase or use software online. Often, the vendor displays the agreement on your computer screen and requires you to click "I agree" or "Accept" before you are allowed to use the software.

Shrink-wrap and click-wrap agreements are both examples of *mass-market licenses*. A mass-market license is a license with set terms that is offered to all consumers who purchase software and are completely non-negotiable. In addition to the above-noted protections, in order to protect against unconscionable (or at least grossly unfair) provisions, if a mass-market license contains a provision that the vendor knows would cause an ordinary consumer not to buy the software in the first place, that term is dropped.

UCITA also addresses the "battle of the forms" problem noted above. If an acceptance to an agreement contains additional terms that don't materially alter the offer, then the same rules apply as for non-computer information contracts. If an acceptance contains terms that materially alter the terms proposed by the person making the offer, then no contract exists unless "other circumstances" show that a contract was formed. Although this may appear to be vague, it really leads back to non-electronic contract principles. If there is no offer and acceptance due to differing terms, but the parties keep on dealing with each other afterwards, then there is probably going to be a contract. Under UCITA, the terms of the deal are all those agreed to, and the terms that materially altered the original offer are deleted.

Electronic "Agents" and Signatures

UCITA doesn't really have a Statute of Frauds. However, it does provide that *authentication,* a process whereby companies confirm that records actually came from the other party to the transaction and not an outside party, will satisfy the signature requirement and that electronic records satisfy writing requirements. UCITA also provides that, if it conflicts with other laws and rules concerning consumer protection, the consumer protection laws will take precedence.

Some companies create contracts called *trading partner agreements* at the outset of their relationship to establish how they will authenticate records during the term of their dealings with each other. The party that does not follow the procedures in the agreement is the party that carries the burden for any mistakes that are made. Trading partner agreements have their shortcomings, however. First of all, they serve only to establish the company's relationship with a single vendor. Secondly, in many instances, companies enter into single transactions, rather than extended relationships, and trading partner agreements are not feasible.

This is where UCITA comes in. The UCITA requires that the parties establish a procedure for authenticating records. Authentication under UCITA involves creating a standard practice for verifying that records did come from the other party. Continuing with our earlier example, if you receive an order from ABC Corp. for 1,000 widgets, there must be some method in place for verifying that ABC Corp. did, in fact, place that order.

Although UCITA notes that authentication should substitute for a signature, where other laws take precedence, or where UCITA is not adopted in its proposed form, some courts may not adhere to this notion. UETA addresses authentication of records as well. However, UETA's authentication requirements focus on substituting electronic records for paper records. Under UETA, where a record must be delivered to another party, electronic delivery will suffice, provided that the recipient can print or otherwise store the record. UETA recognizes digital signatures, in addition to other identifying items, such as passwords and pin numbers, in attributing a document to a party.

Therefore, in many cases, electronic contracts do not contain "signatures" in the traditional sense of the word. Although a signature is any mark intended to validate the parties' intent to form a contract, without a physically signed trading partner agreement, or digital signature legislation like that outlined below, there are still problems meeting the signature requirement. The Statute of Frauds does not apply to contracts for goods under $500, to short-term service contracts, to contracts that have already been performed, etc. Therefore, there are times when a contract formed on the Internet will be enforceable despite one party's contention that electronic signatures don't count. However, where signatures are required, more proof may be necessary.

Many states have enacted digital signature legislation in order to assist with the Statute of Fraud's signature requirement in electronic contracting. In addition, the federal government recently adopted the Electronic Signatures in Global and National Commerce Act ("ESIGN"), which generally applies to all electronic transactions, and preempts any attempt by other laws to deny the enforceability of a signature, or document, simply because it is in electronic form. ESIGN does not apply to family law matters; testamentary matters; documents signed in conjunction with court proceedings; certain notices, including repossession notices under credit agreements, termination of utility services, and similar notices; or to the UCC, except for Articles 2 and 2A and a few other UCC provisions.

There are consumer protection provisions contained in ESIGN that relate to disclosures of information provided electronically. The provisions are rather detailed, and not relevant to this discussion, but it is worth noting that, where a written disclosure of information is required, a consumer is supposed to consent before the information may be disclosed electronically. However, the effectiveness of that provision is undermined by another provision that states that failure to obtain consumer consent does not necessarily void the disclosure. In any event, aside from the affirmative consent requirement, ESIGN is short on security and fraud protection. Considering that the signature requirement was originally developed to avoid fraud in contracts, this could be a major problem.

Another aspect of UCITA has to do with automated transactions. UCITA says that even an automated process is binding on the parties. The computers are "electronic agents" of the parties, so the transaction is treated as if human employees of each of the parties entered into the agreement. UETA recognizes the acts of electronic agents as well.

The Mailbox Rule

The UCITA also changes the mailbox rule. A message is binding upon the recipient when received, not when sent the sender. This may appear to be an unnecessary distinction, since e-mails are usually sent and received almost instantaneously. However, due to the many technical difficulties associated with web usage, there are times when e-mails are delayed or incorrectly routed. In any event, you should note that you don't have to actually read a message for it to be binding on you.

The Perfect Tender Rule

The perfect tender rule is not followed to the letter on the Internet in all circumstances. Almost all software, especially software in its initial edition, has a fair number of *bugs*—that is, glitches in the program that cause errors during operation. Some bugs are fairly major, but most are merely annoying or even largely undetectable. Strictly speaking, a bug in the software would mean that the software was something less than what the purchaser bargained for. However, because bugs are a reality in the industry, UCITA takes them into account.

Where the parties to the contract are businesses, bugs cannot be used to abandon the deal unless the bugs are serious enough to be considered a material breach. However, if a company is selling software to an individual, there are no exceptions for minor defects. This does not mean that the software has to be perfect. It simply means that the software has to conform to the contract between the parties. This is why most software licenses, including those licenses between individuals and Internet Service Providers, include a provision that excuses minor bugs in the program.

Implied Warranties

As we discussed earlier in this chapter, there are certain warranties that are implied in contracts for the sale of goods. UCITA allows express and implied warranties just like the UCC, but it also allows parties to disclaim them. However, UCITA creates a new warranty for computer information transactions, and the parties are not allowed to disclaim it. The parties to the transaction automatically warrant that the information that is the subject of the transaction was not misappropriated and does not infringe on another's rights (such as copyrights). There is, however, an exception if the seller is abiding by specifications provided by the purchaser, unless there is an alternative method that would not infringe and the seller is aware of it.

Logic Bombs

In addition, to what we have already discussed, there are provisions in UCITA that address *logic bombs*. Logic bombs are features of a program that shut it down if the licensing agreement is breached. Payment of the licensing fee is the offense of greatest interest to the licensor. Although it is necessary for software developers to collect their fees in order to stay in business, considering the large amounts of information that some businesses, or even individuals, stand to lose if a program stops functioning, you can see why logic bombs should be used with caution, especially where the breach is unavoidable, immaterial, or inadvertent.

UCITA allows the use of logic bombs, but requires that the breach be a significant one. Sometimes, a contract defines what is to be considered a material breach. UCITA, however, states that definition in the contract is not what will determine what is material—materiality will be determined by industry standards. UCITA also requires express consent to these measures in the original agreement, in addition to requiring detailed notice to a specific person 15 days before shutting the software down and requiring the licensor to exercise his rights without any breach of the peace.

Choice of Law Rules

As we discussed earlier in this chapter, whose rules apply depends largely on the circumstances. As you can imagine, when dealing electronically through several interim servers with a user in another state or country, it is difficult to determine where, exactly, the transaction took place. If your contract does not contain a *choice of law clause* designating whose rules apply, then UCITA sets out a method for determining what jurisdiction's law takes precedence.

Generally, if a contract is for access or delivery of electronic copies, then the jurisdiction of the provider takes precedence. An example of an access agreement would be your contract with your Internet Service Provider. Delivery of electronic copies would be downloads of software, music, videos, or other files. If you are ordering something that will be physically delivered to you, then the laws of your jurisdiction apply. Otherwise, the law of the jurisdiction with the most significant connection to the agreement apply.

WEB DESIGN AGREEMENTS

Web design agreements pose a different set of issues of which you should be aware. The Internet provides you with the capability of contracting online with web designers who will design your site and manage it without you ever meeting them. If you contract with a designer over the web, then all of the considerations we've discussed earlier in this chapter apply. Keep in mind, however, that a web designer is providing you with a service and a program, which is considered to fall into the definition of "goods," so you may have to consider elements of both goods and services contracts, depending upon how your jurisdiction treats mixed agreements.

Aside from the issues previously discussed in this chapter, there are other important considerations involved in web design agreements. Web designers come in all types, with different levels of experience and expertise. Likewise, the specific services offered varies. As in other areas we have discussed, some of the following suggestions regarding agreements with web designers are based on common sense while others are a little more complicated.

When negotiating an agreement for a web design, it is important that you always retain the rights to your domain name, and make sure that the contact information on the site identifies the person who will ultimately be responsible for updating it. This is fairly standard in that most web designers will not want any rights to your domain name. The key is the registration. Once the name is registered, the information is extremely difficult to change. We have experienced difficulty in this area on several fronts; it takes a very long time and a lot of persistence to change information once the domain name registrar has established the account. Changing hosts is difficult as well without changing the administrative contact, because the new host cannot upload the information to the web without the ability to access your account. Therefore, if your web designer will not be serving as your web host, make sure that he or she uses the web host's information when opening your account.

You should also retain the rights to your source code, which is your web site's program. It has been our experience that most web designers will allow you to retain the rights to it, so you can use your site as you please once the design work is complete. When you retain the rights to the source code, the agreement is basically a "work for hire" arrangement, whereby you pay the web designer to do a job on your behalf and the end result (i.e. the copyright to the program) belongs exclusively to you. However, there are some designers who may want to retain the copyright to the source code as their creation and simply issue you a license to use it. This can be problematic if you wish to revise or update your site, since the bundle of rights that a copyright owner holds includes the right to make derivative works. If the designer retains the copyright, only the designer may change it unless the license states otherwise. Therefore, you should not consent

THE LAW OF CONTRACTS   169

to this arrangement unless you have a specific reason for doing so.

There are other aspects of the web site that a designer will want to retain. The *back end functionality* is the programming that allows the web site to function with the host. An example of this programming is the *scripts* (programs) used to compile the information that you get from users—such as name, address, and e-mail address—into a readable form. Think of this as a wall outlet. The program is the extension cord and the host is the wiring in the wall. The back-end functions are the connections between the two or the socket. If you move your web site to another host, there will be a different socket to plug into. Therefore, giving up the rights to this programming is not going to interfere with your ability to change your site or to relocate it to a different server. In any event, these programs are generally developed separately from your web site and are proprietary.

It always makes sense to find out exactly what services your web designer can provide. If the designer is simply developing your site, make sure that he or she can recommend a host, and that your accounts are set up for that host. If your designer plans to provide hosting services, find out what is included. For instance, if you plan on updating your site frequently, find out how many hours of update work are included in the monthly fee you will be charged, find out if e-mail accounts are included and, if so, how many. In addition, you will want to know what the extra cost for non-included services, such as labor for updates above your allotted number of hours, will be.

Make sure that your agreement with the web designer provides you the right to view the site as it is constructed. This is fairly standard. Many contracts allow you periodic reviews and the right to view the *alpha site* and, after approval, the *beta site,* before the site is considered complete. The alpha site is your completed web site run on a stand-alone computer (i.e., a computer not connected to the Internet). The beta site is your completed web site as it is posted on the Internet, but before all of the bugs are worked out.

As you view your web site in its different stages before completion, you should reserve the right to make minor alterations and alterations that will bring the site into compliance with the contract at no additional charge. This is fairly standard practice. Plus, you should reserve the right to make other alterations if, as the site is constructed, you decide that you don't like the way it is turning out. Frequently, you don't know whether you will like the way the site looks until you're able to view it on the computer screen. Since you generally have to pay extra for these alterations, make sure your contract stipulates what the charge will be. Usually there is an hourly charge for labor on top of the work that is covered by the original contract.

Your contract should also designate who holds the copyright to the materials used on the web site. If you provide pictures, music, text, etc., then you will usually be responsible for licenses, if they are necessary, and you will maintain the copyright for original works. However, you usually have to indemnify the designer against any potential infringement liability. The reverse is true if the designer uses his or her own materials on your site. An *indemnity* is simply an agreement to pay back any money that the innocent party has to pay if they get sued due to use of the materials.

Your agreement with your web host, whether it is your designer or another entity, should address service disruption as well. Temporary outages are a given—they will happen sooner or later. You should know what is considered "temporary" and, if the outage goes beyond that time frame, you should know what you are entitled to for compensation. Generally, you are entitled to a pro rata reduction of your monthly fee. Most web hosts are unwilling to be responsible for any monetary damages beyond your monthly payment to them, and if that is the case, you need to be aware of it.

Similarly, web designers and hosts usually limit their liability for damages resulting from any breach of the contract to the amount of money you have paid them. Very seldom will you find a host that agrees to be responsible for extra damages, such as lost profits. If you can negotiate a better deal, by all means, do so. However, if you are stuck with a limitation of liability provision, keep two things in mind. First, the limitation of liability should be as mutual as possible. You should at least disclaim your liability for incidental and consequential damages, which are money damages incurred by the injured party from the breach that are not otherwise a part of the contract.

Secondly, you should exclude copyright infringement liability from the liability limitation if the designer or host is providing any materials for you. As we discussed earlier in this section, there should be an indemnity provision if the designer or host is providing materials, like generic background music or a photograph, for you to use on your web site. If you get sued for copyright infringement over materials that your designer told you he or she had a right to use, then you could be liable for more than what you have paid the host or designer. You want to be sure that you have maximum ability to retrieve the damages from your designer should such a situation arise.

A FINAL WORD OF ADVICE

Most disputes related to contracts, Internet or otherwise, are caused by two fundamental problems, both of which are easily avoided. The first involves the failure of contracting parties to fully and completely work through the deal that will form their contract. If there are potential problems or issues on the horizon, it is much easier and cheaper to address them before the deal is done rather than after. You do yourself no favors by ignoring concerns and hoping for the best. In our experience as lawyers, problems tend to crop up earlier than later. And if a client utters the fateful words, "Don't worry, nothing can go wrong," we are just about one hundred percent sure that trouble is just around the corner. The better approach is to be forthright and direct. If there is something in the deal with which you are uncomfortable, you have two options: fix it or just say no. Unfortunately, too many people choose a third approach: sign the deal and hope everything turns out okay. Because a contract is a consensual arrangement, you have an obligation to yourself to look down the road for potential problems and address them before ever beginning your contractual journey. If that is not possible, you are best advised to look for better terms somewhere else.

Assuming you force yourself to confront difficult issues at the outset, the second problem involves failing to fully and completely describe the respective rights and responsibilities that have been created by your agreement. Paper and ink aren't so expensive that you can't take a little extra time and effort to spell out exactly the expectations, rights, and duties of all parties. Remember that most successful deals are negotiated, drafted, signed, and filed away. The spirit of the deal is guided by mutual respect and good faith while the letter of the deal is determined by what is written in the contract. As long as you have the spirit and the letter of your deal locked up, you will most likely never have to experience the cost and personal agony of nasty and protracted breach of contract litigation. Take the extra time and expend the extra effort even if it means confronting unpleasant or sensitive issues and staying a little later at the office to make sure it is done correctly the first time. You will thank yourself many times over in the ensuing years.

PART FOUR

Business of
the Internet

CHAPTER 15

Taking Care of E-Business

The technological revolution led by the Internet has spawned numerous new terms and attitudes which are thrown around regularly by a new breed of cable news and financial channel anchors and online pundits in eZines devoted to covering the emerging world tech economy. One of our favorites is the "New Economy," where presumably the old rules that governed the management of old line, blue chip companies just don't seem to fit anymore. Of course much of that illusion was fostered prior to the downward spiral of tech stocks and the demise of formerly high-flying dot-com start-up companies in 2000 and 2001. What the market correction has shown is simply this—that business principles are the same, no matter what form the business takes. The fundamental skills taught in business schools regarding planning, organizational structure and management, human resources, and all the rest are as valid as they ever were. The hottest web idea in the world won't fly without a rational, methodically implemented business plan. A business needs profits, not web-site hits or media buzz, in order to survive.

The recent shakeout has made it quite apparent that the New Economy has a great deal in common with the so-called Old Economy. For this reason, we want to spend a little time on some of the basics of business we have not yet covered. As we are witnessing on a daily basis, failure to take account of these tried and true principles can result in disaster and even demise, at least in a business sense. As any NASDAQ investor will tell you—you ignore the basics at your own peril, and that of your investors.

BUSINESS ORGANIZATION

Corporations, limited liability companies, and limited liability partnerships are alive and well on the web. Forming a business entity under which to run your business isn't difficult. If properly created and maintained, your business can operate on a strong foundation and you, your investors, and your employees can avoid a lot of needless headaches.

The Benefits of Forming a Business Entity

The primary benefit of forming one of these organizational models is to gain the considerable benefits of limited legal liability for your business. When you create one of these models and run your web business through it, your maximum exposure—subject, of course, to a few limitations—is the amount of money that you have invested. A simple example serves to illustrate the point.

Suppose you run a web business that sells computer equipment online. You purchase equipment in bulk from a major manufacturer, then resell it on the Net. When you started the business, you and your four business partners each invested $20,000 for construction and maintenance of the web site, an initial order of equipment, and other miscellaneous expenses. Now let's suppose that one of your first customers orders a computer, and, after using it for a few weeks, loses all of its information when the system crashes due to a defective part. The business sues your partnership for the cost of the computer plus profits lost during the down time it took to replace the part and recreate the information, and the cost of their computer technicians and personnel to fix the problem, as well as extra damages that represent the information that was irretrievably lost. This could represent a fairly sizeable sum of money—say, in this case, $250,000. However, you and your partners only invested $100,000 in the company.

If you have not properly limited your liability exposure, either because you didn't attempt to limit it in your contract or because you did so but it was not legally effective, and because you failed to buy insurance, you and each of your partners may be personally liable for the entire judgment. Although the plaintiff cannot collect more than the $250,000 award, on the basis of joint and several liability which is applicable to all partnerships, your former customer and now plaintiff can collect it all from you, leaving it in your lap to attempt to seek contribution from your partners, who may well be on a plane to South America even as you read this. Assuming you don't have a quarter of a million dollars sitting in your personal checking account, or more to the point if you do, this poses a very serious, not to mention expensive, problem.

However, had you incorporated your business, your personal financial situation would look substantially brighter. In this event, the corporation would be the proper party to sue, and although it is liable to the extent of its assets (including the shareholders' $20,000 investments), if you have properly formed and maintained the corporation, none of the shareholders would have to contribute anything further toward the judgment. If the company goes bankrupt because it can't pay the debt, you have only lost your investment.

As you might expect, there are a few exceptions to the rule of limited liability. Suppose you advertise the computers you have for sale as brand-new equipment from a reputable manufacturer, and charge accordingly, but they are, instead, built in your basement from old parts. By your actions you have committed fraud. If you participated in the fraud, then you can be held personally liable for the debt, even if the corporation is properly formed and maintained. But if another officer committed the fraud and you were unaware of it (and had no way of knowing about it), then the corporate shield will probably still protect you.

Organizational Models

There are several different organizational models that you may wish to consider. A description of the different options available to you may be of help. As with other matters we have discussed, however, keep in mind that business organizations are a matter of state law, so the rules may vary from state to state. You should always consult with an attorney and tax advisor to select the organization best for you.

Partnerships or sole proprietorships are the most common forms of business organization. If you and another person, or multiple people, go into business together and take no action to organize yourselves, then you are a partnership. If you go into business by yourself, then you are a sole proprietorship. Although you have the advantage of not having to bother with formality or state filings, there can be some serious disadvantages with these types of businesses. The first, as we have discussed, is liability. If you have not formed an organization that will limit your liability when things go wrong, your personal assets are on the line. Partnerships provide added exposure, as well. Your partners can bind you with their actions in furtherance of the company, even if you don't know what they are doing. If you and your partner have a disagreement about whether the partnership should buy some equipment, then your partner goes out and makes the purchase without your approval, the partnership is liable to pay for the goods—you can't send them back and tell the vendor that you don't want them.

Partnerships can come in different forms, however. A modified version of the partnership is the *limited partnership*. A limited partnership is just like a normal partnership with one exception: partners that are not actively involved in the affairs of the partnership are shielded from liability. This is designed to protect those that buy into partnerships purely for investment purposes. As with other businesses that allow limited liability, however, you must file for protection with the agency in your state that is in charge of business organizations.

Limited liability partnerships are the next step above limited partnerships. Limited liability partnerships provide limited liability for all partners. Similarly, *limited liability companies* (LLCs), provide liability protection for all members, but with a flexibility that allows them to elect to be taxed as either a corporation or a partnership. Again, you must file with your state's agency that oversees business organizations in order to proceed with this form of business. The filing requirements are usually less stringent than they are for corporations, though. LLCs, due to their more advanced protection and structure, require more documentation than partnerships, including an agreement to govern the company's operations, formal documentation of major actions, and regular elections of officers and executive committee members (the executive committee is similar to a board of directors for a corporation).

Perhaps the most well known business organization is the *corporation*. It is also the most complex. A corporation, like an LLC, is a company that the law treats as a separate entity from the person or people who own it. Corporations require an initial charter from your state agency, in addition to yearly update filings. Corporations also require formal documentation of major actions, and yearly shareholder and director meetings.

MAINTAINING LIABILITY PROTECTION

As we have mentioned, proper formation and maintenance are prerequisites for liability protection. In order to have a corporation, you have to adhere to all of the formalities that make a corporation a distinct "person" in the eyes of the law as distinguished from its owner or owners under the law. Those formalities usually include filing a document with your Secretary of State or other designated agency; organizing the business entity, which includes acquiring shares for proper value, electing officers and directors or, in the case of a limited liability company, executive committee members, and issuing shares or membership certificates; approving the acts of the company by vote of the shareholders/members or directors; completing any yearly filing requirements; and separating all company funds from personal funds.

Although all of the corporate formalities are important, failing to separate company funds from personal funds is one of the most common errors. In many cases, especially when the company is owned and operated by one person, an officer may mix company funds with personal funds or pay personal debts directly from company funds. This can get you into trouble fast. When a corporation is determined to be the alter ego of the person running it, the corporate form is disregarded and personal liability is attached to the owner. Spending company money is a sure-fire way to make it appear that the company and the owner are one and the same.

Other seemingly innocent acts can also open the door to personal liability. For instance, if you sign something in your personal capacity, rather than your corporate capacity, then you can be held personally liable. It is usually a good idea to list your title with your signature, just to be sure that it is absolutely clear for whom you are signing. If you incur an obligation before all documents are processed with your state's agency, then you can be personally liable, too.

E-BUSINESS IS STILL BUSINESS

Some people think that forming a business organization is too much trouble and that keeping minutes of every important decision takes too much time. And then there is the matter of separate tax returns for the business. Our response is essentially the same as the IRS—either you are in business or you're not. If indeed you are in business, and as long as you abide by the rules, a business organization can save you a lot of worry if something goes wrong.

Naturally, a web business has different dynamics than a bricks-and-mortar establishment would. You don't have to worry about someone slipping on a wet floor in your lobby or being mugged in your parking lot. But this doesn't mean that you aren't open to exposure. If you sell goods online, there is a risk that the goods won't work like they are supposed to or will cause injury or property damage. Or you may be involved in a contract dispute. Or, for that matter, you may decide to cease operations if your business is losing money. We hope this is not the case, but the track record of a lot of well-heeled dot- coms has not been great.

If any of the above were to happen to you, be assured that your business' creditors will still want their money. If you have employees who work with you, work-related injuries, such as back strain from lifting heavy boxes or injuries from use of equipment, are also a possibility. If you have business partners, the business can be liable for their acts if they are within the course and scope of the enterprise, and if you don't have a business organization, company liability is personal liability. Looking at the possible consequences, it is worth the relatively minor expense and extra paperwork to avoid, or at least limit, your liability exposure.

INSURANCE

Insurance is a simple, and seemingly obvious, precaution that you may want to consider. Thanks to an innovative insurance industry, you can get insurance in just about any amount that will cover you for just about anything from equipment loss and legal judgments to earthquakes and hurricanes. But how much insurance and what kind of insurance do you need? Like most other things, that is entirely dependent upon your business. Coverage for the value of your equipment and inventory is a good idea, because as long as you have physical property, there is always risk of theft or damage due to any number of things, including fire, flood, etc.

Liability coverage is a little different, however. Unlike damage to your own property, which has a set monetary value, liability claims don't generally have any limitations. Personal injury claims from the use of products can go into the millions of dollars. Keep in mind, too, that several states restrict or even eliminate your ability to limit your liability for personal injury, especially if the purchaser is a consumer rather than another business. Therefore, your liability coverage should be substantially greater than your coverage for physical losses. Your insurance agent can recommend coverage that is suitable for your business.

Customer Service

One would think it would go without saying that good customer service is a must—a happy customer is much more likely to be a repeat buyer and much less likely to bring in the lawyers. However, a few recent experiences within the context of managing our law practice demonstrate that not all Internet companies have yet grasped this concept.

One nameless Internet-based company we recently encountered has a "contact information" page that directs customers to different departments for different problems. Most of these departments, including sales and technical support, have e-mail addresses. However, this particular company noted that the specific problem at issue could only be addressed by telephone—no fax number, e-mail address, or regular mail address was provided. When we called the customer service department, the computerized voice on the other end indicated that the wait for a representative would be approximately 120 minutes. Another attempt at a later time indicated that the wait was up to 150 minutes. Does any of this sound familiar?

Another well-known Internet-based company had a phone number for technical support, but the phone was answered by a computer that frequently tells the customer that all representatives are busy, then hangs up. After a week of attempting to call at a time when there happened to be someone available to pick up the phone, a representative took the call, had us change some settings on our computer, then disconnected the call. The changes to the settings did not fix the problem, which led to yet another three days of attempting to get a representative, who couldn't fix the problem either, on the phone.

A third company has a contact section on its web site that provides an e-mail address for problems but, after over a month, has failed to respond to inquiries. We wrote it off to growing pains. But whatever you call it and whatever the reason, it isn't good business.

Some companies, however, have gotten the right idea. A fourth company we recently had dealings with provides three methods of customer service—an e-mail address, instant messaging, and a telephone number. If you use the instant messaging feature, you get an instant response telling you how long the wait will be, and a tone when the representative gets to you so you don't have to sit by the computer. When you call the telephone number, if all of the representatives are busy, you may either wait or enter your phone number. If you enter your phone number, the computer tells you that you are in line and that a representative will call you as soon as one is available. Best of all, one always does.

If you don't make it easy for your customers to bring their problems to your attention, they will find other ways. If you are dealing with a customer that has suffered some personal or financial injury due to your product or service, it is especially important to provide an instant, concerned response. If you try to fix the problem, you may be able to settle the matter for the price of a refund or replaced product, and certainly for less than a judgment and attorneys fees would cost.

Of course, not all matters are suitable for the courts, and many of your users will realize that. There are other ways of making you and your bottom line suffer. As previously noted in Chapter 10, hate pages are a fairly common response to customer service blunders. Many Internet Service Providers give their users space to create their own web pages, and most users won't think twice about using that space to malign your business. Worse yet, many domain name registries provide a domain name and a single page web site for a very low price, meaning that "XYZCorpSucks.com" is just around the corner. A search for your name can pull up some very bad publicity that could just as easily be avoided by anticipating problems and logjams at the outset and finding proactive solutions to head off potential problems.

Good customer service makes good business sense. Answer your e-mails, make yourself easy to get to, and fix problems before they start to erode consumer confidence in your business. If you don't, you're likely to regret it.

THE NECESSITY FOR VIGILANCE AND KNOWLEDGE

If you have read this book from the start, then you know only too well that there are plenty of gray areas where traditional legal principles meet the Internet. As a result, while it's not always easy or fun to be perpetually unsure of where you stand, when you choose to operate in an area you know is unsettled, you should be vigilant in anticipating and avoiding gray areas that can create potential problems. You should also be aware of the consequences if you come out on the losing end. Just ask Napster. If you are operating in a high-risk area where copyright and trademark problems can occur or potential liability exposure is great, it's especially critical that you be able to steer your business operations comfortably away from potential violations or gray areas which might cause disputes. Remember that if you become a defendant in litigation, you are a guaranteed loser in terms of bad publicity, lost time, and attorneys fees to defend your position, even if you are ultimately vindicated.

Even in the areas of Internet business operations that are unclear, there are usually some guidelines. A quick consultation with an attorney who understands Internet-related issues is well worth the consultation fee. Better yet, establishing an ongoing relationship with a lawyer who knows the area and with whom you are comfortable should be a normal expense of doing business, just like marketing costs and insurance premiums. Calculate your pricing scheme to insure these expenses are covered while also allowing for a reasonable profit for yourself. It's just part of doing business, whether you are operating in the New Economy, Old Economy, or somewhere in between.

Know Your Industry

You should know the industry as well. "Everybody does it" is not an effective legal defense. However, industry custom and usage can show good faith on your part, especially where the law is unclear. Procedures and practices that are in line with those of your competitors can provide some security. If competitors haven't been slapped on the hand for a practice, you probably won't be, either. Linking and framing, discussed in Chapters 6 and 9, is a good example. There are generally acceptable ways of linking and framing, and there are ways that a few do it that are likely to get you in trouble.

This brings us to a caveat in the area of industry practice and custom and usage. If you are going to follow your competitors' lead, make sure that their practice is fairly well established in the industry, is followed by a substantial number of companies, and is not otherwise protected. If your only competitor is Napster, then you can see why blindly following others could be a problem. Another good example is the controversy over Amazon.com's 1-Click feature, a process for storing customer information so that, when a customer returns, he or she doesn't have to re-enter the information. Amazon filed suit against Barnes & Noble for patent infringement when Barnes & Noble adopted an ordering process similar to Amazon's. Although many Internet companies use this or similar features, Amazon chose to sue only Barnes & Nobles. You can see how following the pack can be a gamble.

A FINAL WORD OF ADVICE

There is never a way to entirely eliminate risk in business, especially in an area that is developing and changing as rapidly as the Internet. The best advice here is only take calculated risks based on proactive decision making. At the same time, take steps based on established legal principles and common sense to limit your risk as much as possible. Oh yes, and buy insurance. In the final analysis, that is one of the very best things you can do for yourself.

CHAPTER 16

Managing Your Site: E-Marketing, Product Sales, and Other Revenue

Now that you know how to avoid the legal pitfalls of the Internet, let's shift the focus to maximizing your online visibility. As you're surely aware, there are literally millions of web sites on the Internet. Finding ways to stand out in the crowd is essential to your success. Fortunately, there are some very simple and inexpensive things you can do in this regard, along with some not so inexpensive things, to attract users. Depending on your specific goals and the size of your company's bankroll, some or all of these should be incorporated into your e-business plan. If done correctly, you will begin to draw users to your site. Thereafter, it's up to the quality of your site and the consumer demand for your products and services. But before you can get that far, Internet surfers have to know you're out there.

There are wide range of methods you can use—and, not surprisingly, a wide range of price tags to go with them—to get the word out on your business. As with other things we have discussed in this book, many of the principles that work in the real world work in cyberspace as well. However, as you may have also guessed, Internet marketing is a new twist to an old game.

Whether you're selling goods or services or providing information, there are two goals you will want to achieve—get people to your site, and generate enough income for the site to pay for itself. Naturally, your site's purpose will determine the most effective method of promoting it.

GETTING YOUR NAME OUT THERE

As with any good marketing plan, you should know how you plan to promote your site before you begin to design it. Researching your potential audience to plan the most appealing web site and the most effective promotion can save you a great deal of misspent money in the long run. When considering your marketing plan, there are several options available to you.

Meta Tags

The simplest method of steering traffic to your site is through meta tags. As we discussed in Chapter 2, meta tags are words in your web site's programming that characterize your site and what you want people to know about it. For instance, consider our example in Chapter 1. Because they are a retailer that sells music, Music Center's web site might contain meta tags such as "rock," "music," "compact discs," or "CDs." Keep in mind, however, that Music Center should not put the names of popular bands in its meta tags, since that may create a cause of action for trademark infringement.

Meta tags are only a part of what search engines look for, however. Other items, including your site's text, your domain name, and a summary of your web site, are considered when indexing your site. Some search engines do not search meta tags when developing their lists of relevant sites. A few search engines even rule out sites with meta tags. When you decide what search engines to register with, ask for their meta tag policy, and adjust accordingly.

Registering with Search Engines

A good way to bring in traffic is the search engine. It is one of the most common ways for users to locate sites that interest them. Search engines differ in more ways than just their meta tag policy. Although the web search functions are generally referred to as "search engines," there are actually different kinds of providers that accomplish the same purpose, which is to search for sites that match your inquiry. Some search engines have bots (software that searches the web for data) that automatically find new sites, then add those sites to the search engine's database. Some sites require you to submit your site to them for evaluation; they then categorize and list the site manually. Those sites are called *directories*. Specialized search engines are especially likely to require an evaluation of your site.

There are companies you can hire that will submit your site to a number of search engines on your behalf. D2Interactive, 2Submit, SearchRank, and Omaha Webs are just a few of these companies. These outfits commonly offer other services, such as ad placement assistance.

Advertising

Not surprisingly, online advertising can substantially increase traffic to your site. Think about the last time you saw an ad on television. How long did it take for you to forget about it, even if it was for a product you like? Advertising with traditional media is passive. The audience views or hears the ad and, perhaps if they think about it again later, may go out and look for the product.

On the Internet, however, advertising is interactive. If you see an ad for a book you've wanted to read for weeks, you can click on the ad and you are transported to a site where you can buy it. That's the beauty of online advertising. The whole idea behind web surfing is to skip around from one place to another. This, combined with the fact that so many users frequently make online purchases, explains why online advertising can be so effective. A user perusing one site will think nothing of clicking on an ad and being transported to your site. In fact, many ads are designed to open a new window so that you don't lose track of the site you were visiting when you saw the ad.

In many respects, though, Internet advertising is much like advertising everywhere else. You have to place your ad where it will be of greatest benefit to you. A common approach to advertising on the Internet is the *banner ad*. Banner ads appear on web pages, usually across the top of the page. A user can click on the ad and be transported to the advertiser's site. These ads are on web pages all over the Internet—search engines, Internet retailers, newspapers and eZines, and even on personal web pages. Again, there are many companies, including those mentioned above, that can assist you with placing your banner ads in places that have audiences who would be interested in your site.

Keyword Purchases, Search Engine Lists, and Banner Ads

Banner ads work best when used in conjunction with the concept of keywords, which are words that describe your business that can be purchased from *Pay-for-Position* search engines (i.e., search engines that use keywords to place web sites). Keywords are used in a number of ways. Returning to our example of Music Center, let's assume that the company wants to increase traffic to its site. It might purchase the keywords "music" and "compact discs" at a major search engine. For this purchase, when a user enters the word "music" in the search, the search engine may return Music Center as the first name on its list, or perhaps as a featured site. Or it may return other names on the list, but display Music Center's banner ad at the top of the page. In either case, you can see the value of purchasing keywords. When a user enters the right words, your site is the first thing he or she sees.

Banner ads are also effective when placed on sites that offer services or information complementing what you have to offer. This flexibility is one of the key advantages to Internet advertising. For instance, a banner ad for a sporting goods company would be more likely to interest you if you're accessing the scores from last night's ball game than if you're accessing your stock portfolio.

There are numerous ways to use the Net for advertising. There's no "standard" Internet ad campaign. Think in broader terms than simply transporting someone to your web site. For many advertisers, it's not even necessary, or prudent, to have a site. According to the Internet Advertising Bureau, people who use computers in their leisure time displace television watching more than any other activity. Therefore, it makes sense to advertise on the Net even if you don't have a web site since more and more people are migrating to the Internet from television watching. You might think your local business doesn't need international web advertising because you can't service beyond your region. However, think in terms of local web sites. Many local television stations, newspapers, football, baseball, and hockey teams, as well as other local businesses and organizations, have web sites. Purchasing an ad on their web sites, or in the case of local organizations sponsoring their web site, will put your ad in front of local users.

Although you don't have to have a web site to advertise, interactive banner ads are better than just a blurb on a site's home page. Again, giving the user something to do, such as play a game, enter to win a prize, or answer an opinion poll, is more likely to attract their interest. You don't have to develop a six-figure web site—a "micro" site that exists just for the purpose of receiving banner ad traffic could serve you well.

Cross-Linking

Cross-linking is an agreement between two sites to provide links to each other. You can cross link with sites that provide related goods or services and each site will benefit from the other's traffic. There are many instances of sites displaying links to other sites on their web pages—which is mostly what makes the web operate. Cross-linking is similar, except it is a mutual effort.

As with advertising in general, cross-linking is all in the presentation. Let's assume that Music Center settles its differences with Iliad, and they make an agreement to cross-link to each other's web page. If Iliad simply posts a link that says "Click here for Music Center," there probably won't be that many people that will click the link. Although many people would realize that Music Center is a music store because of its name, this is not always the case. Even if they know what goods or services the cross-linked site offers, there is little motivation for users to click on the cross-link. However, if Iliad were to develop a mini-ad that has Music Center's logo and says something like "Like our music? Click here to buy our CDs and t-shirts at Music Center," more people are likely to follow the link.

Customer Lists

As with any other business, you may want to consider purchasing *customer lists* from other companies. Internet "direct mail" is less expensive than traditional mail because you don't have production costs for brochures and the like, and you don't have to pay postage when sending information by e-mail. Keep in mind, however, that people are sensitive about spamming, to the point that most ISPs have policies against it and the federal government is considering legislation and regulations to control it. Before you purchase a customer list, verify that the company that compiled the list provided users a chance to opt out of having their names included. This is usually accomplished by including a check box on the screen that informs users that their names are being provided to companies that offer other services unless they uncheck the box. The policy for most European countries is that the user must affirmatively consent to having his or her name included on a list, rather than assuming consent unless the user indicates otherwise.

When sending e-mail solicitations, you should provide a statement that you are sending the e-mail because the customer indicated an interest in receiving special offers. You should also provide the user with the opportunity to unsubscribe to future mailings if requested.

PAYING THE BILLS

As with any other venture, you can expect that there will be certain expenses involved. Monthly fees to your ISP, computer software and hardware costs, and licensing fees are basic costs for any web site. If you are running a full-service Internet business, you need to consider other business costs, such as inventory, employee expenses, taxes, and insurance.

It goes without saying that you can recover some costs by selling merchandise. We'll discuss that a bit more below. But there are some other income streams that you may wish to consider as well.

In the same way that you can pay other web sites to advertise your business, you can charge for advertising space on your own site. Before doing this, though, you should have an idea of who your audience is and how much traffic you have so that your rates can be set at a reasonable level.

Many sites charge a subscription fee. Although this is not the best choice for raising revenue for most sites, it works well for sites that provide members with instant access to materials such as photographs, music, or legal forms. For a monthly fee, you can access whatever the site has to offer.

Becoming affiliated with other sites can also generate income. Amazon, ubid, and CDNow are a few sites that offer this opportunity to anyone who wishes to take advantage of it. The programs operate by placing an advertisement on your site. When your users click on the link, then make a purchase at the affiliate site during their visit, you receive a portion of the proceeds.

SALES AND DISTRIBUTION

Selling merchandise on the web may seem like a totally different prospect than selling merchandise from a bricks-and-mortar storefront. However, many aspects are the same. You offer a product, your customer expresses an interest in buying it, you accept payment, then you deliver the product, either by mail or by download.

As you might expect, there are considerations here that are unique to the Internet. Once you bring a customer to your site, how do you offer the product? That's fairly simple, although you can add features that really give your products appeal. A picture and a description is the standard method of showcasing what you have to sell. Many sites add sound or video, giving you the ability to "rotate" your product so that it can be seen from all angles. Others give you the

ability to "custom build" your product. For example, several major car manufacturers' sites offer you the opportunity to pick the model and features you
want, including color and add-ons, then show you the result and the price. Your
only limitation is your imagination.

After you have created the presentation your customers can't resist, you should
be ready to accept orders. Although some sites allow you to print order forms
and fax or mail them in, this is not the best method. Internet users want instant
gratification—they want to click a button and be done with it. If they have to
print it out and either mail it or find a fax machine and pay long-distance
charges, they may lose interest.

Although it is more expensive to set up, accepting online orders is the method
of choice for most users. Most major sites use them, including Amazon, CDNow,
L. L. Bean, and the list goes on. Customers can click a button to place the item
in their online cart, proceed to checkout, then sit back and wait for the product
to arrive (for physical products, you should consider an express shipping option
to speed the process even more). We won't even begin to tell you how to set this
up. Your web designer should have all of the details. Just be aware that, from an
online consumer's perspective, this is the best method for accepting orders.

You may wonder if accepting orders by e-mail is a good compromise. Not
really. There is still the matter of payment. If you accept orders any way other
than online, your customer still has to drop the check in the mail or call you
with a credit card number, although you should note that some customers
would prefer calling you rather than transmitting their credit card number online.
There are many companies that can help you set up online credit card payments.
Many of these companies, including efilldirect.com, fulfillnetinc.com, and
jcplogistics.com, will handle all aspects of order fulfillment for you, including
accepting and processing orders, processing payments, distributing your products,
and even customer service. Please note that we are providing these companies as
examples, and we do not necessarily recommend their services. We have neither
researched these companies' history or service record. When deciding who you
want to handle these financial aspects of your business, you should conduct your
own research and ask for recommendations from your web designer.

For online purchases, there is a modified credit card payment system available. These are generally called *wallet services,* although the specific brand name
may be dissimilar. These systems provide a central database where you enter
your name, billing and/or shipping address, and a credit card number. Then,
whenever you make a purchase at a site that honors whatever payment method
you are using, you click a button and all of the information is there.

As has been discussed, privacy and security are major concerns for most
Internet users. Many sites accommodate wary users by offering secure and non-
secure options for certain transactions. Regardless, you should always secure any

transmissions that involve personal and financial information, and you should never store your customers' financial information on a computer that has Internet access. You should also clearly display your privacy policy on your site, and give users an opportunity to remove their information from your customer list.

OUR LAST FINAL WORD OF ADVICE

When it comes to mastering the Internet, it is probably helpful to remember that you are dealing with an unprecedented medium of communication that is both instantaneous and has a global reach. Add to this the fact that utilizing the Internet is deceptively easy and amazingly inexpensive in light of the power it brings to our homes and offices for the price of a computer, modem, and ISP. That's some combination. But as with any traditional medium of communication, the relevant legal, business, or technical dimensions can be disarmingly simple or incomprehensibly complex depending on your specific goals, aspirations, and needs. Whether you are an online consumer, a principal in a multimillion-dollar Internet start-up company, or someone in between, you need to be aware of the relevant factors that can affect you and your use of the Internet.

As has become quite evident, this book is in effect an ambitious mirror of the emerging and evolving online business and legal culture. We acknowledge that, while it hopefully clears up many online issues you were uncertain or even unaware of, it probably raises more questions than it answers. Although certainly frustrating, it is also an unavoidable fact of life. The law of the Internet is moving fast; technical innovation is moving even faster. Unfortunately, we as lawyers and authors and you as businesspeople and consumers have no choice but to hang on for the roller coaster ride that shows no sign of ending anytime soon. All any of us can do is to make an effort to keep up with new developments and react accordingly. For us, that means constant monitoring of case and statutory law as well as governmental regulations, industry practice, and consumer trends. For you, it means keeping up with the latest legal developments while also keeping abreast of your particular industry in order to make informed decisions which incorporate the latest information and a healthy dose of common sense to stay in the game and ahead of the competition. We pledge to do our part and trust you will do the same.

At the very least, it is our hope that we have heightened your level of online awareness when it comes to basic issues of law, business, and technology. At the end of the day, that awareness, combined with creative and innovative decision making, are the keys that will allow you to take maximum advantage of a technological revolution that is indeed changing the world and its citizens in ways so fundamental and at speeds so unprecedented that none of us will ever again be as we were only a few short years ago. We offer you every best wish as you log on for your own cyber-adventure.

Appendices

Glossary

alpha site A completed web site run on a stand-alone computer (i.e., a computer not connected to the Internet).

back-end functionality The programming that allows the web site to function with the host.

beta site A completed web site as it is posted on the Internet, but before all of the bugs are worked out.

bots Software that searches the Web for data and compiles the data for easy use.

browsers The software that allows you to move around on the web.

carnivore An "e-mail sniffer" that peruses e-mails for certain keywords that are set by the program.

clickstream data Data collected concerning the activity of the user.

click-wrap agreements An online license that the software vendor displays for you when you purchase or use software online.

compulsory licenses Licenses that the copyright owner is required to give at pre-set rates.

cookies Files used to collect data from visitors to a site without any deliberate action from the user.

copyright notice A statement of ownership by an author.

crackers Individuals who break into computer systems to cause serious damage or steal information.

defamation An injury to a person's good name or reputation.

deep linking Occurs when a link delivers you directly to a certain spot on another web site without stopping at that web site's home page.

domain name An address that the web site owner registers with one of several registration companies.

download To copy files from another source onto your computer.

e-mail A method of communication that involves typing a message into your computer, then transmitting it to another person's account for pickup at that person's leisure.

encryption A way of coding messages so that, if someone intercepts the message, he or she cannot understand what it says unless he or she can break the code.

flame An angry, even offensive, message directed at an offending user.

framing A method of displaying several pages on the screen at one time.

hackers Individuals who break into computer systems for the purpose of mischief making. Generally, their chief goal in breaking in is to prove that they can do it.

hyperlink A picture, graphic, or line of text, usually colored and underlined, that takes you to another section of the current web site, or to another web site entirely.

hypertext markup language (HTML) Standard Internet programming language.

in personam jurisdiction A court's jurisdiction over you, as a person.

in rem jurisdiction A court's jurisdiction over property.

instant messaging A service provided by some of the larger ISPs, and some other online companies, that allows users to hold real-time conversations with each other from their respective computers.

Internet A series of computers linked together to form a large network.

Internet Service Provider (ISP) A company that provides both individuals and companies with access to the Internet through its own servers and high speed connections to other servers.

license Permission from the copyright owner or proprietor to use a protected work.

linking Occurs when a link delivers the user to another site.

logic bombs Features of a program that will shut the program down if the licensing agreement is breached.

Loi Toubon A French law that requires that materials directed at French users be written in French.

long-arm statute A state statute that will allow a state to take jurisdiction over someone who does not live within that state's borders.

master-use license A license to use a specific, pre-recorded version of a composition.

mechanical license Gives an artist or record label the right to record a copyrighted composition and then to distribute the recording to the public.

meta tags Words or phrases in a web page's program used to give information about the page.

MP3 Stands for MPEG 1 layer 3. This technology allows you to compress audio tracks down into smaller, more manageable files.

newsgroups Very large discussion groups centered around a discrete topic.

print license A license to reproduce printed copies of music and lyrics (such as sheet music).

search engine A feature of a web page that searches the web in order to find material that is similar to the terms you tell it to look for.

serial copying Making copies from copies.

servers Computers that provide other computers in a network with access to computer services, such as Internet access, programs, common files, etc.

service mark A word, name, symbol, device, or other designation that is distinctive of a person's services and that is used to identify those services and distinguish them from the services of others.

shareware Computer software offered for free use and/or distribution.

shrinkwrap agreements Licenses that come with software that dictate the terms of your use.

source code The computer program underlying a web site.

spamming Sending unsolicited e-mails to very large numbers of users.

statutory licenses Licenses that the copyright holder is required to give.

streaming Real-time transmission of an audio or video file.

synchronization license License to use a musical composition in conjunction with video.

top-level domain names Web address extensions, such as .com, .org, .edu, etc.

trademark A word, name, symbol, device, or other designation that is distinctive of a person's goods and that is used to identify those goods and distinguish them from the goods of others.

Trojan horse A type of computer virus in the form of a destructive file that appears to be harmless.

videogram license License that allows the synchronized work itself to be copied and distributed to the public.

virus The general term for a destructive computer program that is designed to reproduce and/or transmit itself to other computers.

webcasts Internet broadcasts.

webmaster A person, or group of people, who maintains a web site.

web site A document on the Internet where individuals, businesses, and other organizations store information for others to access.

worm A virus that creates a large amount of useless information, with the goal of filling the computer's memory and crashing the computer.

Summary of Statues

Audio Home Recording Act of 1992

The Audio Home Recording Act was developed to counteract home recording by consumers. The Act allows consumers to make copies of their own cassettes and compact discs for personal use, such as to maintain in storage. The Act requires that manufacturers of digital audio recording devices, such as cassette recorders and blank cassettes, collect a royalty (called a "DART" royalty) that is then distributed to various types of recording industry participants, such as record labels, artists, and songwriters. The Act also requires that the manufacturers include technology within the device that is designed to prevent serial copying.

This Act specifically excludes objects "in which one or more computer programs are fixed" from the definition of digital musical recording. The Ninth Circuit Court of Appeals used this language to decide that MP3 players do not fall under this Act. A digital audio recording device must record from a digital musical recording in order to fall under this Act's requirements and protections. The court decided that, since MP3 players record from a computer, MP3 players must not be digital audio recording devices. This ignores the theory that MP3 players actually record from sound files, rather than from computers, but it is the leading case interpreting the statute.

If the Act applies to MP3 technology, then you may make MP3 files for your own personal use from your own tapes and compact discs. However, if the Act does not apply to MP3 technology, then copying of tapes and compact discs into MP3 files is not legal unless you are otherwise licensed.

Digital Performance Rights in Sound Recordings Act of 1995

The Digital Performance Rights in Sound Recordings Act created a "digital performance right" for copyright owners of sound recordings. Until this Act, copyright owners of sound recordings, such as record companies, could not restrict the performance of their recordings—performance rights belonged exclusively to the composers of the underlying composition. The "digital performance right" gives the copyright holder of rights in sound recordings the ability to restrict the digital performance of his or her recordings, thereby requiring those that would digitally perform the recording (that is, play the recording via satellite, Internet, or cable transmission) to acquire a license. These licenses were strictly voluntary and could be withheld by the copyright owner. Only noninteractive subscription services were subject to the licensing requirements, exempting most webcasting services due to their nonsubcription nature. This Act was later supplemented and clarified by the Digital Millennium Copyright Act.

Digital Millennium Copyright Act

Enacted in 1998, the Digital Millennium Copyright Act (DMCA) adopted the World Intellectual Property Organization (WIPO) Copyright Treaty and the WIPO Performances and Phonograms Treaty. It also extended safe harbors to Internet Service Providers (ISPs) and to those who repair and maintain computers (some previous court rulings had found individuals who repair or maintain computers liable for copyright infringement based on the fact that a copy of the computer program was created in the computer's memory simply by turning the machine on). In addition, the DMCA limited the exclusion from the digital performance license requirements to nonsubscription broadcast transmissions, meaning that webcasters are now required to obtain a digital performance license from the copyright owner of a sound recording. However, the DMCA also added compulsory license provisions. These provisions require copyright owners of sound recordings to issue licenses to webcasters that meet certain criteria.

Lanham Act

The Lanham Act governs trademarks and service marks. This Act grants protection to distinctive marks, allowing those who have rights in certain marks to prevent others from using the marks in connection with similar goods and services. The Act also allows those who have rights in famous marks to prevent others from using the marks in connection with any goods or services.

Anticybersquatting Consumer Protection Act

In 1999, Congress amended the Lanham Act to include sanctions for so-called "cybersquatting" (that is, the registration of a domain name containing the trademark or service mark of another for the purpose of preventing its use by the mark holder or for the purpose of acquiring money in exchange for the domain name's transfer).

Computer Fraud and Abuse Act

The Computer Fraud and Abuse Act (CFAA) protects seven specific areas from abuses associated with computer crime. Those areas are classified information, financial information, trespasses against government computers, trespasses against computers used by the government (even if the computer is not actually owned by the government) in order to take property, damage to computers used by the government, distribution of passwords used to access computers, and extortion.

No Electronic Theft Act

The No Electronic Theft Act created criminal penalties for willful copyright infringement. The Act designates penalties for copyright infringement for commercial advantage; private financial gain (including through receipt of other copyrighted works); or through reproduction or distribution of a copy or copies of a work or works where the total retail value is in excess of $1,000 during any 180-day period (stiffer penalties apply where ten or more copies and more than a $2,500 value are involved). The Act also extended the statute of limitations from three to five years.

Electronic Communications Privacy Act

The Electronic Communications Privacy Act was enacted in 1986 to amend the federal anti-wiretapping statute. Among other things, the Act protects electronic mail and voice messages (both in transit and stored messages) from interception or disclosure by anyone except online operators in the performance of their duties. Generally speaking, these communications cannot be accessed without a properly obtained search warrant or consent of one of the parties.

Privacy Protection Act of 1980

The Privacy Protection Act protects publishers from the seizure of materials. The Act was designed to encourage the free flow of information to the press. Therefore, unless a publisher is suspected of committing a crime related to the materials that are to be seized, law enforcement officials are not allowed to search or seize such materials.

Uniform Commercial Code (Articles 2 and 2A)

Articles 2 and 2A of the Uniform Commercial Code (UCC) are proposed sets of rules that apply to contracts for the sale of goods and the leasing of goods, respectively. Because contracts are a matter of state law, laws concerning contracts vary from state to state. The American Law Institute proposed a uniform set of rules that would apply to contracts for the sale or lease of goods in order to promote stability in commerce. Most states have adopted the UCC in some form, meaning that the laws in most states concerning contracts for the sales of goods are similar. However, because uniform laws are merely proposals, states may change provisions before adopting them.

Uniform Computer Information Transactions Act

The Uniform Computer Information Transactions Act (UCITA) is a proposed set of rules that applies to contracts involving computer information. If computer information is only a portion of the entire contract's subject matter, then the Act applies only to that portion. UCITA applies to electronic contracts for services delivered through electronic transfer and for services delivered in the more traditional sense.

Uniform Electronic Transactions Act

The Uniform Electronic Transactions Act (UETA) is designed to ensure that electronic records or signatures are still legally valid even though they are electronic. However, the Act only applies if the parties expressly agree to conduct their transactions electronically and if they are able to retain the electronic documents in some form, whether it be printouts or on disk. In essence, UETA contains four provisions that accomplish this purpose:

1. Records and signatures cannot be declared legally ineffective simply because they are electronic.
2. Contracts formed with electronic records cannot be declared legally ineffective simply because they are electronic.
3. If a document must be in writing, then an electronic writing will suffice.
4. If a document must be signed, then an electronic signature will suffice.

UETA does not apply in situations where UCITA would apply (that is, it doesn't apply to computer information transactions); where state law expressly overrides it; or to any provisions of the Uniform Commercial Code (UCC) other than Articles 2 and 2A (that is, those portions of the UCC that apply to the sale or leasing of goods), and a couple of other general provisions.

Electronic Signatures in Global and National Commerce Act

The Electronic Signatures in Global and National Commerce Act (ESIGN) generally applies to all electronic transactions and preempts any attempt by other laws to deny the enforceability of a signature, or document, simply because it is in electronic form. ESIGN does not apply to family law matters; testamentary matters; documents signed in conjunction with court proceedings; certain notices, including repossession notices under credit agreements, termination of utility services, and similar notices; or to the UCC, except for Articles 2 and 2A and a few other UCC provisions.

Selected Statutory Provisions

Selected Provisions of the
AUDIO HOME RECORDING ACT OF 1992

17 U.S.C. 1001
Sec. 1001 Definitions

As used in this chapter, the following terms have the following meanings:

(1)   A "digital audio copied recording" is a reproduction in a digital recording format of a digital musical recording, whether that reproduction is made directly from another digital musical recording or indirectly from a transmission.

(2)   A "digital audio interface device" is any machine or device that is designed specifically to communicate digital audio information and related interface data to a digital audio recording device through a nonprofessional interface.

(3)   A "digital audio recording device" is any machine or device of a type commonly distributed to individuals for use by individuals, whether or not included with or as part of some other machine or device, the digital recording function of which is designed or marketed for the primary purpose of, and that is capable of, making a digital audio copied recording for private use, except for—

(A)   professional model products, and

(B)   dictation machines, answering machines, and other audio recording equipment that is designed and marketed primarily for the creation of sound recordings resulting from the fixation of nonmusical sounds.

(4)   (A)   A "digital audio recording medium" is any material object in a form commonly distributed for use by individuals, that is primarily marketed or most commonly used by consumers for the purpose of making digital audio copied recordings by use of a digital audio recording device.

(B) Such term does not include any material object—

(i)   that embodies a sound recording at the time it is first distributed by the importer or manufacturer; or

(ii)   that is primarily marketed and most commonly used by consumers either for the purpose of making copies of motion pictures or other audiovisual works or for the purpose of making copies of nonmusical literary works, including computer programs or data bases.

(5)   (A)   A "digital musical recording" is a material object—

(i)   in which are fixed, in a digital recording format, only sounds, and material, statements, or instructions incidental to those fixed sounds, if any, and

(ii)   from which the sounds and material can be perceived, reproduced, or otherwise communicated, either directly or with the aid of a machine or device.

(B)   A "digital musical recording" does not include a material object—

(i)   in which the fixed sounds consist entirely of spoken word recordings, or

(ii)   in which one or more computer programs are fixed, except that a digital musical recording may contain statements or instructions constituting the fixed sounds and incidental material, and statements or instructions to be used directly or indirectly in order to bring about the perception, reproduction, or communication of the fixed sounds and incidental material.

(C)   For purposes of this paragraph—

(i)   a "spoken word recording" is a sound recording in which are fixed only a series of spoken words, except that the spoken words may be accompanied by incidental musical or other sounds, and

(ii)   the term "incidental" means related to and relatively minor by comparison.

(6)   "Distribute" means to sell, lease, or assign a product to consumers in the United States, or to sell, lease, or assign a product in the United States for ultimate transfer to consumers in the United States.

(7)   An "interested copyright party" is—

(A)   the owner of the exclusive right under section 106(1) of this title to reproduce a sound recording of a musical work that has been embodied in a digital musical recording or analog musical recording lawfully made under this title that has been distributed;

(B)   the legal or beneficial owner of, or the person that controls, the right to reproduce in a digital musical recording or analog musical recording a musical work that has been embodied in a digital musical recording or analog musical recording lawfully made under this title that has been distributed;

(C)   a featured recording artist who performs on a sound recording that has been distributed; or

(D)   any association or other organization—

(i)   representing persons specified in subparagraph (A), (B), or (C), or

(ii)   engaged in licensing rights in musical works to music users on behalf of writers and publishers.

(8)   To "manufacture" means to produce or assemble a product in the United States. A "manufacturer" is a person who manufactures.

(9)   A "music publisher" is a person that is authorized to license the reproduction of a particular musical work in a sound recording.

(10)   A "professional model product" is an audio recording device that is designed, manufactured, marketed, and intended for use by recording professionals in the ordinary course of a lawful business, in accordance with such

requirements as the Secretary of Commerce shall establish by regulation.

(11)   The term "serial copying" means the duplication in a digital format of a copyrighted musical work or sound recording from a digital reproduction of a digital musical recording. The term "digital reproduction of a digital musical recording" does not include a digital musical recording as distributed, by authority of the copyright owner, for ultimate sale to consumers.

(12)   The "transfer price" of a digital audio recording device or a digital audio recording medium—

(A)   is, subject to subparagraph (B)—

(i)   in the case of an imported product, the actual entered value at United States Customs (exclusive of any freight, insurance, and applicable duty), and

(ii)   in the case of a domestic product, the manufacturer's transfer price (FOB the manufacturer, and exclusive of any direct sales taxes or excise taxes incurred in connection with the sale); and

(B)   shall, in a case in which the transferor and transferee are related entities or within a single entity, not be less than a reasonable arms-length price under the principles of the regulations adopted pursuant to section 482 of the Internal Revenue Code of 1986, or any successor provision to such section.

(13)   A "writer" is the composer or lyricist of a particular musical work.

17 U.S.C. 1002
Sec. 1002 Incorporation of copying controls

(a)   Prohibition on Importation, Manufacture, and Distribution.—No person shall import, manufacture, or distribute any digital audio recording device or digital audio interface device that does not conform to—

(1)   the Serial Copy Management System;

(2)   a system that has the same functional characteristics as the Serial Copy Management System and requires that copyright and generation status information be accurately sent, received, and acted upon between devices using the system's method of serial copying regulation and devices using the Serial Copy Management System; or

(3)   any other system certified by the Secretary of Commerce as prohibiting unauthorized serial copying.

(b)   Development of Verification Procedure.—The Secretary of Commerce shall establish a procedure to verify, upon the petition of an interested party, that a system meets the standards set forth in subsection (a)(2).

(c)   Prohibition on Circumvention of the System.—No person shall import, manufacture, or distribute any device, or offer or perform any service, the primary purpose or effect of which is to avoid, bypass, remove, deactivate, or otherwise circumvent any program or circuit which implements, in whole or in part, a system described in subsection (a).

(d)   Encoding of Information on Digital Musical Recordings.—

(1)   Prohibition on encoding inaccurate information.—No person shall encode a digital musical recording of a sound recording with inaccurate information relating to the category code, copyright status, or generation status of the source material for the recording.

(2)   Encoding of copyright status not required.—Nothing in this chapter requires any person engaged in the importation or manufacture of digital musical recordings to encode any such digital musical recording with respect to its copyright status.

(e)   Information Accompanying Transmissions in Digital Format.—Any person who transmits or otherwise communicates to the public any sound recording in digital format is not required under this chapter to transmit or otherwise communicate the information relating to the copyright status of the sound recording. Any such person who does transmit or otherwise communicate such copyright status information shall transmit or communicate such information accurately.

17 U.S.C. 1003
Sec. 1003 Obligation to make royalty payments

(a)   Prohibition on Importation and Manufacture.—No person shall import into and distribute, or manufacture and distribute, any digital audio recording device or digital audio recording medium unless such person records the notice specified by this section and subsequently deposits the statements of account and applicable royalty payments for such device or medium specified in section 1004.

(b)   Filing of Notice.—The importer or manufacturer of any digital audio recording device or digital audio recording medium, within a product category or utilizing a technology with respect to which such manufacturer or importer has not previously filed a notice under this subsection, shall file with the Register of Copyrights a notice with respect to such device or medium, in such form and content as the Register shall prescribe by regulation.

(c)   Filing of Quarterly and Annual Statements of Account.—

(1)   Generally.—Any importer or manufacturer that distributes any digital audio recording device or digital audio recording medium that it manufactured or imported shall file with the Register of Copyrights, in such form and content as the Register shall prescribe by regulation, such quarterly and annual statements of account with respect to such distribution as the Register shall prescribe by regulation.

(2)   Certification, verification, and confidentiality.—Each such statement

shall be certified as accurate by an authorized officer or principal of the importer or manufacturer. The Register shall issue regulations to provide for the verification and audit of such statements and to protect the confidentiality of the information contained in such statements. Such regulations shall provide for the disclosure, in confidence, of such statements to interested copyright parties.
(3)   Royalty payments.—Each such statement shall be accompanied by the royalty payments specified in section 1004.

17 U.S.C. 1004
Sec. 1004. Royalty payments

(a)   Digital Audio Recording Devices.—
(1)   Amount of payment.—The royalty payment due under section 1003 for each digital audio recording device imported into and distributed in the United States, or manufactured and distributed in the United States, shall be 2 percent of the transfer price. Only the first person to manufacture and distribute or import and distribute such device shall be required to pay the royalty with respect to such device.
(2)   Calculation for devices distributed with other devices.—With respect to a digital audio recording device first distributed in combination with one or more devices, either as a physically integrated unit or as separate components, the royalty payment shall be calculated as follows:
(A)   If the digital audio recording device and such other devices are part of a physically integrated unit, the royalty payment shall be based on the transfer price of the unit, but shall be reduced by any royalty payment made on any digital audio recording device included within the unit that was not first distributed in combination with the unit.
(B)   If the digital audio recording device is not part of a physically integrated unit and substantially similar devices have been distributed separately at any time during the preceding 4 calendar quarters, the royalty payment shall be based on the average transfer price of such devices during those 4 quarters.
(C)   If the digital audio recording device is not part of a physically integrated unit and substantially similar devices have not been distributed separately at any time during the preceding 4 calendar quarters, the royalty payment shall be based on a constructed price reflecting the proportional value of such device to the combination as a whole.
(3)   Limits on royalties.—Notwithstanding paragraph (1) or (2), the amount of the royalty payment for each digital audio recording device shall not be less than $1 nor more than the royalty maximum. The royalty maximum shall be $8 per device, except that in the case of a physically integrated unit containing more than 1 digital audio recording device, the royalty maximum for such unit

shall be $12. During the 6th year after the effective date of this chapter, and not more than once each year thereafter, any interested copyright party may petition the Librarian of Congress to increase the royalty maximum and, if more than 20 percent of the royalty payments are at the relevant royalty maximum, the Librarian of Congress shall prospectively increase such royalty maximum with the goal of having no more than 10 percent of such payments at the new royalty maximum; however the amount of any such increase as a percentage of the royalty maximum shall in no event exceed the percentage increase in the Consumer Price Index during the period under review.

(b)　　　Digital Audio Recording Media.—The royalty payment due under section 1003 for each digital audio recording medium imported into and distributed in the United States, or manufactured and distributed in the United States, shall be 3 percent of the transfer price. Only the first person to manufacture and distribute or import and distribute such medium shall be required to pay the royalty with respect to such medium.

17 U.S.C. 1005
Sec. 1005. Deposit of royalty payments and deduction of expenses

The Register of Copyrights shall receive all royalty payments deposited under this chapter and, after deducting the reasonable costs incurred by the Copyright Office under this chapter, shall deposit the balance in the Treasury of the United States as offsetting receipts, in such manner as the Secretary of the Treasury directs. All funds held by the Secretary of the Treasury shall be invested in interest-bearing United States securities for later distribution with interest under section 1007. The Register may, in the Register's discretion, 4 years after the close of any calendar year, close out the royalty payments account for that calendar year, and may treat any funds remaining in such account and any subsequent deposits that would otherwise be attributable to that calendar year as attributable to the succeeding calendar year.

17 U.S.C. 1006
Sec. 1006. Entitlement to royalty payments

(a)　　　Interested Copyright Parties.—The royalty payments deposited pursuant to section 1005 shall, in accordance with the procedures specified in section 1007, be distributed to any interested copyright party—
(1)　　　whose musical work or sound recording has been—
(A)　　　embodied in a digital musical recording or an analog musical recording lawfully made under this title that has been distributed, and
(B)　　　distributed in the form of digital musical recordings or analog musical

recordings or disseminated to the public in transmissions, during the period to which such payments pertain; and

(2)   who has filed a claim under section 1007.

(b)   Allocation of Royalty Payments to Groups.—The royalty payments shall be divided into 2 funds as follows:

(1)   The Sound Recordings Fund.—66⅔ percent of the royalty payments shall be allocated to the Sound Recordings Fund. 2⅝ percent of the royalty payments allocated to the Sound Recordings Fund shall be placed in an escrow account managed by an independent administrator jointly appointed by the interested copyright parties described in section 1001(7)(A) and the American Federation of Musicians (or any successor entity) to be distributed to nonfeatured musicians (whether or not members of the American Federation of Musicians or any successor entity) who have performed on sound recordings distributed in the United States. 1⅜ percent of the royalty payments allocated to the Sound Recordings Fund shall be placed in an escrow account managed by an independent administrator jointly appointed by the interested copyright parties described in section 1001(7)(A) and the American Federation of Television and Radio Artists (or any successor entity) to be distributed to nonfeatured vocalists (whether or not members of the American Federation of Television and Radio Artists or any successor entity) who have performed on sound recordings distributed in the United States. 40 percent of the remaining royalty payments in the Sound Recordings Fund shall be distributed to the interested copyright parties described in section 1001(7)(C), and 60 percent of such remaining royalty payments shall be distributed to the interested copyright parties described in section 1001(7)(A).

(2)   The Musical Works Fund.—

(A)   33⅓ percent of the royalty payments shall be allocated to the Musical Works Fund for distribution to interested copyright parties described in section 1001(7)(B).

(B)(i) Music publishers shall be entitled to 50 percent of the royalty payments allocated to the Musical Works Fund.

(ii)   Writers shall be entitled to the other 50 percent of the royalty payments allocated to the Musical Works Fund.

(c)   Allocation of Royalty Payments Within Groups.—If all interested copyright parties within a group specified in subsection (b) do not agree on a voluntary proposal for the distribution of the royalty payments within each group, the Librarian of Congress shall convene a copyright arbitration royalty panel which shall, pursuant to the procedures specified under section 1007(c), allocate royalty payments under this section based on the extent to which, during the relevant period—

(1)   for the Sound Recordings Fund, each sound recording was distributed

in the form of digital musical recordings or analog musical recordings; and

(2)   for the Musical Works Fund, each musical work was distributed in the form of digital musical recordings or analog musical recordings or disseminated to the public in transmissions.

17 U.S.C. 1007
Sec. 1007. Procedures for distributing royalty payments

(a)   Filing of Claims and Negotiations.—

(1)   Filing of claims.—During the first 2 months of each calendar year after calendar year 1992, every interested copyright party seeking to receive royalty payments to which such party is entitled under section 1006 shall file with the Librarian of Congress a claim for payments collected during the preceding year in such form and manner as the Librarian of Congress shall prescribe by regulation.

(2)   Negotiations.—Notwithstanding any provision of the antitrust laws, for purposes of this section interested copyright parties within each group specified in section 1006(b) may agree among themselves to the proportionate division of royalty payments, may lump their claims together and file them jointly or as a single claim, or may designate a common agent, including any organization described in section 1001(7)(D), to negotiate or receive payment on their behalf; except that no agreement under this subsection may modify the allocation of royalties specified in section 1006(b).

(b)   Distribution of Payments in the Absence of a Dispute.—After the period established for the filing of claims under subsection (a), in each year after 1992, the Librarian of Congress shall determine whether there exists a controversy concerning the distribution of royalty payments under section 1006(c). If the Librarian of Congress determines that no such controversy exists, the Librarian of Congress shall, within 30 days after such determination, authorize the distribution of the royalty payments as set forth in the agreements regarding the distribution of royalty payments entered into pursuant to subsection (a), after deducting its reasonable administrative costs under this section.

(c)   Resolution of Disputes.—If the Librarian of Congress finds the existence of a controversy, the Librarian shall, pursuant to chapter 8 of this title, convene a copyright arbitration royalty panel to determine the distribution of royalty payments. During the pendency of such a proceeding, the Librarian of Congress shall withhold from distribution an amount sufficient to satisfy all claims with respect to which a controversy exists, but shall, to the extent feasible, authorize the distribution of any amounts that are not in controversy. The Librarian of Congress shall, before authorizing the distribution of such royalty payments, deduct the reasonable administrative costs incurred by the Librarian under this section.

Selected provisions of the DIGITAL PERFORMANCE RIGHTS IN SOUND RECORDINGS ACT and the DIGITAL MILLENNIUM COPYRIGHT ACT

17 U.S.C. 114
Sec. 114. Scope of exclusive rights in sound recordings

(a)   The exclusive rights of the owner of copyright in a sound recording are limited to the rights specified by clauses (1), (2), (3) and (6) of section 106, and do not include any right of performance under section 106(4).

(b)   The exclusive right of the owner of copyright in a sound recording under clause (1) of section 106 is limited to the right to duplicate the sound recording in the form of phonorecords or copies that directly or indirectly recapture the actual sounds fixed in the recording. The exclusive right of the owner of copyright in a sound recording under clause (2) of section 106 is limited to the right to prepare a derivative work in which the actual sounds fixed in the sound recording are rearranged, remixed, or otherwise altered in sequence or quality. The exclusive rights of the owner of copyright in a sound recording under clauses (1) and (2) of section 106 do not extend to the making or duplication of another sound recording that consists entirely of an independent fixation of other sounds, even though such sounds imitate or simulate those in the copyrighted sound recording. The exclusive rights of the owner of copyright in a sound recording under clauses (1), (2), and (3) of section 106 do not apply to sound recordings included in educational television and radio programs (as defined in section 397 of title 47) distributed or transmitted by or through public broadcasting entities (as defined by section 118(g)): Provided, That copies or phonorecords of said programs are not commercially distributed by or through public broadcasting entities to the general public.

(c)   This section does not limit or impair the exclusive right to perform publicly, by means of a phonorecord, any of the works specified by section 106(4).

(d)   Limitations on exclusive right.—Notwithstanding the provisions of section 106(6)—

(1)   Exempt transmissions and retransmissions.—The performance of a sound recording publicly by means of a digital audio transmission, other than as a part of an interactive service, is not an infringement of section 106(6) if the performance is part of—

(A)   a nonsubscription broadcast transmission;

(B)   a retransmission of a nonsubscription broadcast transmission: Provided, That, in the case of a retransmission of a radio station's broadcast transmission—

(i)   the radio station's broadcast transmission is not willfully or repeatedly retransmitted more than a radius of 150 miles from the site of the radio broadcast transmitter, however—

(I)　　the 150-mile limitation under this clause shall not apply when a nonsubscription broadcast transmission by a radio station licensed by the Federal Communications Commission is retransmitted on a nonsubscription basis by a terrestrial broadcast station, terrestrial translator, or terrestrial repeater licensed by the Federal Communications Commission; and

(II)　　in the case of a subscription retransmission of a nonsubscription broadcast retransmission covered by subclause (I), the 150-mile radius shall be measured from the transmitter site of such broadcast retransmitter;

(ii)　　the retransmission is of radio station broadcast transmissions that are—

(I)　　obtained by the retransmitter over the air;

(II)　　not electronically processed by the retransmitter to deliver separate and discrete signals; and

(III)　　retransmitted only within the local communities served by the retransmitter;

(iii)　　the radio station's broadcast transmission was being retransmitted to cable systems (as defined in section 111(f)) by a satellite carrier on January 1, 1995, and that retransmission was being retransmitted by cable systems as a separate and discrete signal, and the satellite carrier obtains the radio station's broadcast transmission in an analog format: Provided, That the broadcast transmission being retransmitted may embody the programming of no more than one radio station; or

(iv)　　the radio station's broadcast transmission is made by a noncommercial educational broadcast station funded on or after January 1, 1995, under section 396(k) of the Communications Act of 1934 (47 U.S.C. 396(k)), consists solely of noncommercial educational and cultural radio programs, and the retransmission, whether or not simultaneous, is a nonsubscription terrestrial broadcast retransmission; or

(C)　　a transmission that comes within any of the following categories—

(i)　　a prior or simultaneous transmission incidental to an exempt transmission, such as a feed received by and then retransmitted by an exempt transmitter: Provided, That such incidental transmissions do not include any subscription transmission directly for reception by members of the public;

(ii)　　a transmission within a business establishment, confined to its premises or the immediately surrounding vicinity;

(iii)　　a retransmission by any retransmitter, including a multichannel video programming distributor as defined in section 602(12) of the Communications Act of 1934 (47 U.S.C. 522(12)), of a transmission by a transmitter licensed to publicly perform the sound recording as a part of that transmission, if the retransmission is simultaneous with the licensed transmission and authorized by the transmitter; or

(iv)   a transmission to a business establishment for use in the ordinary course of its business: Provided, That the business recipient does not retransmit the transmission outside of its premises or the immediately surrounding vicinity, and that the transmission does not exceed the sound recording performance complement. Nothing in this clause shall limit the scope of the exemption in clause (ii).

(2)   Statutory licensing of certain transmissions.—The performance of a sound recording publicly by means of a subscription digital audio transmission not exempt under paragraph (1), an eligible nonsubscription transmission, or a transmission not exempt under paragraph (1) that is made by a preexisting satellite digital audio radio service shall be subject to statutory licensing, in accordance with subsection (f) if—

(A)   (i)   the transmission is not part of an interactive service;

(ii)   except in the case of a transmission to a business establishment, the transmitting entity does not automatically and intentionally cause any device receiving the transmission to switch from one program channel to another; and

(iii)   except as provided in section 1002(e), the transmission of the sound recording is accompanied, if technically feasible, by the information encoded in that sound recording, if any, by or under the authority of the copyright owner of that sound recording, that identifies the title of the sound recording, the featured recording artist who performs on the sound recording, and related information, including information concerning the underlying musical work and its writer;

(B)   in the case of a subscription transmission not exempt under paragraph (1) that is made by a preexisting subscription service in the same transmission medium used by such service on July 31, 1998, or in the case of a transmission not exempt under paragraph (1) that is made by a preexisting satellite digital audio radio service—

(i)   the transmission does not exceed the sound recording performance complement; and

(ii)   the transmitting entity does not cause to be published by means of an advance program schedule or prior announcement the titles of the specific sound recordings or phonorecords embodying such sound recordings to be transmitted; and

(C)   in the case of an eligible nonsubscription transmission or a subscription transmission not exempt under paragraph (1) that is made by a new subscription service or by a preexisting subscription service other than in the same transmission medium used by such service on July 31, 1998—

(i)   the transmission does not exceed the sound recording performance complement, except that this requirement shall not apply in the case of a retransmission of a broadcast transmission if the retransmission is made by a transmitting entity that does not have the right or ability to control the programming of the broadcast station making the broadcast transmission, unless—

(I)   the broadcast station makes broadcast transmissions—

(aa)   in digital format that regularly exceed the sound recording performance complement; or

(bb)   in analog format, a substantial portion of which, on a weekly basis, exceed the sound recording performance complement; and

(II)   the sound recording copyright owner or its representative has notified the transmitting entity in writing that broadcast transmissions of the copyright owner's sound recordings exceed the sound recording performance complement as provided in this clause;

(ii)   the transmitting entity does not cause to be published, or induce or facilitate the publication, by means of an advance program schedule or prior announcement, the titles of the specific sound recordings to be transmitted, the phonorecords embodying such sound recordings, or, other than for illustrative purposes, the names of the featured recording artists, except that this clause does not disqualify a transmitting entity that makes a prior announcement that a particular artist will be featured within an unspecified future time period, and in the case of a retransmission of a broadcast transmission by a transmitting entity that does not have the right or ability to control the programming of the broadcast transmission, the requirement of this clause shall not apply to a prior oral announcement by the broadcast station, or to an advance program schedule published, induced, or facilitated by the broadcast station, if the transmitting entity does not have actual knowledge and has not received written notice from the copyright owner or its representative that the broadcast station publishes or induces or facilitates the publication of such advance program schedule, or if such advance program schedule is a schedule of classical music programming published by the broadcast station in the same manner as published by that broadcast station on or before September 30, 1998;

(iii)   the transmission—

(I)   is not part of an archived program of less than 5 hours duration;

(II)   is not part of an archived program of 5 hours or greater in duration that is made available for a period exceeding 2 weeks;

(III)   is not part of a continuous program which is of less than 3 hours duration; or

(IV)   is not part of an identifiable program in which performances of sound recordings are rendered in a predetermined order, other than an archived or continuous program, that is transmitted at—

(aa)   more than 3 times in any 2-week period that have been publicly announced in advance, in the case of a program of less than 1 hour in duration, or (bb) more than 4 times in any 2-week period that have been publicly announced in advance, in the case of a program of 1 hour or more in duration, except that the requirement of this subclause shall not apply in the case of a retransmission of a broadcast transmission by a transmitting entity that does not have the right or ability to control the programming of the broadcast transmission, unless the transmitting entity is given notice in writing by the copyright owner of the sound recording that the broadcast station makes broadcast transmissions that regularly violate such requirement;

(iv)   the transmitting entity does not knowingly perform the sound recording, as part of a service that offers transmissions of visual images contemporaneously with transmissions of sound recordings, in a manner that is likely to cause confusion, to cause mistake, or to deceive, as to the affiliation, connection, or association of the copyright owner or featured recording artist with the transmitting entity or a particular product or service advertised by the transmitting entity, or as to the origin, sponsorship, or approval by the copyright owner or featured recording artist of the activities of the transmitting entity other than the performance of the sound recording itself;

(v)   the transmitting entity cooperates to prevent, to the extent feasible without imposing substantial costs or burdens, a transmission recipient or any other person or entity from automatically scanning the transmitting entity's transmissions alone or together with transmissions by other transmitting entities in order to select a particular sound recording to be transmitted to the transmission recipient, except that the requirement of this clause shall not apply to a satellite digital audio service that is in operation, or that is licensed by the Federal Communications Commission, on or before July 31, 1998;

(vi)   the transmitting entity takes no affirmative steps to cause or induce the making of a phonorecord by the transmission recipient, and if the technology used by the transmitting entity enables the transmitting entity to limit the making by the transmission recipient of phonorecords of the transmission directly in a digital format, the transmitting entity sets such technology to limit such making of phonorecords to the extent permitted by such technology;

(vii)   phonorecords of the sound recording have been distributed to the public under the authority of the copyright owner or the copyright owner authorizes the transmitting entity to transmit the sound recording, and the transmitting entity makes the transmission from a phonorecord lawfully made under the authority of the copyright owner, except that the requirement of this clause shall not apply to a retransmission of a broadcast transmission by a transmitting entity that does not have the right or ability to control the programming of the broadcast transmission, unless the transmitting entity is given notice in writing by the copyright owner of the sound recording that the broadcast station makes broadcast transmissions that regularly violate such requirement;

(viii)   the transmitting entity accommodates and does not interfere with the transmission of technical measures that are widely used by sound recording copyright owners to identify or protect copyrighted works, and that are technically feasible of being transmitted by the transmitting entity without imposing substantial costs on the transmitting entity or resulting in perceptible aural or visual degradation of the digital signal, except that the requirement of this clause shall not apply to a satellite digital audio service that is in operation, or that is licensed under the authority of the Federal Communications Commission, on or before July 31, 1998, to the extent that such service has designed, developed, or made commitments to procure equipment or technology that is not compatible with such technical measures before such technical measures are widely adopted by sound recording copyright owners; and

(ix)   the transmitting entity identifies in textual data the sound recording during, but not before, the time it is performed, including the title of the sound recording, the title of the phonorecord embodying such sound recording, if any, and the featured recording artist, in a manner to permit it to be displayed to the transmission recipient by the device or technology intended for receiving the service provided by the transmitting entity, except that the obligation in this clause shall not take effect until 1 year after the date of the enactment of the Digital Millennium Copyright Act and shall not apply in the case of a retransmission of a broadcast transmission by a transmitting entity that does not have the right or ability to control the programming of the broadcast transmission, or in the case in which devices or technology intended for receiving the service provided by the transmitting entity that have the capability to display such textual data are not common in the marketplace.

(3)   Licenses for transmissions by interactive services.—

(A)   No interactive service shall be granted an exclusive license under section 106(6) for the performance of a sound recording publicly by means of digital audio transmission for a period in excess of 12 months, except that with respect to an exclusive license granted to an interactive service by a licensor that holds the copyright to 1,000 or fewer sound recordings, the period of such license shall not exceed 24 months; Provided, however, That the grantee of such exclusive license shall be ineligible to receive another exclusive license for the performance of that sound recording for a period of 13 months from the expiration of the prior exclusive license.

(B)   The limitation set forth in subparagraph (A) of this paragraph shall not apply if—

(i)   the licensor has granted and there remain in effect licenses under section 106(6) for the public performance of sound recordings by means of digital audio transmission by at least 5 different interactive services: Provided, however, That each such license must be for a minimum of 10 percent of the copyrighted sound recordings owned by the licensor that have been licensed to interactive services, but in no event less than 50 sound recordings; or

(ii)   the exclusive license is granted to perform publicly up to 45 seconds of a sound recording and the sole purpose of the performance is to promote the distribution or performance of that sound recording.

(C)   Notwithstanding the grant of an exclusive or nonexclusive license of the right of public performance under section 106(6), an interactive service may not publicly perform a sound recording unless a license has been granted for the public performance of any copyrighted musical work contained in the sound recording: Provided, That such license to publicly perform the copyrighted musical work may be granted either by a performing rights society representing the copyright owner or by the copyright owner.

(D)   The performance of a sound recording by means of a retransmission of a digital audio transmission is not an infringement of section 106(6) if—

(i)   the retransmission is of a transmission by an interactive service licensed to publicly perform the sound recording to a particular member of the public as part of that transmission; and

(ii)   the retransmission is simultaneous with the licensed transmission, authorized by the transmitter, and limited to that particular member of the public intended by the interactive service to be the recipient of the transmission.

(E)   For the purposes of this paragraph—

(i)   a "licensor" shall include the licensing entity and any other entity under any material degree of common ownership, management, or control that owns copyrights in sound recordings; and

(ii)   a "performing rights society" is an association or corporation that licenses the public performance of nondramatic musical works on behalf of the copyright owner, such as the American Society of Composers, Authors and Publishers, Broadcast Music, Inc., and SESAC, Inc.

(4)   Rights not otherwise limited.—

(A)   Except as expressly provided in this section, this section does not limit or impair the exclusive right to perform a sound recording publicly by means of a digital audio transmission under section 106(6).

(B)   Nothing in this section annuls or limits in any way—

(i)   the exclusive right to publicly perform a musical work, including by means of a digital audio transmission, under section 106(4);

(ii)   the exclusive rights in a sound recording or the musical work embodied therein under sections 106(1), 106(2) and 106(3); or

(iii)   any other rights under any other clause of section 106, or remedies available under this title, as such rights or remedies exist either before or after the date of enactment of the Digital Performance Right in Sound Recordings Act of 1995.

(C)   Any limitations in this section on the exclusive right under section 106(6) apply only to the exclusive right under section 106(6) and not to any other exclusive rights under section 106. Nothing in this section shall be construed to annul, limit, impair or otherwise affect in any way the ability of the owner of a copyright in a sound recording to exercise the rights under sections 106(1), 106(2) and 106(3), or to obtain the remedies available under this title pursuant to such rights, as such rights and remedies exist either before or after the date of enactment of the Digital Performance Right in Sound Recordings Act of 1995.

(e)   Authority for negotiations.—

(1)   Notwithstanding any provision of the antitrust laws, in negotiating statutory licenses in accordance with subsection (f), any copyright owners of sound recordings and any entities performing sound recordings affected by this section may negotiate and agree upon the royalty rates and license terms and conditions for the performance of such sound recordings and the proportionate division of fees paid among copyright owners, and may designate common agents on a nonexclusive basis to negotiate, agree to, pay, or receive payments.

(2)   For licenses granted under section 106(6), other than statutory licenses, such as for performances by interactive services or performances that exceed the sound recording performance complement—

(A)   copyright owners of sound recordings affected by this section may designate common agents to act on their behalf to grant licenses and receive and remit royalty payments: Provided, That each copyright owner shall establish the royalty rates and material license terms and conditions unilaterally, that is, not in agreement, combination, or concert with other copyright owners of sound recordings; and

(B)   entities performing sound recordings affected by this section may designate common agents to act on their behalf to obtain licenses and collect and pay royalty fees: Provided, That each entity performing sound recordings shall determine the royalty rates and material license terms and conditions unilaterally, that is, not in agreement, combination, or concert with other entities performing sound recordings.

(f) Licenses for certain nonexempt transmissions.—

(1)   (A)   No later than 30 days after the enactment of the Digital Performance Right in Sound Recordings Act of 1995, the Librarian of Congress shall cause notice to be published in the Federal Register of the initiation of voluntary negotiation proceedings for the purpose of determining reasonable terms and rates of royalty payments for subscription transmissions by preexisting subscription services and transmissions by preexisting satellite digital audio radio services specified by subsection (d)(2) of this section during the

period beginning on the effective date of such Act and ending on December 31, 2001, or, if a copyright arbitration royalty panel is convened, ending 30 days after the Librarian issues and publishes in the Federal Register an order adopting the determination of the copyright arbitration royalty panel or an order setting the terms and rates (if the Librarian rejects the panel's determination). Such terms and rates shall distinguish among the different types of digital audio transmission services then in operation. Any copyright owners of sound recordings, preexisting subscription services, or preexisting satellite digital audio radio services may submit to the Librarian of Congress licenses covering such subscription transmissions with respect to such sound recordings.

(B)   In the absence of license agreements negotiated under subparagraph (A), during the 60-day period commencing 6 months after publication of the notice specified in subparagraph (A), and upon the filing of a petition in accordance with section 803(a)(1), the Librarian of Congress shall, pursuant to chapter 8, convene a copyright arbitration royalty panel to determine and publish in the Federal Register a schedule of rates and terms which, subject to paragraph (3), shall be binding on all copyright owners of sound recordings and entities performing sound recordings affected by this paragraph. In establishing rates and terms for preexisting subscription services and preexisting satellite digital audio radio services, in addition to the objectives set forth in section 801(b)(1), the copyright arbitration royalty panel may consider the rates and terms for comparable types of subscription digital audio transmission services and comparable circumstances under voluntary license agreements negotiated as provided in subparagraph (A).

(C)   (i)   Publication of a notice of the initiation of voluntary negotiation proceedings as specified in subparagraph (A) shall be repeated, in accordance with regulations that the Librarian of Congress shall prescribe—

(I)   no later than 30 days after a petition is filed by any copyright owners of sound recordings, any preexisting subscription services, or any preexisting satellite digital audio radio services indicating that a new type of subscription digital audio transmission service on which sound recordings are performed is or is about to become operational; and

(II)   in the first week of January 2001, and at 5-year intervals thereafter.

(ii)   The procedures specified in subparagraph (B) shall be repeated, in accordance with regulations that the Librarian of Congress shall prescribe, upon filing of a petition in accordance with section 803(a)(1) during a 60-day period commencing—

(I) 6 months after publication of a notice of the initiation of voluntary negotiation proceedings under subparagraph (A) pursuant to a petition under clause (i)(I) of this subparagraph; or

(II) on July 1, 2001, and at 5-year intervals thereafter.

(iii)   The procedures specified in subparagraph (B) shall be concluded in accordance with section 802.

(2)   (A)   No later than 30 days after the date of the enactment of the Digital Millennium Copyright Act, the Librarian of Congress shall cause notice to be published in the Federal Register of the initiation of voluntary negotiation proceedings for the purpose of determining reasonable terms and rates of royalty payments for public performances of sound recordings by means of eligible nonsubscription transmissions and transmissions by new subscription services specified by subsection (d)(2) during the period beginning on the date of the enactment of such Act and ending on December 31, 2000, or such other date as the parties may agree. Such rates and terms shall distinguish among the different types of eligible nonsubscription transmission services and new subscription services then in operation and shall include a minimum fee for each such type of service. Any copyright owners of sound recordings or any entities performing sound recordings affected by this paragraph may submit to the Librarian of Congress licenses covering such eligible nonsubscription transmissions and new subscription services with respect to such sound recordings. The parties to each negotiation proceeding shall bear their own costs.

(B)   In the absence of license agreements negotiated under subparagraph (A), during the 60-day period commencing 6 months after publication of the notice specified in subparagraph (A), and upon the filing of a petition in accordance with section 803(a)(1), the Librarian of Congress shall, pursuant to chapter 8, convene a copyright arbitration royalty panel to determine and publish in the Federal Register a schedule of rates and terms which, subject to paragraph (3), shall be binding on all copyright owners of sound recordings and entities performing sound recordings affected by this paragraph during the period beginning on the date of the enactment of the Digital Millennium Copyright Act and ending on December 31, 2000, or such other date as the parties may agree. Such rates and terms shall distinguish among the different types of eligible nonsubscription transmission services then in operation and shall include a minimum fee for each such type of service, such differences to be based on criteria including, but not limited to, the quantity and nature of the use of sound recordings and the degree to which use of the service may substitute for or may promote the purchase of phonorecords by consumers. In establishing rates and terms for transmissions by eligible nonsubscription services and new subscription services, the copyright arbitration royalty panel shall establish rates and terms that most clearly represent the rates and terms that would have been negotiated in the marketplace between a willing buyer and a willing seller. In determining such rates and terms, the copyright arbitration royalty panel shall base its decision on economic, competitive and programming information presented by the parties, including—

(i)   whether use of the service may substitute for or may promote the sales of phonorecords or otherwise may interfere with or may enhance the sound recording copyright owner's other streams of revenue from its sound recordings; and

(ii)   the relative roles of the copyright owner and the transmitting entity in the copyrighted work and the service made available to the public with respect to relative creative contribution, technological contribution, capital investment, cost, and risk. In establishing such rates and terms, the copyright arbitration royalty panel may consider the rates and terms for comparable types of digital audio transmission services and comparable circumstances under voluntary license agreements negotiated under subparagraph (A).

(C)   (i)   Publication of a notice of the initiation of voluntary negotiation proceedings as specified in subparagraph (A) shall be repeated in accordance with regulations that the Librarian of Congress shall prescribe—

(I)   no later than 30 days after a petition is filed by any copyright owners of sound recordings or any eligible nonsubscription service or new subscription service indicating that a new type of eligible nonsubscription service or new subscription service on which sound recordings are performed is or is about to become operational; and

(II)   in the first week of January 2000, and at 2-year intervals thereafter, except to the extent that different years for the repeating of such proceedings may be determined in accordance with subparagraph (A).

(ii)   The procedures specified in subparagraph (B) shall be repeated, in accordance with regulations that the Librarian of Congress shall prescribe, upon filing of a petition in accordance with section 803(a)(1) during a 60-day period commencing—

(I)   6 months after publication of a notice of the initiation of voluntary negotiation proceedings under subparagraph (A) pursuant to a petition under clause (i)(I); or

(II)   on July 1, 2000, and at 2-year intervals thereafter, except to the extent that different years for the repeating of such proceedings may be determined in accordance with subparagraph (A).

(iii)   The procedures specified in subparagraph (B) shall be concluded in accordance with section 802.

(3)   License agreements voluntarily negotiated at any time between 1 or more copyright owners of sound recordings and 1 or more entities performing sound recordings shall be given effect in lieu of any determination by a copyright arbitration royalty panel or decision by the Librarian of Congress.

(4)   (A)   The Librarian of Congress shall also establish requirements by which copyright owners may receive reasonable notice of the use of their sound recordings under this section, and under which records of such use shall be kept

and made available by entities performing sound recordings.

(B)   Any person who wishes to perform a sound recording publicly by means of a transmission eligible for statutory licensing under this subsection may do so without infringing the exclusive right of the copyright owner of the sound recording—

(i)   by complying with such notice requirements as the Librarian of Congress shall prescribe by regulation and by paying royalty fees in accordance with this subsection; or

(ii)   if such royalty fees have not been set, by agreeing to pay such royalty fees as shall be determined in accordance with this subsection.

(C)   Any royalty payments in arrears shall be made on or before the twentieth day of the month next succeeding the month in which the royalty fees are set.

(5)   Repealed. Pub.L. 105-304, Title IV, § 405(a)(2)(C), Oct. 28, 1998, 112 Stat. 2894.

(g)   Proceeds from licensing of transmissions.—

(1)   Except in the case of a transmission licensed under a statutory license in accordance with subsection (f) of this section—

(A)   a featured recording artist who performs on a sound recording that has been licensed for a transmission shall be entitled to receive payments from the copyright owner of the sound recording in accordance with the terms of the artist's contract; and

(B)   a nonfeatured recording artist who performs on a sound recording that has been licensed for a transmission shall be entitled to receive payments from the copyright owner of the sound recording in accordance with the terms of the nonfeatured recording artist's applicable contract or other applicable agreement.

(2)   The copyright owner of the exclusive right under section 106(6) of this title to publicly perform a sound recording by means of a digital audio transmission shall allocate to recording artists in the following manner its receipts from the statutory licensing of transmission performances of the sound recording in accordance with subsection (f) of this section:

(A)   2 ½ percent of the receipts shall be deposited in an escrow account managed by an independent administrator jointly appointed by copyright owners of sound recordings and the American Federation of Musicians (or any successor entity) to be distributed to nonfeatured musicians (whether or not members of the American Federation of Musicians) who have performed on sound recordings.

(B)   2 ½ percent of the receipts shall be deposited in an escrow account managed by an independent administrator jointly appointed by copyright owners of sound recordings and the American Federation of Television and Radio Artists (or any successor entity) to be distributed to nonfeatured vocalists (whether or not members of the American Federation of Television and Radio Artists) who have performed on sound recordings.

(C)   45 percent of the receipts shall be allocated, on a per sound recording basis, to the recording artist or artists featured on such sound recording (or the persons conveying rights in the artists' performance in the sound recordings).

(h)   Licensing to affiliates.—

(1)   If the copyright owner of a sound recording licenses an affiliated entity the right to publicly perform a sound recording by means of a digital audio transmission under section 106(6), the copyright owner shall make the licensed sound recording available under section 106(6) on no less favorable terms and conditions to all bona fide entities that offer similar services, except that, if there are material differences in the scope of the requested license with respect to the type of service, the particular sound recordings licensed, the frequency of use, the number of subscribers served, or the duration, then the copyright owner may establish different terms and conditions for such other services.

(2)   The limitation set forth in paragraph (1) of this subsection shall not apply in the case where the copyright owner of a sound recording licenses—

(A)   an interactive service; or

(B)   an entity to perform publicly up to 45 seconds of the sound recording and the sole purpose of the performance is to promote the distribution or performance of that sound recording.

(i)   No effect on royalties for underlying works.—License fees payable for the public performance of sound recordings under section 106(6) shall not be taken into account in any administrative, judicial, or other governmental proceeding to set or adjust the royalties payable to copyright owners of musical works for the public performance of their works. It is the intent of Congress that royalties payable to copyright owners of musical works for the public performance of their works shall not be diminished in any respect as a result of the rights granted by section 106(6).

(j)   Definitions.—As used in this section, the following terms have the following meanings:

(1)   An "affiliated entity" is an entity engaging in digital audio transmissions covered by section 106(6), other than an interactive service, in which the licensor has any direct or indirect partnership or any ownership interest amounting to 5 percent or more of the outstanding voting or non-voting stock.

(2)   An "archived program" is a predetermined program that is available repeatedly on the demand of the transmission recipient and that is performed in the same order from the beginning, except that an archived program shall not include a recorded event or broadcast transmission that makes no more than an incidental use of sound recordings, as long as such recorded event or broadcast transmission does not contain an entire sound recording or feature a particular sound recording.

(3)   A "broadcast" transmission is a transmission made by a terrestrial broadcast station licensed as such by the Federal Communications Commission.

(4)   A "continuous program" is a predetermined program that is continuously performed in the same order and that is accessed at a point in the program that is beyond the control of the transmission recipient.

(5)   A "digital audio transmission" is a digital transmission as defined in section 101, that embodies the transmission of a sound recording. This term does not include the transmission of any audiovisual work.

(6)   An "eligible nonsubscription transmission" is a noninteractive nonsubscription digital audio transmission not exempt under subsection (d)(1) that is made as part of a service that provides audio programming consisting, in whole or in part, of performances of sound recordings, including retransmissions of broadcast transmissions, if the primary purpose of the service is to provide to the public such audio or other entertainment programming, and the primary purpose of the service is not to sell, advertise, or promote particular products or services other than sound recordings, live concerts, or other music-related events.

(7)   An "interactive service" is one that enables a member of the public to receive a transmission of a program specially created for the recipient, or on request, a transmission of a particular sound recording, whether or not as part of a program, which is selected by or on behalf of the recipient. The ability of individuals to request that particular sound recordings be performed for reception by the public at large, or in the case of a subscription service, by all subscribers of the service, does not make a service interactive, if the programming on each channel of the service does not substantially consist of sound recordings that are performed within 1 hour of the request or at a time designated by either the transmitting entity or the individual making such request. If an entity offers both interactive and noninteractive services (either concurrently or at different times), the noninteractive component shall not be treated as part of an interactive service.

(8)   A "new subscription service" is a service that performs sound recordings by means of noninteractive subscription digital audio transmissions and that is not a preexisting subscription service or a preexisting satellite digital audio radio service.

(9)   A "nonsubscription" transmission is any transmission that is not a subscription transmission.

(10)   A "preexisting satellite digital audio radio service" is a subscription satellite digital audio radio service provided pursuant to a satellite digital audio radio service license issued by the Federal Communications Commission on or before July 31, 1998, and any renewal of such license to the extent of the scope of the original license, and may include a limited number of sample channels representative of the subscription service that are made available on a non-

subscription basis in order to promote the subscription service.

(11)   A "preexisting subscription service" is a service that performs sound recordings by means of noninteractive audio-only subscription digital audio transmissions, which was in existence and was making such transmissions to the public for a fee on or before July 31, 1998, and may include a limited number of sample channels representative of the subscription service that are made available on a nonsubscription basis in order to promote the subscription service.

(12)   A "retransmission" is a further transmission of an initial transmission, and includes any further retransmission of the same transmission. Except as provided in this section, a transmission qualifies as a "retransmission" only if it is simultaneous with the initial transmission. Nothing in this definition shall be construed to exempt a transmission that fails to satisfy a separate element required to qualify for an exemption under section 114(d)(1).

(13)   The "sound recording performance complement" is the transmission during any 3-hour period, on a particular channel used by a transmitting entity, of no more than—

(A)   3 different selections of sound recordings from any one phonorecord lawfully distributed for public performance or sale in the United States, if no more than 2 such selections are transmitted consecutively; or

(B)   4 different selections of sound recordings—

(i)   by the same featured recording artist; or

(ii)   from any set or compilation of phonorecords lawfully distributed together as a unit for public performance or sale in the United States, if no more than three such selections are transmitted consecutively: Provided, That the transmission of selections in excess of the numerical limits provided for in clauses (A) and (B) from multiple phonorecords shall nonetheless qualify as a sound recording performance complement if the programming of the multiple phonorecords was not willfully intended to avoid the numerical limitations prescribed in such clauses.

(14)   A "subscription" transmission is a transmission that is controlled and limited to particular recipients, and for which consideration is required to be paid or otherwise given by or on behalf of the recipient to receive the transmission or a package of transmissions including the transmission.

(15)   A "transmission" is either an initial transmission or a retransmission.

Selected Provisions of the LANHAM TRADEMARK ACT and the ANTICYBERSQUATTING CONSUMER PROTECTION ACT

15. U.S.C. 1125

Sec. 1125 False designations of origin, false descriptions, and dilution forbidden

(a)   Civil action

(1)   Any person who, on or in connection with any goods or services, or any container for goods, uses in commerce any word, term, name, symbol, or device, or any combination thereof, or any false designation of origin, false or misleading description of fact, or false or misleading representation of fact, which—

(A)   is likely to cause confusion, or to cause mistake, or to deceive as to the affiliation, connection, or association of such person with another person, or as to the origin, sponsorship, or approval of his or her goods, services, or commercial activities by another person, or

(B)   in commercial advertising or promotion, misrepresents the nature, characteristics, qualities, or geographic origin of his or her or another person's goods, services, or commercial activities, shall be liable in a civil action by any person who believes that he or she is or is likely to be damaged by such act.

(2)   As used in this subsection, the term "any person" includes any State, instrumentality of a State or employee of a State or instrumentality of a State acting in his or her official capacity. Any State, and any such instrumentality, officer, or employee, shall be subject to the provisions of this chapter in the same manner and to the same extent as any nongovernmental entity.

(3)   In a civil action for trade dress infringement under this chapter for trade dress not registered on the principal register, the person who asserts trade dress protection has the burden of proving that the matter sought to be protected is not functional.

(b)   Importation

Any goods marked or labeled in contravention of the provisions of this section shall not be imported into the United States or admitted to entry at any customhouse of the United States. The owner, importer, or consignee of goods refused entry at any customhouse under this section may have any recourse by protest or appeal that is given under the customs revenue laws or may have the remedy given by this chapter in cases involving goods refused entry or seized.

(c)   Remedies for dilution of famous marks

(1)   The owner of a famous mark shall be entitled, subject to the principles of equity and upon such terms as the court deems reasonable, to an injunction against another person's commercial use in commerce of a mark or trade name, if such use begins after the mark has become famous and causes dilution of the distinctive quality of the mark, and to obtain such other relief as is provided in this subsection. In determining whether a mark is distinctive and famous, a court may consider factors such as, but not limited to—

(A)   the degree of inherent or acquired distinctiveness of the mark;

(B)   the duration and extent of use of the mark in connection with the goods or services with which the mark is used;

(C)   the duration and extent of advertising and publicity of the mark;

(D)   the geographical extent of the trading area in which the mark is used;

(E)   the channels of trade for the goods or services with which the mark is used;

(F)   the degree of recognition of the mark in the trading areas and channels of trade used by the marks' owner and the person against whom the injunction is sought;

(G)   the nature and extent of use of the same or similar marks by third parties; and

(H)   whether the mark was registered under the Act of March 3, 1881, or the Act of February 20, 1905, or on the principal register.

(2)   In an action brought under this subsection, the owner of the famous mark shall be entitled only to injunctive relief as set forth in section 1116 of this title unless the person against whom the injunction is sought willfully intended to trade on the owner's reputation or to cause dilution of the famous mark. If such willful intent is proven, the owner of the famous mark shall also be entitled to the remedies set forth in sections 1117(a) and 1118 of this title, subject to the discretion of the court and the principles of equity.

(3)   The ownership by a person of a valid registration under the Act of March 3, 1881, or the Act of February 20, 1905, or on the principal register shall be a complete bar to an action against that person, with respect to that mark, that is brought by another person under the common law or a statute of a State and that seeks to prevent dilution of the distinctiveness of a mark, label, or form of advertisement.

(4)   The following shall not be actionable under this section:

(A)   Fair use of a famous mark by another person in comparative commercial advertising or promotion to identify the competing goods or services of the owner of the famous mark.

(B)   Noncommercial use of a mark.

(C)   All forms of news reporting and news commentary.

(d)   Cyberpiracy prevention

(1)   (A)   A person shall be liable in a civil action by the owner of a mark, including a personal name which is protected as a mark under this section, if, without regard to the goods or services of the parties, that person

(i)   has a bad faith intent to profit from that mark, including a personal name which is protected as a mark under this section; and

(ii)   registers, traffics in, or uses a domain name that—

(I)   in the case of a mark that is distinctive at the time of registration of the domain name, is identical or confusingly similar to that mark;

(II)   in the case of a famous mark that is famous at the time of registration of the domain name, is identical or confusingly similar to or dilutive of that mark; or

(III)   is a trademark, word, or name protected by reason of section 706 of Title 18 or section 220506 of Title 36.

(B)   (i)   In determining whether a person has a bad faith intent described under subparagraph (a), a court may consider factors such as, but not limited to

(I)   the trademark or other intellectual property rights of the person, if any, in the domain name;

(II)   the extent to which the domain name consists of the legal name of the person or a name that is otherwise commonly used to identify that person;

(III)   the person's prior use, if any, of the domain name in connection with the bona fide offering of any goods or services;

(IV)   the person's bona fide noncommercial or fair use of the mark in a site accessible under the domain name;

(V)   the person's intent to divert consumers from the mark owner's online location to a site accessible under the domain name that could harm the good-will represented by the mark, either for commercial gain or with the intent to tarnish or disparage the mark, by creating a likelihood of confusion as to the source, sponsorship, affiliation, or endorsement of the site;

(VI)   the person's offer to transfer, sell, or otherwise assign the domain name to the mark owner or any third party for financial gain without having used, or having an intent to use, the domain name in the bona fide offering of any goods or services, or the person's prior conduct indicating a pattern of such conduct;

(VII)   the person's provision of material and misleading false contact information when applying for the registration of the domain name, the person's intentional failure to maintain accurate contact information, or the person's prior conduct indicating a pattern of such conduct;

(VIII)   the person's registration or acquisition of multiple domain names which the person knows are identical or confusingly similar to marks of others that are distinctive at the time of registration of such domain names, or dilutive of famous marks of others that are famous at the time of registration of such domain names, without regard to the goods or services of the parties; and

(IX)   the extent to which the mark incorporated in the person's domain name registration is or is not distinctive and famous within the meaning of subsection (c)(1) of this section.

(ii)   Bad faith intent described under subparagraph (A) shall not be found in any case in which the court determines that the person believed and had reasonable grounds to believe that the use of the domain name was a fair use or otherwise lawful.

(C)   In any civil action involving the registration, trafficking, or use of a domain name under this paragraph, a court may order the forfeiture or cancellation of the domain name or the transfer of the domain name to the owner of the mark.

(D)   A person shall be liable for using a domain name under subparagraph (A) only if that person is the domain name registrant or that registrant's authorized licensee.

(E)   As used in this paragraph, the term "traffics in" refers to transactions that include, but are not limited to, sales, purchases, loans, pledges, licenses, exchanges of currency, and any other transfer for consideration or receipt in exchange for consideration.

(2)   (A)   The owner of a mark may file an in rem civil action against a domain name in the judicial district in which the domain name registrar, domain name registry, or other domain name authority that registered or assigned the domain name is located if

(i)   the domain name violates any right of the owner of a mark registered in the Patent and Trademark Office, or protected under subsection (a) or (c); and

(ii)   the court finds that the owner—

(I)   is not able to obtain in personam jurisdiction over a person who would have been a defendant in a civil action under paragraph (1); or

(II)   through due diligence was not able to find a person who would have been a defendant in a civil action under paragraph (1) by—

(aa)   sending a notice of the alleged violation and intent to proceed under this paragraph to the registrant of the domain name at the postal and e-mail address provided by the registrant to the registrar; and

(bb)   publishing notice of the action as the court may direct promptly after filing the action.

(B)   The actions under subparagraph (A)(ii) shall constitute service of process.

(C)   In an in rem action under this paragraph, a domain name shall be deemed to have its situs in the judicial district in which

(i)   the domain name registrar, registry, or other domain name authority that registered or assigned the domain name is located; or

(ii)   documents sufficient to establish control and authority regarding the disposition of the registration and use of the domain name are deposited with the court.

(D)   (i)   The remedies in an in rem action under this paragraph shall be limited to a court order for the forfeiture or cancellation of the domain name or the transfer of the domain name to the owner of the mark. upon receipt of written notification of a filed, stamped copy of a complaint filed by the owner of a mark in a United States district court under this paragraph, the domain name registrar, domain name registry, or other domain name authority shall

(I)   expeditiously deposit with the court documents sufficient to establish the court's control and authority regarding the disposition of the registration and use of the domain name to the court; and

(II)   not transfer, suspend, or otherwise modify the domain name during the pendency of the action, except upon order of the court.

(ii)   The domain name registrar or registry or other domain name authority shall not be liable for injunctive or monetary relief under this paragraph except in the case of bad faith or reckless disregard, which includes a willful failure to comply with any such court order.

(3)   The civil action established under paragraph (1) and the in rem action established under paragraph (2), and any remedy available under either such action, shall be in addition to any other civil action or remedy otherwise applicable.

(4)   The in rem jurisdiction established under paragraph (2) shall be in addition to any other jurisdiction that otherwise exists, whether in rem or in personam.

15 U.S.C. 1129
Sec. 1129. Cyberpiracy protections for individuals

(1)   In general
(A)   Civil liability. Any person who registers a domain name that consists of the name of another living person, or a name substantially and confusingly similar thereto, without that person's consent, with the specific intent to profit from such name by selling the domain name for financial gain to that person or any third party, shall be liable in a civil action by such person.

(B)   Exception. A person who in good faith registers a domain name consisting of the name of another living person, or a name substantially and confusingly similar thereto, shall not be liable under this paragraph if such name is used in, affiliated with, or related to a work of authorship protected under title 17, including a work made for hire as defined in section 101 of title 17, and if the person registering the domain name is the copyright owner or licensee of the work, the person intends to sell the domain name in conjunction with the lawful exploitation of the work, and such registration is not prohibited by a contract between the registrant and the named person. The exception under this subparagraph shall apply only to a civil action brought under paragraph (1) and shall in no manner limit the protections afforded under the Trademark Act of 1946 (15 U.S.C. 1051 et seq.) or other provision of Federal or State law.

(2)   Remedies. In any civil action brought under paragraph (1), a court may award injunctive relief, including the forfeiture or cancellation of the domain name or the transfer of the domain name to the plaintiff. The court may also, in its discretion, award costs and attorneys fees to the prevailing party.

(3)   Definition. In this section, the term "domain name" has the meaning

given that term in section 45 of the Trademark Act of 1946 (15 U.S.C. 1127).
(4)   Effective date. This section shall apply to domain names registered on
or after November 29, 1999.

Selected Provisions of the
COMPUTER FRAUD AND ABUSE ACT

18 U.S.C. 1030
Sec. 1030. Fraud and related activity in connection with computers

(a)   Whoever—
(1)   having knowingly accessed a computer without authorization or
exceeding authorized access, and by means of such conduct having obtained
information that has been determined by the United States Government
pursuant to an Executive order or statute to require protection against unauthorized disclosure for reasons of national defense or foreign relations, or any
restricted data, as defined in paragraph y of section 11 of the Atomic Energy
Act of 1954, with reason to believe that such information so obtained could be
used to the injury of the United States, or to the advantage of any foreign
nation willfully communicates, delivers, transmits, or causes to be communicated, delivered, or transmitted, or attempts to communicate, deliver, transmit or
cause to be communicated, delivered, or transmitted the same to any person not
entitled to receive it, or willfully retains the same and fails to deliver it to the
officer or employee of the United States entitled to receive it;
(2)   intentionally accesses a computer without authorization or exceeds
authorized access, and thereby obtains—
(A)   information contained in a financial record of a financial institution, or
of a card issuer as defined in section 1602(n) of title 15, or contained in a file
of a consumer reporting agency on a consumer, as such terms are defined in the
Fair Credit Reporting Act (15 U.S.C. 1681 et seq.);
(B)   information from any department or agency of the United States; or
(C)   information from any protected computer if the conduct involved an
interstate or foreign communication;
(3)   intentionally, without authorization to access any nonpublic computer
of a department or agency of the United States, accesses such a computer of
that department or agency that is exclusively for the use of the Government of
the United States or, in the case of a computer not exclusively for such use, is
used by or for the Government of the United States and such conduct affects
that use by or for the Government of the United States;
(4)   knowingly and with intent to defraud, accesses a protected computer

without authorization, or exceeds authorized access, and by means of such conduct furthers the intended fraud and obtains anything of value, unless the object of the fraud and the thing obtained consists only of the use of the computer and the value of such use is not more than $5,000 in any 1-year period;

(5)   (A)   knowingly causes the transmission of a program, information, code, or command, and as a result of such conduct, intentionally causes damage without authorization, to a protected computer;

(B)   intentionally accesses a protected computer without authorization, and as a result of such conduct, recklessly causes damage; or

(C)   intentionally accesses a protected computer without authorization, and as a result of such conduct, causes damage;

(6)   knowingly and with intent to defraud traffics (as defined in section 1029) in any password or similar information through which a computer may be accessed without authorization, if—

(A)   such trafficking affects interstate or foreign commerce; or

(B)   such computer is used by or for the Government of the United States;

(7)   with intent to extort from any person, firm, association, educational institution, financial institution, government entity, or other legal entity, any money or other thing of value, transmits in interstate or foreign commerce any communication containing any threat to cause damage to a protected computer;

shall be punished as provided in subsection (c) of this section.

(b)   Whoever attempts to commit an offense under subsection (a) of this section shall be punished as provided in subsection (c) of this section.

(c)   The punishment for an offense under subsection (a) or (b) of this section is—

(1)   (A)   a fine under this title or imprisonment for not more than ten years, or both, in the case of an offense under subsection (a)(1) of this section which does not occur after a conviction for another offense under this section, or an attempt to commit an offense punishable under this subparagraph; and

(B)   a fine under this title or imprisonment for not more than twenty years, or both, in the case of an offense under subsection (a)(1) of this section which occurs after a conviction for another offense under this section, or an attempt to commit an offense punishable under this subparagraph;

(2)   (A)   a fine under this title or imprisonment for not more than one year, or both, in the case of an offense under subsection (a)(2), (a)(3), (a)(5)(C), or (a)(6) of this section which does not occur after a conviction for another offense under this section, or an attempt to commit an offense punishable under this subparagraph; and

(B)   a fine under this title or imprisonment for not more than 5 years, or both, in the case of an offense under subsection (a)(2), if—

(i)   the offense was committed for purposes of commercial advantage or private financial gain;

(ii)   the offense was committed in furtherance of any criminal or tortious act in violation of the Constitution or laws of the United States or of any State; or

(iii)   the value of the information obtained exceeds $5,000;

(C)   a fine under this title or imprisonment for not more than ten years, or both, in the case of an offense under subsection (a)(2), (a)(3) or (a)(6) of this section which occurs after a conviction for another offense under this section, or an attempt to commit an offense punishable under this subparagraph; and

(3)   (A)   a fine under this title or imprisonment for not more than five years, or both, in the case of an offense under subsection (a)(4), (a)(5)(A), (a)(5)(B), or (a)(7) of this section which does not occur after a conviction for another offense under this section, or an attempt to commit an offense punishable under this subparagraph; and

(B)   a fine under this title or imprisonment for not more than ten years, or both, in the case of an offense under subsection (a)(4), (a)(5)(A), (a)(5)(B), (a)(5)(C), or (a)(7) of this section which occurs after a conviction for another offense under this section, or an attempt to commit an offense punishable under this subparagraph; and

(d)   The United States Secret Service shall, in addition to any other agency having such authority, have the authority to investigate offenses under subsections (a)(2)(A), (a)(2)(B), (a)(3), (a)(4), (a)(5), and (a)(6) of this section. Such authority of the United States Secret Service shall be exercised in accordance with an agreement which shall be entered into by the Secretary of the Treasury and the Attorney General.

(e)   As used in this section—

(1)   the term "computer" means an electronic, magnetic, optical, electro-chemical, or other high speed data processing device performing logical, arithmetic, or storage functions, and includes any data storage facility or communications facility directly related to or operating in conjunction with such device, but such term does not include an automated typewriter or type-setter, a portable hand held calculator, or other similar device;

(2)   the term "protected computer" means a computer—

(A)   exclusively for the use of a financial institution or the United States Government, or, in the case of a computer not exclusively for such use, used by or for a financial institution or the United States Government and the conduct constituting the offense affects that use by or for the financial institution or the Government; or

(B)   which is used in interstate or foreign commerce or communication;

(3)   the term "State" includes the District of Columbia, the Commonwealth of Puerto Rico, and any other commonwealth, possession or territory of the United States;

(4)   the term "financial institution" means—

(A)   an institution with deposits insured by the Federal Deposit Insurance Corporation;

(B)   the Federal Reserve or a member of the Federal Reserve including any Federal Reserve Bank;

(C)   a credit union with accounts insured by the National Credit Union Administration;

(D)   a member of the Federal home loan bank system and any home loan bank;

(E)   any institution of the Farm Credit System under the Farm Credit Act of 1971;

(F)   a broker-dealer registered with the Securities and Exchange Commission pursuant to section 15 of the Securities Exchange Act of 1934;

(G)   the Securities Investor Protection Corporation;

(H)   a branch or agency of a foreign bank (as such terms are defined in paragraphs (1) and (3) of section 1(b) of the International Banking Act of 1978); and

(I)   an organization operating under section 25 or section 25(a) of the Federal Reserve Act.

(5)   the term "financial record" means information derived from any record held by a financial institution pertaining to a customer's relationship with the financial institution;

(6)   the term "exceeds authorized access" means to access a computer with authorization and to use such access to obtain or alter information in the computer that the accesser is not entitled so to obtain or alter;

(7)   the term "department of the United States" means the legislative or judicial branch of the Government or one of the executive departments enumerated in section 101 of title 5; and

(8)   the term "damage" means any impairment to the integrity or availability of data, a program, a system, or information, that—

(A)   causes loss aggregating at least $5,000 in value during any 1-year period to one or more individuals;

(B)   modifies or impairs, or potentially modifies or impairs, the medical examination, diagnosis, treatment, or care of one or more individuals;

(C)   causes physical injury to any person; or

(D)   threatens public health or safety; and

(9)   the term "government entity" includes the Government of the United States, any State or political subdivision of the United States, any foreign

country, and any state, province, municipality, or other political subdivision of a foreign country.

(f)   This section does not prohibit any lawfully authorized investigative, protective, or intelligence activity of a law enforcement agency of the United States, a State, or a political subdivision of a State, or of an intelligence agency of the United States.

(g)   Any person who suffers damage or loss by reason of a violation of this section may maintain a civil action against the violator to obtain compensatory damages and injunctive relief or other equitable relief. Damages for violations involving damage as defined in subsection (e)(8)(A) are limited to economic damages. No action may be brought under this subsection unless such action is begun within 2 years of the date of the act complained of or the date of the discovery of the damage.

(h)   The Attorney General and the Secretary of the Treasury shall report to the Congress annually, during the first 3 years following the date of the enactment of this subsection, concerning investigations and prosecutions under subsection (a)(5).

Selected Provisions of the NO ELECTRONIC THEFT ACT

17 U.S.C. 506
Sec. 506. Criminal offenses

(a)   Criminal Infringement.—Any person who infringes a copyright willfully either—

(1)   for purposes of commercial advantage or private financial gain, or

(2)   by the reproduction or distribution, including by electronic means, during any 180-day period, of 1 or more copies or phonorecords of 1 or more copyrighted works, which have a total retail value of more than $1,000, shall be punished as provided under section 2319 of title 18, United States Code. For purposes of this subsection, evidence of reproduction or distribution of a copyrighted work, by itself, shall not be sufficient to establish willful infringement.

(b)   Forfeiture and Destruction.—When any person is convicted of any violation of subsection (a), the court in its judgment of conviction shall, in addition to the penalty therein prescribed, order the forfeiture and destruction or other disposition of all infringing copies or phonorecords and all implements, devices, or equipment used in the manufacture of such infringing copies or phonorecords.

(c)   Fraudulent Copyright Notice.—Any person who, with fraudulent intent, places on any article a notice of copyright or words of the same purport that such person knows to be false, or who, with fraudulent intent, publicly distributes or imports for public distribution any article bearing such notice or words that such person knows to be false, shall be fined not more than $2,500.

(d)   Fraudulent Removal of Copyright Notice.—Any person who, with fraudulent intent, removes or alters any notice of copyright appearing on a copy of a copyrighted work shall be fined not more than $2,500.

(e)   False Representation.—Any person who knowingly makes a false representation of a material fact in the application for copyright registration provided for by section 409, or in any written statement filed in connection with the application, shall be fined not more than $2,500.

(f)   Rights of Attribution and Integrity.—Nothing in this section applies to infringement of the rights conferred by section 106A(a).

18 U.S.C. 2319
Sec. 2319. Criminal infringement of a copyright

(a)   Whoever violates section 506(a) (relating to criminal offenses) of title 17 shall be punished as provided in subsections (b) and (c) of this section and such penalties shall be in addition to any other provisions of title 17 or any other law.

(b)   Any person who commits an offense under section 506(a)(1) of title 17—

(1)   shall be imprisoned not more than 5 years, or fined in the amount set forth in this title, or both, if the offense consists of the reproduction or distribution, including by electronic means, during any 180-day period, of at least 10 copies or phonorecords, of 1 or more copyrighted works, which have a total retail value of more than $2,500;

(2)   shall be imprisoned not more than 10 years, or fined in the amount set forth in this title, or both, if the offense is a second or subsequent offense under paragraph (1); and

(3)   shall be imprisoned not more than 1 year, or fined in the amount set forth in this title, or both, in any other case.

(c)   Any person who commits an offense under section 506(a)(2) of title 17, United States Code—

(1)   shall be imprisoned not more than 3 years, or fined in the amount set forth in this title, or both, if the offense consists of the reproduction or distribution of 10 or more copies or phonorecords of 1 or more copyrighted works, which have a total retail value of $2,500 or more;

(2)   shall be imprisoned not more than 6 years, or fined in the amount set

forth in this title, or both, if the offense is a second or subsequent offense under paragraph (1); and

(3)   shall be imprisoned not more than 1 year, or fined in the amount set forth in this title, or both, if the offense consists of the reproduction or distribution of 1 or more copies or phonorecords of 1 or more copyrighted works, which have a total retail value of more than $1,000.

(d)   (1)   During preparation of the presentence report pursuant to Rule 32(c) of the Federal Rules of Criminal Procedure, victims of the offense shall be permitted to submit, and the probation officer shall receive, a victim impact statement that identifies the victim of the offense and the extent and scope of the injury and loss suffered by the victim, including the estimated economic impact of the offense on that victim.

(2)   Persons permitted to submit victim impact statements shall include—

(A)   producers and sellers of legitimate works affected by conduct involved in the offense;

(B)   holders of intellectual property rights in such works; and

(C)   the legal representatives of such producers, sellers, and holders.

(e)   As used in this section—

(1)   the terms "phonorecord" and "copies" have, respectively, the meanings set forth in section 101 (relating to definitions) of title 17; and

(2)   the terms "reproduction" and "distribution" refer to the exclusive rights of a copyright owner under clauses (1) and (3) respectively of section 106 (relating to exclusive rights in copyrighted works), as limited by sections 107 through 120, of title 17.

Selected Provisions of the
ELECTRONIC COMMUNICATIONS PRIVACY ACT

18 U.S.C. 2511
Sec. 2511. Interception and disclosure of wire, oral, or electronic communications

(1)   Except as otherwise specifically provided in this chapter any person who—

(a)   intentionally intercepts, endeavors to intercept, or procures any other person to intercept or endeavor to intercept, any wire, oral, or electronic communication;

(b)   intentionally uses, endeavors to use, or procures any other person to use or endeavor to use any electronic, mechanical, or other device to intercept any oral communication when—

(i)   such device is affixed to, or otherwise transmits a signal through, a wire, cable, or other like connection used in wire communication; or

(ii) such device transmits communications by radio, or interferes with the transmission of such communication; or

(iii) such person knows, or has reason to know, that such device or any component thereof has been sent through the mail or transported in interstate or foreign commerce; or

(iv) such use or endeavor to use (A) takes place on the premises of any business or other commercial establishment the operations of which affect interstate or foreign commerce; or (B) obtains or is for the purpose of obtaining information relating to the operations of any business or other commercial establishment the operations of which affect interstate or foreign commerce; or

(v) such person acts in the District of Columbia, the Commonwealth of Puerto Rico, or any territory or possession of the United States;

(c)   intentionally discloses, or endeavors to disclose, to any other person the contents of any wire, oral, or electronic communication, knowing or having reason to know that the information was obtained through the interception of a wire, oral, or electronic communication in violation of this subsection;

(d)   intentionally uses, or endeavors to use, the contents of any wire, oral, or electronic communication, knowing or having reason to know that the information was obtained through the interception of a wire, oral, or electronic communication in violation of this subsection; or

(e)   (i)   intentionally discloses, or endeavors to disclose, to any other person the contents of any wire, oral, or electronic communication, intercepted by means authorized by sections 2511(2)(a)(ii), 2511(2)(b) to (c), 2511(2)(e), 2516, and 2518 of this chapter,

(ii) knowing or having reason to know that the information was obtained through the interception of such a communication in connection with a criminal investigation,

(iii) having obtained or received the information in connection with a criminal investigation, and

(iv) with intent to improperly obstruct, impede, or interfere with a duly authorized criminal investigation,

shall be punished as provided in subsection (4) or shall be subject to suit as provided in subsection (5).

(2)   (a)   (i)   It shall not be unlawful under this chapter for an operator of a switchboard, or an officer, employee, or agent of a provider of wire or electronic communication service, whose facilities are used in the transmission of a wire or electronic communication, to intercept, disclose, or use that communication in the normal course of his employment while engaged in any activity which is a necessary incident to the rendition of his service or to the protection of the rights or property of the provider of that service, except that

a provider of wire communication service to the public shall not utilize service observing or random monitoring except for mechanical or service quality control checks.

(ii)   Notwithstanding any other law, providers of wire or electronic communication service, their officers, employees, and agents, landlords, custodians, or other persons, are authorized to provide information, facilities, or technical assistance to persons authorized by law to intercept wire, oral, or electronic communications or to conduct electronic surveillance, as defined in section 101 of the Foreign Intelligence Surveillance Act of 1978, if such provider, its officers, employees, or agents, landlord, custodian, or other specified person, has been provided with—

(A)   a court order directing such assistance signed by the authorizing judge, or

(B)   a certification in writing by a person specified in section 2518(7) of this title or the Attorney General of the United States that no warrant or court order is required by law, that all statutory requirements have been met, and that the specified assistance is required, setting forth the period of time during which the provision of the information, facilities, or technical assistance is authorized and specifying the information, facilities, or technical assistance required. No provider of wire or electronic communication service, officer, employee, or agent thereof, or landlord, custodian, or other specified person shall disclose the existence of any interception or surveillance or the device used to accomplish the interception or surveillance with respect to which the person has been furnished a court order or certification under this chapter, except as may otherwise be required by legal process and then only after prior notification to the Attorney General or to the principal prosecuting attorney of a State or any political subdivision of a State, as may be appropriate. Any such disclosure, shall render such person liable for the civil damages provided for in section 2520. No cause of action shall lie in any court against any provider of wire or electronic communication service, its officers, employees, or agents, landlord, custodian, or other specified person for providing information, facilities, or assistance in accordance with the terms of a court order or certification under this chapter.

(b)   It shall not be unlawful under this chapter for an officer, employee, or agent of the Federal Communications Commission, in the normal course of his employment and in discharge of the monitoring responsibilities exercised by the Commission in the enforcement of chapter 5 of title 47 of the United States Code, to intercept a wire or electronic communication, or oral communication transmitted by radio, or to disclose or use the information thereby obtained.

(c)   It shall not be unlawful under this chapter for a person acting under color of law to intercept a wire, oral, or electronic communication, where such person is a party to the communication or one of the parties to the communication has given prior consent to such interception.

(d)   It shall not be unlawful under this chapter for a person not acting under color of law to intercept a wire, oral, or electronic communication where such person is a party to the communication or where one of the parties to the communication has given prior consent to such interception unless such communication is intercepted for the purpose of committing any criminal or tortious act in violation of the Constitution or laws of the United States or of any State.

(e)   Notwithstanding any other provision of this title or section 705 or 706 of the Communications Act of 1934, it shall not be unlawful for an officer, employee, or agent of the United States in the normal course of his official duty to conduct electronic surveillance, as defined in section 101 of the Foreign Intelligence Surveillance Act of 1978, as authorized by that Act.

(f)   Nothing contained in this chapter or chapter 121, or section 705 of the Communications Act of 1934, shall be deemed to affect the acquisition by the United States Government of foreign intelligence information from international or foreign communications, or foreign intelligence activities conducted in accordance with otherwise applicable Federal law involving a foreign electronic communications system, utilizing a means other than electronic surveillance as defined in section 101 of the Foreign Intelligence Surveillance Act of 1978, and procedures in this chapter and the Foreign Intelligence Surveillance Act of 1978 shall be the exclusive means by which electronic surveillance, as defined in section 101 of such Act, and the interception of domestic wire and oral communications may be conducted.

(g)   It shall not be unlawful under this chapter or chapter 121 of this title for any person—

(i)   to intercept or access an electronic communication made through an electronic communication system that is configured so that such electronic communication is readily accessible to the general public;

(ii)   to intercept any radio communication which is transmitted—

(I)   by any station for the use of the general public, or that relates to ships, aircraft, vehicles, or persons in distress;

(II)   by any governmental, law enforcement, civil defense, private land mobile, or public safety communications system, including police and fire, readily accessible to the general public;

(III)   by a station operating on an authorized frequency within the bands allocated to the amateur, citizens band, or general mobile radio services; or

(IV)   by any marine or aeronautical communications system;

(iii)   to engage in any conduct which—

(I)   is prohibited by section 633 of the Communications Act of 1934; or

(II)   is excepted from the application of section 705(a) of the Communications Act of 1934 by section 705(b) of that Act;

(iv)   to intercept any wire or electronic communication the transmission of which is causing harmful interference to any lawfully operating station or consumer electronic equipment, to the extent necessary to identify the source of such interference; or

(v)   for other users of the same frequency to intercept any radio communication made through a system that utilizes frequencies monitored by individuals engaged in the provision or the use of such system, if such communication is not scrambled or encrypted.

(h)   It shall not be unlawful under this chapter—

(i)   to use a pen register or a trap and trace device (as those terms are defined for the purposes of chapter 206 (relating to pen registers and trap and trace devices) of this title); or

(ii)   for a provider of electronic communication service to record the fact that a wire or electronic communication was initiated or completed in order to protect such provider, another provider furnishing service toward the completion of the wire or electronic communication, or a user of that service, from fraudulent, unlawful or abusive use of such service.

(3)   (a)   Except as provided in paragraph (b) of this subsection, a person or entity providing an electronic communication service to the public shall not intentionally divulge the contents of any communication (other than one to such person or entity, or an agent thereof) while in transmission on that service to any person or entity other than an addressee or intended recipient of such communication or an agent of such addressee or intended recipient.

(b)   A person or entity providing electronic communication service to the public may divulge the contents of any such communication—

(i)   as otherwise authorized in section 2511(2)(a) or 2517 of this title;

(ii)   with the lawful consent of the originator or any addressee or intended recipient of such communication;

(iii)   to a person employed or authorized, or whose facilities are used, to forward such communication to its destination; or

(iv)   which were inadvertently obtained by the service provider and which appear to pertain to the commission of a crime, if such divulgence is made to a law enforcement agency.

(4)   (a)   Except as provided in paragraph (b) of this subsection or in subsection (5), whoever violates subsection (1) of this section shall be fined under this title or imprisoned not more than five years, or both.

(b)   If the offense is a first offense under paragraph (a) of this subsection and is not for a tortious or illegal purpose or for purposes of direct or indirect commercial advantage or private commercial gain, and the wire or electronic communication with respect to which the offense under paragraph (a) is a radio communication that is not scrambled, encrypted, or transmitted using modulation techniques the essential parameters of which have been withheld from the public with the intention of preserving the privacy of such communication, then—

(i)   if the communication is not the radio portion of a cellular telephone communication, a cordless telephone communication that is transmitted between the cordless telephone handset and the base unit, a public land mobile radio service communication or a paging service communication, and the conduct is not that described in subsection (5), the offender shall be fined under this title or imprisoned not more than one year, or both; and

(ii)   if the communication is the radio portion of a cellular telephone communication, a cordless telephone communication that is transmitted between the cordless telephone handset and the base unit, a public land mobile radio service communication or a paging service communication, the offender shall be fined under this title.

(c)   Conduct otherwise an offense under this subsection that consists of or relates to the interception of a satellite transmission that is not encrypted or scrambled and that is transmitted—

(i)   to a broadcasting station for purposes of retransmission to the general public; or

(ii)   as an audio subcarrier intended for redistribution to facilities open to the public, but not including data transmissions or telephone calls,

is not an offense under this subsection unless the conduct is for the purposes of direct or indirect commercial advantage or private financial gain.

(5)   (a)   (i)   If the communication is—

(A)   a private satellite video communication that is not scrambled or encrypted and the conduct in violation of this chapter is the private viewing of that communication and is not for a tortious or illegal purpose or for purposes of direct or indirect commercial advantage or private commercial gain; or

(B)   a radio communication that is transmitted on frequencies allocated under subpart D of part 74 of the rules of the Federal Communications Commission that is not scrambled or encrypted and the conduct in violation of this chapter is not for a tortious or illegal purpose or for purposes of direct or indirect commercial advantage or private commercial gain,

then the person who engages in such conduct shall be subject to suit by the Federal Government in a court of competent jurisdiction.

(ii)   In an action under this subsection—

(A)   if the violation of this chapter is a first offense for the person under paragraph (a) of subsection (4) and such person has not been found liable in a civil action under section 2520 of this title, the Federal Government shall be entitled to appropriate injunctive relief; and

(B)   if the violation of this chapter is a second or subsequent offense under paragraph (a) of subsection (4) or such person has been found liable in any prior civil action under section 2520, the person shall be subject to a mandatory $500 civil fine.

(b)   The court may use any means within its authority to enforce an injunction issued under paragraph (ii)(A), and shall impose a civil fine of not less than $500 for each violation of such an injunction.

Selected Provisions of the
PRIVACY PROTECTION ACT OF 1980

42 U.S.C. 2000aa

Sec. 2000aa. Searches and seizures by government officers and employees in connection with investigation or prosecution of criminal offenses

(a)   Work product materials

Notwithstanding any other law, it shall be unlawful for a government officer or employee, in connection with the investigation or prosecution of a criminal offense, to search for or seize any work product materials possessed by a person reasonably believed to have a purpose to disseminate to the public a newspaper, book, broadcast, or other similar form of public communication, in or affecting interstate or foreign commerce; but this provision shall not impair or affect the ability of any government officer or employee, pursuant to otherwise applicable law, to search for or seize such materials, if—

(1)   there is probable cause to believe that the person possessing such materials has committed or is committing the criminal offense to which the materials relate: Provided, however, That a government officer or employee may not search for or seize such materials under the provisions of this paragraph if the offense to which the materials relate consists of the receipt, possession, communication, or withholding of such materials or the information contained therein (but such a search or seizure may be conducted under the provisions of this paragraph if the offense consists of the receipt, possession, or communication of information relating to the national defense, classified information, or restricted data under the provisions of section 793, 794, 797, or 798 of Title 18, or section 2274, 2275 or 2277 of this title, or section 783 of Title 50, or if the offense involves the production, possession, receipt, mailing, sale, distribution, shipment, or transportation of child pornography, the sexual exploitation of children, or the sale or purchase of children under section 2251, 2251A, 2252, or 2252A of Title 18); or

(2)   there is reason to believe that the immediate seizure of such materials is necessary to prevent the death of, or serious bodily injury to, a human being.

(b)   Other documents

Notwithstanding any other law, it shall be unlawful for a government officer or employee, in connection with the investigation or prosecution of a criminal offense, to search for or seize documentary materials, other than work product materials, possessed by a person in connection with a purpose to disseminate to the public a newspaper, book, broadcast, or other similar form of public communication, in or affecting interstate or foreign commerce; but this provision shall not impair or affect the ability of any government officer or employee, pursuant to otherwise applicable law, to search for or seize such materials, if—

(1)   there is probable cause to believe that the person possessing such materials has committed or is committing the criminal offense to which the materials relate: Provided, however, That a government officer or employee may not search for or seize such materials under the provisions of this paragraph if the offense to which the materials relate consists of the receipt, possession, communication, or withholding of such materials or the information contained therein (but such a search or seizure may be conducted under the provisions of this paragraph if the offense consists of the receipt, possession, or communication of information relating to the national defense, classified information, or restricted data under the provisions of section 793, 794, 797, or 798 of Title 18, or section 2274, 2275, or 2277 of this title, or section 783 of Title 50, or if the offense involves the production, possession, receipt, mailing, sale, distribution, shipment, or transportation of child pornography, the sexual exploitation of children, or the sale or purchase of children under section 2251, 2251A, 2252, or 2252A of Title 18);

(2)   there is reason to believe that the immediate seizure of such materials is necessary to prevent the death of, or serious bodily injury to, a human being;

(3)   there is reason to believe that the giving of notice pursuant to a subpena duces tecum would result in the destruction, alteration, or concealment of such materials; or

(4)   such materials have not been produced in response to a court order directing compliance with a subpena duces tecum, and—

(A)   all appellate remedies have been exhausted; or

(B)   there is reason to believe that the delay in an investigation or trial occasioned by further proceedings relating to the subpena would threaten the interests of justice.

(c)   Objections to court ordered subpoenas; affidavits

In the event a search warrant is sought pursuant to paragraph (4)(B) of subsection (b) of this section, the person possessing the materials shall be afforded adequate opportunity to submit an affidavit setting forth the basis for any contention that the materials sought are not subject to seizure.

Selected Provisions of the UNIFORM COMPUTER INFORMATION TRANSACTIONS ACT

Sec. 104. Mixed transactions: agreement to opt-in or opt-out.

The parties may agree that this [Act], including contract-formation rules, governs the transaction, in whole or part, or that other law governs the transaction and this [Act] does not apply, if a material part of the subject matter to which the agreement applies is computer information or informational rights in it that are within the scope of this [Act], or is subject matter within this [Act] under Section 103(b), or is subject matter excluded by Section 103(d)(1) or (3). However, any agreement to do so is subject to the following rules:

(1)   An agreement that this [Act] governs a transaction does not alter the applicability of any statute, rule, or procedure that may not be varied by agreement of the parties or that may be varied only in a manner specified by the statute, rule or procedure, including a consumer protection statute [or administrative rule]. In addition, in a mass-market transaction, the agreement does not alter the applicability of a law applicable to a copy of information in printed form.

(2)   An agreement that this [Act] does not govern a transaction:

(A)   does not alter the applicability of Section 214 or 816; and

(B)   in a mass-market transaction, does not alter the applicability under [this Act] of the doctrine of unconscionability or fundamental public policy or the obligation of good faith.

(3)   In a mass-market transaction, any term under this section which changes the extent to which this [Act] governs the transaction must be conspicuous.

(4)   A copy of a computer program contained in and sold or leased as part of goods and which is excluded from this [Act] by Section 103(b)(1) cannot provide the basis for an agreement under this section that this [Act] governs the transaction.

Sec. 105. Relation to federal law; fundamental public policy; transactions subject to other state law.

(a)   A provision of this [Act] which is preempted by federal law is unenforceable to the extent of the preemption.

(b)   If a term of a contract violates a fundamental public policy, the court may refuse to enforce the contract, enforce the remainder of the contract without the impermissible term, or limit the application of the impermissible term so as to avoid a result contrary to public policy, in each case to the extent that the interest in enforcement is clearly outweighed by a public policy against enforcement of the term.

(c)   Except as otherwise provided in subsection (d), if this [Act] or a term of a contract under this [Act] conflicts with a consumer protection statute [or administrative rule], the consumer protection statute [or rule] governs.

(d)   If a law of this State in effect on the effective date of this [Act] applies to a transaction governed by this [Act], the following rules apply:

(1)   A requirement that a term, waiver, notice, or disclaimer be in a writing is satisfied by a record.

(2)   A requirement that a record, writing, or term be signed is satisfied by an authentication.

(3)   A requirement that a term be conspicuous, or the like, is satisfied by a term that is conspicuous under this [Act].

(4)   A requirement of consent or agreement to a term is satisfied by a manifestation of assent to the term in accordance with this [Act].

[(e)   The following laws govern in the case of a conflict between this [Act] and the other law:]

Legislative Note: The purpose of subsection (c) is to make clear that this Act does not alter the application to computer information transactions of the substantive provisions of a State's consumer protection statutes or rules (including rules about the timing and content of required disclosures) and does not alter application of the State's statutes giving regulatory authority to a state agency such as the Office of the Attorney General. It may be appropriate, for purposes of clarity, in subsection (c) to cross reference particular statutes such as the State's Unfair and Deceptive Practices Act by inserting "including [cite the statute]." Subject to the federal Electronic Signatures Global and National Commerce Act, if certain consumer protection laws should be appropriately excepted from the electronic commerce rules in subsection (d), those laws should be excluded from the operation of subsection (d).

Sec. 107. Legal recognition of electronic record and authentication; use of electronic agents.

(a)   A record or authentication may not be denied legal effect or enforceability solely because it is in electronic form.

(b)   This [Act] does not require that a record or authentication be generated, stored, sent, received, or otherwise processed by electronic means or in electronic form.

(c)   In any transaction, a person may establish requirements regarding the type of authentication or record acceptable to it.

(d)   A person that uses an electronic agent that it has selected for making an authentication, performance, or agreement, including manifestation of assent, is bound by the operations of the electronic agent, even if no individual was aware of or reviewed the agent's operations or the results of the operations.

Sec. 108. Proof and effect of authentication.

(a)   Authentication may be proven in any manner, including a showing that a party made use of information or access that could have been available only if it engaged in conduct or operations that authenticated the record or term.

(b)   Compliance with a commercially reasonable attribution procedure agreed to or adopted by the parties or established by law for authenticating a record authenticates the record as a matter of law.

Sec. 109. Choice of law.

(a)   The parties in their agreement may choose the applicable law. However, the choice is not enforceable in a consumer contract to the extent it would vary a rule that may not be varied by agreement under the law of the jurisdiction whose law would apply under subsections (b) and (c) in the absence of the agreement.

(b)   In the absence of an enforceable agreement on choice of law, the following rules determine which jurisdiction's law governs in all respects for purposes of contract law:

(1)   An access contract or a contract providing for electronic delivery of a copy is governed by the law of the jurisdiction in which the licensor was located when the agreement was entered into.

(2)   A consumer contract that requires delivery of a copy on a tangible medium is governed by the law of the jurisdiction in which the copy is or should have been delivered to the consumer.

(3)   In all other cases, the contract is governed by the law of the jurisdiction having the most significant relationship to the transaction.

(c)   In cases governed by subsection (b), if the jurisdiction whose law governs is outside the United States, the law of that jurisdiction governs only if it provides substantially similar protections and rights to a party not located in that jurisdiction as are provided under this [Act]. Otherwise, the law of the State that has the most significant relationship to the transaction governs.

(d)   For purposes of this section, a party is located at its place of business if it has one place of business, at its chief executive office if it has more than one place of business, or at its place of incorporation or primary registration if it does not have a physical place of business. Otherwise, a party is located at its primary residence.

Sec. 110. Contractual choice of forum.

(a)   The parties in their agreement may choose an exclusive judicial forum unless the choice is unreasonable and unjust.
(b)   A judicial forum specified in an agreement is not exclusive unless the agreement expressly so provides.

Sec. 203. Offer and acceptance in general.

Unless otherwise unambiguously indicated by the language or the circumstances:
(1)   An offer to make a contract invites acceptance in any manner and by any medium reasonable under the circumstances.
(2)   An order or other offer to acquire a copy for prompt or current delivery invites acceptance by either a prompt promise to ship or a prompt or current shipment of a conforming or nonconforming copy. However, a shipment of a nonconforming copy is not an acceptance if the licensor seasonably notifies the licensee that the shipment is offered only as an accommodation to the licensee.
(3)   If the beginning of a requested performance is a reasonable mode of acceptance, an offeror that is not notified of acceptance or performance within a reasonable time may treat the offer as having lapsed before acceptance.
(4)   If an offer in an electronic message evokes an electronic message accepting the offer, a contract is formed:
(A)   when an electronic acceptance is received; or
(B)   if the response consists of beginning performance, full performance, or giving access to information, when the performance is received or the access is enabled and necessary access materials are received.

Sec. 204. Acceptance with varying terms.

(a)   In this section, an acceptance materially alters an offer if it contains a term that materially conflicts with or varies a term of the offer or that adds a material term not contained in the offer.
(b)   Except as otherwise provided in Section 205, a definite and seasonable expression of acceptance operates as an acceptance, even if the acceptance

contains terms that vary from the terms of the offer, unless the acceptance materially alters the offer.

(c)   If an acceptance materially alters the offer, the following rules apply:

(1)   A contract is not formed unless:

(A)   a party agrees, such as by manifesting assent, to the other party's offer or acceptance; or

(B)   all the other circumstances, including the conduct of the parties, establish a contract.

(2)   If a contract is formed by the conduct of both parties, the terms of the contract are determined under Section 210.

(d)   If an acceptance varies from but does not materially alter the offer, a contract is formed based on the terms of the offer. In addition, the following rules apply:

(1)   Terms in the acceptance which conflict with terms in the offer are not part of the contract.

(2)   An additional nonmaterial term in the acceptance is a proposal for an additional term. Between merchants, the proposed additional term becomes part of the contract unless the offeror gives notice of objection before, or within a reasonable time after, it receives the proposed terms.

Sec. 206. Offer and acceptance: electronic agents.

(a)   A contract may be formed by the interaction of electronic agents. If the interaction results in the electronic agents' engaging in operations that under the circumstances indicate acceptance of an offer, a contract is formed, but a court may grant appropriate relief if the operations resulted from fraud, electronic mistake, or the like.

(b)   A contract may be formed by the interaction of an electronic agent and an individual acting on the individual's own behalf or for another person. A contract is formed if the individual takes an action or makes a statement that the individual can refuse to take or say and that the individual has reason to know will:

(1)   cause the electronic agent to perform, provide benefits, or allow the use or access that is the subject of the contract, or send instructions to do so; or

(2)   indicate acceptance, regardless of other expressions or actions by the individual to which the individual has reason to know the electronic agent cannot react.

(c)   The terms of a contract formed under subsection (b) are determined under Section 208 or 209 but do not include a term provided by the individual if the individual had reason to know that the electronic agent could not react to the term.

Sec. 209. Mass-market license.

(a)   A party adopts the terms of a mass-market license for purposes of Section 208 only if the party agrees to the license, such as by manifesting assent, before or during the party's initial performance or use of or access to the information. A term is not part of the license if:
(1)   the term is unconscionable or is unenforceable under Section 105(a) or (b); or
(2)   subject to Section 301, the term conflicts with a term to which the parties to the license have expressly agreed.
(b)   If a mass-market license or a copy of the license is not available in a manner permitting an opportunity to review by the licensee before the licensee becomes obligated to pay and the licensee does not agree, such as by manifesting assent, to the license after having an opportunity to review, the licensee is entitled to a return under Section 112 and, in addition, to:
(1)   reimbursement of any reasonable expenses incurred in complying with the licensor's instructions for returning or destroying the computer information or, in the absence of instructions, expenses incurred for return postage or similar reasonable expense in returning the computer information; and
(2)   compensation for any reasonable and foreseeable costs of restoring the licensee's information processing system to reverse changes in the system caused by the installation, if:
(A)   the installation occurs because information must be installed to enable review of the license; and
(B)   the installation alters the system or information in it but does not restore the system or information after removal of the installed information because the licensee rejected the license.
(c)   In a mass-market transaction, if the licensor does not have an opportunity to review a record containing proposed terms from the licensee before the licensor delivers or becomes obligated to deliver the information, and if the licensor does not agree, such as by manifesting assent, to those terms after having that opportunity, the licensor is entitled to a return.

Sec. 215. Electronic message: when effective; effect of acknowledgment.

(a)   Receipt of an electronic message is effective when received even if no individual is aware of its receipt.
(b)   Receipt of an electronic acknowledgment of an electronic message establishes that the message was received but by itself does not establish that the content sent corresponds to the content received.

Sec. 403. Implied warranty: merchantability of computer program.

(a)   Unless the warranty is disclaimed or modified, a licensor that is a merchant with respect to computer programs of the kind warrants:
(1)   to the end user that the computer program is fit for the ordinary purposes for which such computer programs are used;
(2)   to the distributor that:
(A)   the program is adequately packaged and labeled as the agreement requires; and
(B)   in the case of multiple copies, the copies are within the variations permitted by the agreement, of even kind, quality, and quantity within each unit and among all units involved; and
(3)   that the program conforms to any promises or affirmations of fact made on the container or label.
(b)   Unless disclaimed or modified, other implied warranties with respect to computer programs may arise from course of dealing or usage of trade.
(c)   No warranty is created under this section with respect to informational content, but an implied warranty may arise under Section 404.

Sec. 404. Implied warranty: informational content.

(a)   Unless the warranty is disclaimed or modified, a merchant that, in a special relationship of reliance with a licensee, collects, compiles, processes, provides, or transmits informational content warrants to that licensee that there is no inaccuracy in the informational content caused by the merchant's failure to perform with reasonable care.
(b)   A warranty does not arise under subsection (a) with respect to:
(1)   published informational content; or
(2)   a person that acts as a conduit or provides no more than editorial serv-ices in collecting, compiling, distributing, processing, providing, or transmitting informational content that under the circumstances can be identified as that of a third person.
(c)   The warranty under this section is not subject to the preclusion in Section 113(a) (1) on disclaiming obligations of diligence, reasonableness, or care.

Sec. 405. Implied warranty: licensee's purpose; system integration.

(a)   Unless the warranty is disclaimed or modified, if a licensor at the time of contracting has reason to know any particular purpose for which the computer information is required and that the licensee is relying on the licensor's skill or judgment to select, develop, or furnish suitable information, the following rules apply:

(1)   Except as otherwise provided in paragraph (2), there is an implied warranty that the information is fit for that purpose.

(2)   If from all the circumstances it appears that the licensor was to be paid for the amount of its time or effort regardless of the fitness of the resulting information, the warranty under paragraph (1) is that the information will not fail to achieve the licensee's particular purpose as a result of the licensor's lack of reasonable effort.

(b)   There is no warranty under subsection (a) with regard to:

(1)   the aesthetics, appeal, suitability to taste, or subjective quality of informational content; or

(2)   published informational content, but there may be a warranty with regard to the licensor's selection among published informational content from different providers if the selection is made by an individual acting as or on behalf of the licensor.

(c)   If an agreement requires a licensor to provide or select a system consisting of computer programs and goods, and the licensor has reason to know that the licensee is relying on the skill or judgment of the licensor to select the components of the system, there is an implied warranty that the components provided or selected will function together as a system.

(d)   The warranty under this section is not subject to the preclusion in Section 113(a)(1) on disclaiming diligence, reasonableness, or care.

Sec. 406. Disclaimer or modification of warranty.

(a)   Words or conduct relevant to the creation of an express warranty and words or conduct tending to disclaim or modify an express warranty must be construed wherever reasonable as consistent with each other. Subject to Section 301 with regard to parol or extrinsic evidence, the disclaimer or modification is inoperative to the extent that such construction is unreasonable.

(b)   Except as otherwise provided in subsections (c), (d), and (e), to disclaim or modify an implied warranty or any part of it, but not the warranty in Section 401, the following rules apply:

(1)   Except as otherwise provided in this subsection:

(A)   To disclaim or modify the implied warranty arising under Section 403, language must mention "merchantability" or "quality" or use words of similar import and, if in a record, must be conspicuous.

(B)   To disclaim or modify the implied warranty arising under Section 404, language in a record must mention "accuracy" or use words of similar import.

(2)   Language to disclaim or modify the implied warranty arising under Section 405 must be in a record and be conspicuous. It is sufficient to state

"There is no warranty that this information, our efforts, or the system will fulfill any of your particular purposes or needs", or words of similar import.

(3)   Language in a record is sufficient to disclaim all implied warranties if it individually disclaims each implied warranty or, except for the warranty in Section 401, if it is conspicuous and states "Except for express warranties stated in this contract, if any, this 'information' 'computer program' is provided with all faults, and the entire risk as to satisfactory quality, performance, accuracy, and effort is with the user", or words of similar import.

(4)   A disclaimer or modification sufficient under [Article 2 or 2A of the Uniform Commercial Code] to disclaim or modify an implied warranty of merchantability is sufficient to disclaim or modify the warranties under Sections 403 and 404. A disclaimer or modification sufficient under [Article 2 or 2A of the Uniform Commercial Code] to disclaim or modify an implied warranty of fitness for a particular purpose is sufficient to disclaim or modify the warranties under Section 405.

(c)   Unless the circumstances indicate otherwise, all implied warranties, but not the warranty under Section 401, are disclaimed by expressions like "as is" or "with all faults" or other language that in common understanding calls the licensee's attention to the disclaimer of warranties and makes plain that there are no implied warranties.

(d)   If a licensee before entering into a contract has examined the information or the sample or model as fully as it desired or has refused to examine the information, there is no implied warranty with regard to defects that an examination ought in the circumstances to have revealed to the licensee.

(e)   An implied warranty may also be disclaimed or modified by course of performance, course of dealing, or usage of trade.

(f)   If a contract requires ongoing performance or a series of performances by the licensor, language of disclaimer or modification which complies with this section is effective with respect to all performances under the contract.

(g)   Remedies for breach of warranty may be limited in accordance with this [Act] with respect to liquidation or limitation of damages and contractual modification of remedy.

Sec. 704. Copy: refusal of defective tender.

(a)   Subject to subsection (b) and Section 705, tender of a copy that is a material breach of contract permits the party to which tender is made to:
(1)   refuse the tender;
(2)   accept the tender; or
(3)   accept any commercially reasonable units and refuse the rest.

(b)   In a mass-market transaction that calls for only a single tender of a copy, a licensee may refuse the tender if the tender does not conform to the contract.

(c)   Refusal of a tender is ineffective unless:

(1)   it is made before acceptance;

(2)   it is made within a reasonable time after tender or completion of any permitted effort to cure; and

(3)   the refusing party seasonably notifies the tendering party of the refusal.

(d)   Except in a case governed by subsection (b), a party that rightfully refuses tender of a copy may cancel the contract only if the tender was a material breach of the whole contract or the agreement so provides.

Sec. 814. Discontinuing access.

On material breach of an access contract or if the agreement so provides, a party may discontinue all contractual rights of access of the party in breach and direct any person that is assisting the performance of the contract to discontinue its performance.

Sec. 816. Limitations on electronic self-help.

(a)   In this section, "electronic self-help" means the use of electronic means to exercise a licensor's rights under Section 815(b).

(b)   On cancellation of a license, electronic self-help is not permitted, except as provided in this section. Electronic self-help is prohibited in mass-market transactions.

(c)   If the parties agree to permit electronic self-help, the licensee shall separately manifest assent to a term authorizing use of electronic self-help. The term must:

(1)   provide for notice of exercise as provided in subsection (d);

(2)   state the name of the person designated by the licensee to which notice of exercise must be given and the manner in which notice must be given and place to which notice must be sent to that person; and

(3)   provide a simple procedure for the licensee to change the designated person or place.

(d)   Before resorting to electronic self-help authorized by a term of the license, the licensor shall give notice in a record to the person designated by the licensee stating:

(1)   that the licensor intends to resort to electronic self-help as a remedy on or after 15 days following receipt by the licensee of the notice;

(2)   the nature of the claimed breach that entitles the licensor to resort to self-help; and

(3)   the name, title, and address, including direct telephone number, facsimile number, or e-mail address, to which the licensee may communicate concerning the claimed breach.

(e)   A licensee may recover direct and incidental damages caused by wrongful use of electronic self-help. The licensee may also recover consequential damages for wrongful use of electronic self-help, whether or not those damages are excluded by the terms of the license, if:

(1)   within the period specified in subsection (d)(1), the licensee gives notice to the licensor's designated person describing in good faith the general nature and magnitude of damages;

(2)   the licensor has reason to know the damages of the type described in subsection (f) may result from the wrongful use of electronic self-help; or

(3)   the licensor does not provide the notice required in subsection (d).

(f)   Even if the licensor complies with subsections (c) and (d), electronic self-help may not be used if the licensor has reason to know that its use will result in substantial injury or harm to the public health or safety or grave harm to the public interest substantially affecting third persons not involved in the dispute.

(g)   A court of competent jurisdiction of this State shall give prompt consideration to a petition for injunctive relief and may enjoin, temporarily or permanently, the licensor from exercising electronic self-help even if authorized by a license term or enjoin the licensee from misappropriation or misuse of computer information, as may be appropriate, upon consideration of the following:

(1)   grave harm of the kinds stated in subsection (f), or the threat thereof, whether or not the licensor has reason to know of those circumstances;

(2)   irreparable harm or threat of irreparable harm to the licensee or licensor;

(3)   that the party seeking the relief is more likely than not to succeed under its claim when it is finally adjudicated;

(4)   that all of the conditions to entitle a person to the relief under the laws of this State have been fulfilled; and

(5)   that the party that may be adversely affected is adequately protected against loss, including a loss because of misappropriation or misuse of computer information, that it may suffer because the relief is granted under this [Act].

(h)   Before breach of contract, rights or obligations under this section may not be waived or varied by an agreement, but the parties may prohibit use of electronic self-help, and the parties, in the term referred to in subsection (c), may specify additional provisions more favorable to the licensee.

(i)   This section does not apply if the licensor obtains possession of a copy without a breach of the peace and the electronic self-help is used solely with respect to that copy.

Selected Provisions of the
UNIFORM ELECTRONIC TRANSACTIONS ACT

Sec. 7. Legal recognition of electronic records, electronic signatures, and electronic contracts.

(a)   A record or signature may not be denied legal effect or enforceability solely because it is in electronic form.

(b)   A contract may not be denied legal effect or enforceability solely because an electronic record was used in its formation.

(c)   If a law requires a record to be in writing, an electronic record satisfies the law.

(d)   If a law requires a signature, an electronic signature satisfies the law.

Sec. 8. Provision of information in writing; presentation of records.

(a)   If parties have agreed to conduct a transaction by electronic means and a law requires a person to provide, send, or deliver information in writing to another person, the requirement is satisfied if the information is provided, sent, or delivered, as the case may be, in an electronic record capable of retention by the recipient at the time of receipt. An electronic record is not capable of retention by the recipient if the sender or its information processing system inhibits the ability of the recipient to print or store the electronic record.

(b)   If a law other than this [Act] requires a record (i) to be posted or displayed in a certain manner, (ii) to be sent, communicated, or transmitted by a specified method, or (iii) to contain information that is formatted in a certain manner, the following rules apply:

(1)   The record must be posted or displayed in the manner specified in the other law.

(2)   Except as otherwise provided in subsection (d)(2), the record must be sent, communicated, or transmitted by the method specified in the other law.

(3)   The record must contain the information formatted in the manner specified in the other law.

(c)   If a sender inhibits the ability of a recipient to store or print an electronic record, the electronic record is not enforceable against the recipient.

(d)   The requirements of this section may not be varied by agreement, but:

(1)   to the extent a law other than this [Act] requires information to be provided, sent, or delivered in writing but permits that requirement to be varied by agreement, the requirement under subsection (a) that the information be in the form of an electronic record capable of retention may also be varied by agreement; and

(2)   a requirement under a law other than this [Act] to send, communicate, or transmit a record by [first-class mail, postage prepaid] [regular United States mail], may be varied by agreement to the extent permitted by the other law.

Sec. 9. Attribution and effect of electronic record and electronic signature.

(a)   An electronic record or electronic signature is attributable to a person if it was the act of the person. The act of the person may be shown in any manner, including a showing of the efficacy of any security procedure applied to determine the person to which the electronic record or electronic signature was attributable.
(b)   The effect of an electronic record or electronic signature attributed to a person under subsection (a) is determined from the context and surrounding circumstances at the time of its creation, execution, or adoption, including the parties' agreement, if any, and otherwise as provided by law.

Sec. 12. Retention of electronic records; originals.

(a)   If a law requires that a record be retained, the requirement is satisfied by retaining an electronic record of the information in the record which:
(1)   accurately reflects the information set forth in the record after it was first generated in its final form as an electronic record or otherwise; and
(2)   remains accessible for later reference.
(b)   A requirement to retain a record in accordance with subsection (a) does not apply to any information the sole purpose of which is to enable the record to be sent, communicated, or received.
(c)   A person may satisfy subsection (a) by using the services of another person if the requirements of that subsection are satisfied.
(d)   If a law requires a record to be presented or retained in its original form, or provides consequences if the record is not presented or retained in its original form, that law is satisfied by an electronic record retained in accordance with subsection (a).
(e)   If a law requires retention of a check, that requirement is satisfied by retention of an electronic record of the information on the front and back of the check in accordance with subsection (a).
(f)   A record retained as an electronic record in accordance with subsection (a) satisfies a law requiring a person to retain a record for evidentiary, audit, or like purposes, unless a law enacted after the effective date of this [Act] specifically prohibits the use of an electronic record for the specified purpose.
(g)   This section does not preclude a governmental agency of this State from specifying additional requirements for the retention of a record subject to the agency's jurisdiction.

Sec. 14. Automated transaction.

In an automated transaction, the following rules apply:

(1)   A contract may be formed by the interaction of electronic agents of the parties, even if no individual was aware of or reviewed the electronic agents' actions or the resulting terms and agreements.

(2)   A contract may be formed by the interaction of an electronic agent and an individual, acting on the individual's own behalf or for another person, including by an interaction in which the individual performs actions that the individual is free to refuse to perform and which the individual knows or has reason to know will cause the electronic agent to complete the transaction or performance.

(3)   The terms of the contract are determined by the substantive law applicable to it.

Selected Provisions of the ELECTRONIC SIGNATURES IN GLOBAL AND NATIONAL COMMERCE ACT

15 U.S.C. 7001

Sec. 7001. General rule of validity

(a)   In general

Notwithstanding any statute, regulation, or other rule of law (other than this subchapter and subchapter II of this chapter), with respect to any transaction in or affecting interstate or foreign commerce—

(1)   a signature, contract, or other record relating to such transaction may not be denied legal effect, validity, or enforceability solely because it is in electronic form; and

(2)   a contract relating to such transaction may not be denied legal effect, validity, or enforceability solely because an electronic signature or electronic record was used in its formation.

(b)   Preservation of rights and obligations

This subchapter does not—

(1)   limit, alter, or otherwise affect any requirement imposed by a statute, regulation, or rule of law relating to the rights and obligations of persons under such statute, regulation, or rule of law other than a requirement that contracts or other records be written, signed, or in nonelectronic form; or

(2)   require any person to agree to use or accept electronic records or electronic signatures, other than a governmental agency with respect to a record other than a contract to which it is a party.

(c)   Consumer disclosures

(1)   Consent to electronic records

Notwithstanding subsection (a), if a statute, regulation, or other rule of law requires that information relating to a transaction or transactions in or affecting interstate or foreign commerce be provided or made available to a consumer in writing, the use of an electronic record to provide or make available (whichever is required) such information satisfies the requirement that such information be in writing if—

(A)   the consumer has affirmatively consented to such use and has not withdrawn such consent;

(B)   the consumer, prior to consenting, is provided with a clear and conspicuous statement—

(i)   informing the consumer of (I) any right or option of the consumer to have the record provided or made available on paper or in nonelectronic form, and (II) the right of the consumer to withdraw the consent to have the record provided or made available in an electronic form and of any conditions, consequences (which may include termination of the parties' relationship), or fees in the event of such withdrawal;

(ii)   informing the consumer of whether the consent applies (I) only to the particular transaction which gave rise to the obligation to provide the record, or (II) to identified categories of records that may be provided or made available during the course of the parties' relationship;

(iii)   describing the procedures the consumer must use to withdraw consent as provided in clause (i) and to update information needed to contact the consumer electronically; and

(iv)   informing the consumer (I) how, after the consent, the consumer may, upon request, obtain a paper copy of an electronic record, and (II) whether any fee will be charged for such copy;

(C)   the consumer—

(i)   prior to consenting, is provided with a statement of the hardware and software requirements for access to and retention of the electronic records; and

(ii)   consents electronically, or confirms his or her consent electronically, in a manner that reasonably demonstrates that the consumer can access information in the electronic form that will be used to provide the information that is the subject of the consent; and

(D)   after the consent of a consumer in accordance with subparagraph (A), if a change in the hardware or software requirements needed to access or retain electronic records creates a material risk that the consumer will not be able to access or retain a subsequent electronic record that was the subject of the consent, the person providing the electronic record—

(i)   provides the consumer with a statement of (I) the revised hardware and software requirements for access to and retention of the electronic records, and

(II) the right to withdraw consent without the imposition of any fees for such withdrawal and without the imposition of any condition or consequence that was not disclosed under subparagraph (B)(i); and

(ii)   again complies with subparagraph (C).

(2)   Other rights

(A)   Preservation of consumer protections

Nothing in this subchapter affects the content or timing of any disclosure or other record required to be provided or made available to any consumer under any statute, regulation, or other rule of law.

(B)   Verification or acknowledgment

If a law that was enacted prior to this chapter expressly requires a record to be provided or made available by a specified method that requires verification or acknowledgment of receipt, the record may be provided or made available electronically only if the method used provides verification or acknowledgment of receipt (whichever is required).

(3)   Effect of failure to obtain electronic consent or confirmation of consent

The legal effectiveness, validity, or enforceability of any contract executed by a consumer shall not be denied solely because of the failure to obtain electronic consent or confirmation of consent by that consumer in accordance with paragraph (1)(C)(ii).

(4)   Prospective effect

Withdrawal of consent by a consumer shall not affect the legal effectiveness, validity, or enforceability of electronic records provided or made available to that consumer in accordance with paragraph (1) prior to implementation of the consumer's withdrawal of consent. A consumer's withdrawal of consent shall be effective within a reasonable period of time after receipt of the withdrawal by the provider of the record. Failure to comply with paragraph (1)(D) may, at the election of the consumer, be treated as a withdrawal of consent for purposes of this paragraph.

(5)   Prior consent

This subsection does not apply to any records that are provided or made available to a consumer who has consented prior to the effective date of this subchapter to receive such records in electronic form as permitted by any statute, regulation, or other rule of law.

(6)   Oral communications

An oral communication or a recording of an oral communication shall not qualify as an electronic record for purposes of this subsection except as otherwise provided under applicable law.

(d)   Retention of contracts and records

(1)   Accuracy and accessibility

If a statute, regulation, or other rule of law requires that a contract or other record relating to a transaction in or affecting interstate or foreign commerce be retained, that requirement is met by retaining an electronic record of the information in the contract or other record that—

(A)   accurately reflects the information set forth in the contract or other record; and

(B)   remains accessible to all persons who are entitled to access by statute, regulation, or rule of law, for the period required by such statute, regulation, or rule of law, in a form that is capable of being accurately reproduced for later reference, whether by transmission, printing, or otherwise.

(2)   Exception

A requirement to retain a contract or other record in accordance with paragraph (1) does not apply to any information whose sole purpose is to enable the contract or other record to be sent, communicated, or received.

(3)   Originals

If a statute, regulation, or other rule of law requires a contract or other record relating to a transaction in or affecting interstate or foreign commerce to be provided, available, or retained in its original form, or provides consequences if the contract or other record is not provided, available, or retained in its original form, that statute, regulation, or rule of law is satisfied by an electronic record that complies with paragraph (1).

(4)   Checks

If a statute, regulation, or other rule of law requires the retention of a check, that requirement is satisfied by retention of an electronic record of the information on the front and back of the check in accordance with paragraph (1).

(e)   Accuracy and ability to retain contracts and other records

Notwithstanding subsection (a), if a statute, regulation, or other rule of law requires that a contract or other record relating to a transaction in or affecting interstate or foreign commerce be in writing, the legal effect, validity, or enforceability of an electronic record of such contract or other record may be denied if such electronic record is not in a form that is capable of being retained and accurately reproduced for later reference by all parties or persons who are entitled to retain the contract or other record.

(f)   Proximity

Nothing in this subchapter affects the proximity required by any statute, regulation, or other rule of law with respect to any warning, notice, disclosure, or other record required to be posted, displayed, or publicly affixed.

(g)   Notarization and acknowledgment

If a statute, regulation, or other rule of law requires a signature or record relating to a transaction in or affecting interstate or foreign commerce to be notarized, acknowledged, verified, or made under oath, that requirement is satisfied if the electronic signature of the person authorized to perform those acts, together with all other information required to be included by other applicable statute, regulation, or rule of law, is attached to or logically associated with the signature or record.

(h)   Electronic agents

A contract or other record relating to a transaction in or affecting interstate or foreign commerce may not be denied legal effect, validity, or enforceability solely because its formation, creation, or delivery involved the action of one or more electronic agents so long as the action of any such electronic agent is legally attributable to the person to be bound.

(i)   Insurance

It is the specific intent of the Congress that this subchapter and subchapter II of this chapter apply to the business of insurance.

(j)   Insurance agents and brokers

An insurance agent or broker acting under the direction of a party that enters into a contract by means of an electronic record or electronic signature may not be held liable for any deficiency in the electronic procedures agreed to by the parties under that contract if—

(1)   the agent or broker has not engaged in negligent, reckless, or intentional tortious conduct;

(2)   the agent or broker was not involved in the development or establishment of such electronic procedures; and

(3)   the agent or broker did not deviate from such procedures.

This appendix does not contain the entire text of the referenced Acts. For more information concerning federal law visit http://uscode.house.gov/. For more information concerning Uniform Acts visit www.nccusl.org.

Index